Constantin Brancusi (1876-1957) is the key sculptor of the modern period – even more than Auguste Rodin, Henry Moore, Pablo Picasso, Barbara Hepworth, Marcel Duchamp, Alberto Giacometti or others. This book explores some of the reasons why Brancusi's art is so enduring, and how his influence can be discerned in much of contemporary art.

SCULPTURE BOOKS FROM CRESCENT MOON PUBLISHING

CONSTANTIN BRANCUSI

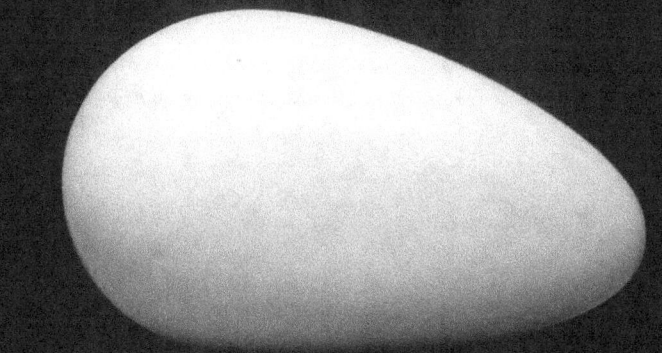

CONSTANTIN BRANCUSI

Sculpting the Essence of Things

James Pearson

Crescent Moon

Crescent Moon Publishing
P.O. Box 393
Maidstone
Kent
ME14 5XU, U.K.

First published 1994. Second edition 2008. Third edition 2011.
© James Pearson 1994, 2008, 2011.

Printed and bound in the U.S.A.
Set in Rotis Semi Sans,10 on 16pt.
Designed by Radiance Graphics.

British Library Cataloguing in Publication data

Pearson, James
Constantin Brancusi: Sculpting the Essence of Things
I. Title
730.92

ISBN-13 9781861712844

Contents

NOTE

Many of Constantin Brancusi's sculptures are housed in the Brancusi Collection at the Musée Nationale d'Art Moderne, Paris. The Museum of Modern Art in New York City and Philadelphia Museum of Art also have important collections.

ABBREVIATIONS

Paris = Musée Nationale d'Art Moderne, Paris, France

Philadelphia = Philadelphia Museum of Art, Philadelphia, USA

New York = Museum of Modern Art, New York

I am no longer of this world. I am far from myself, I am no longer a part of my own person. I am within the essence of things themselves.

Constantin Brancusi

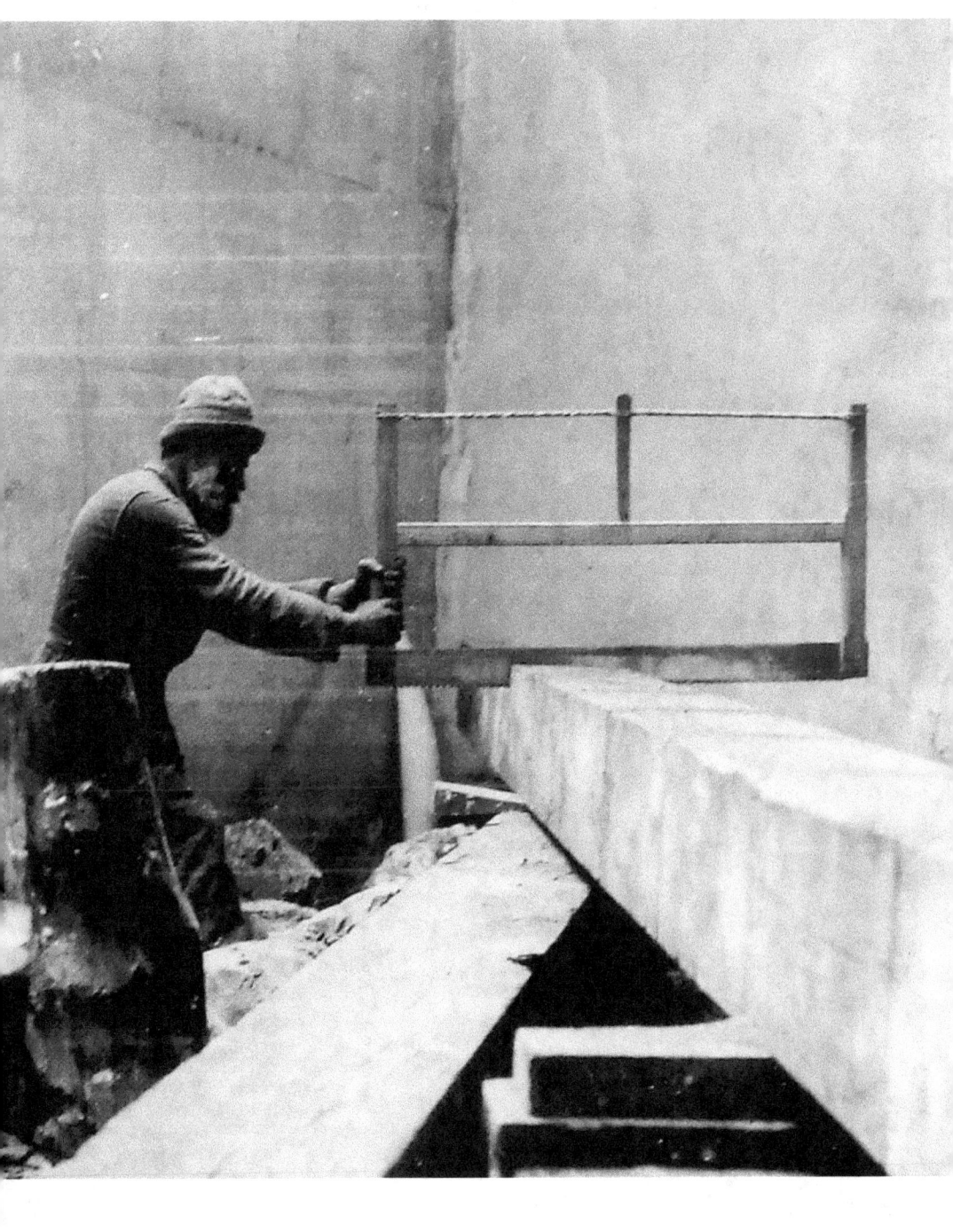

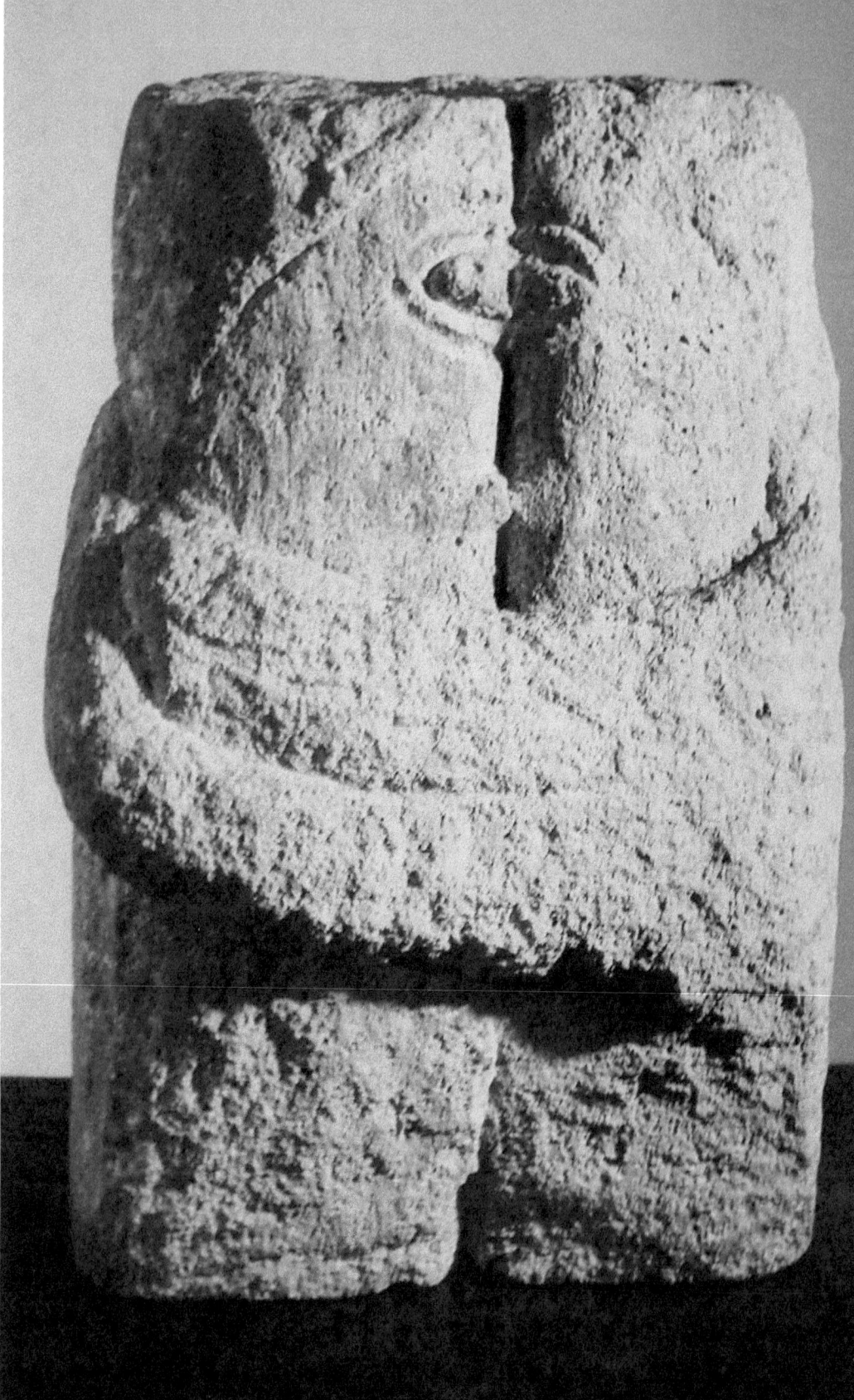

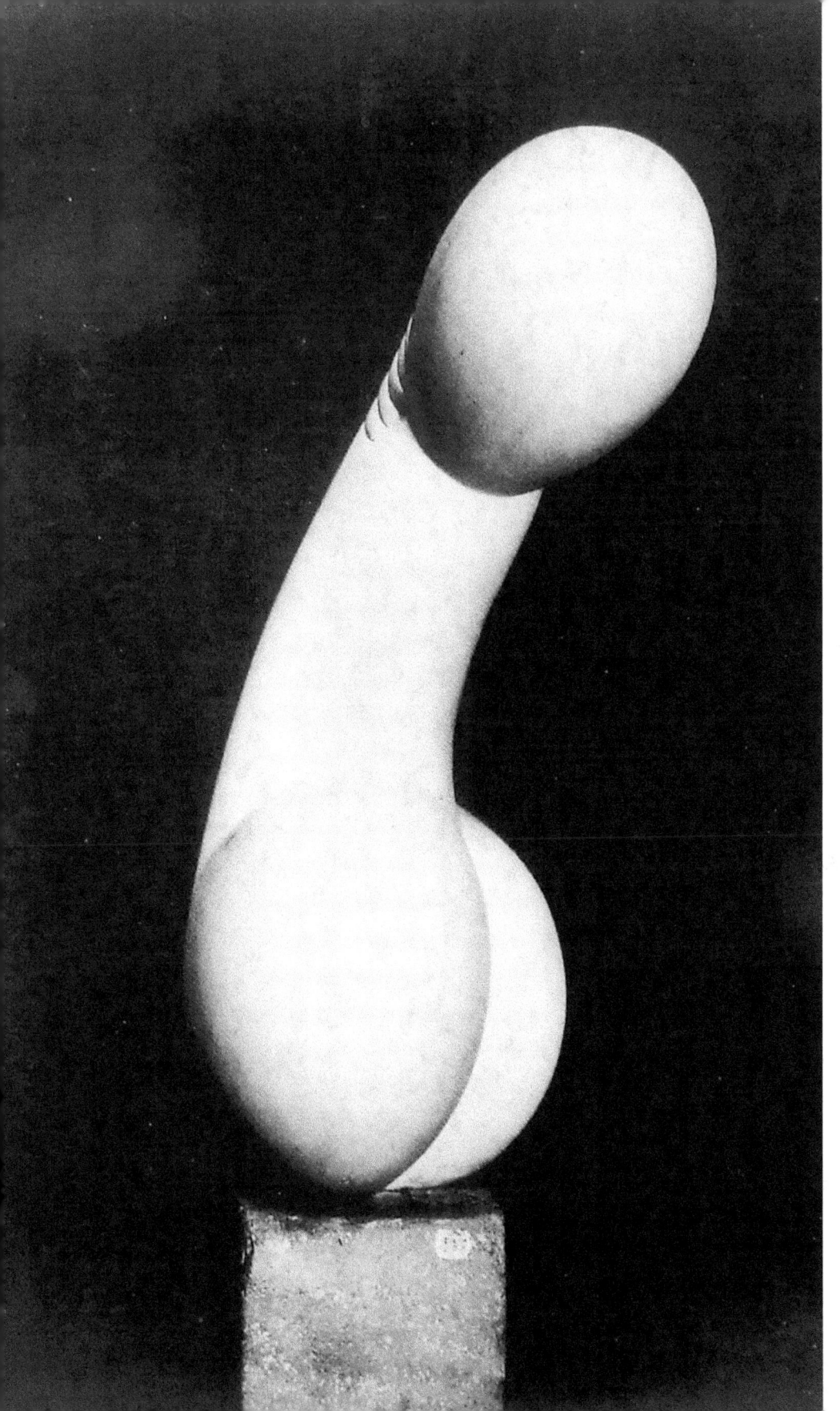

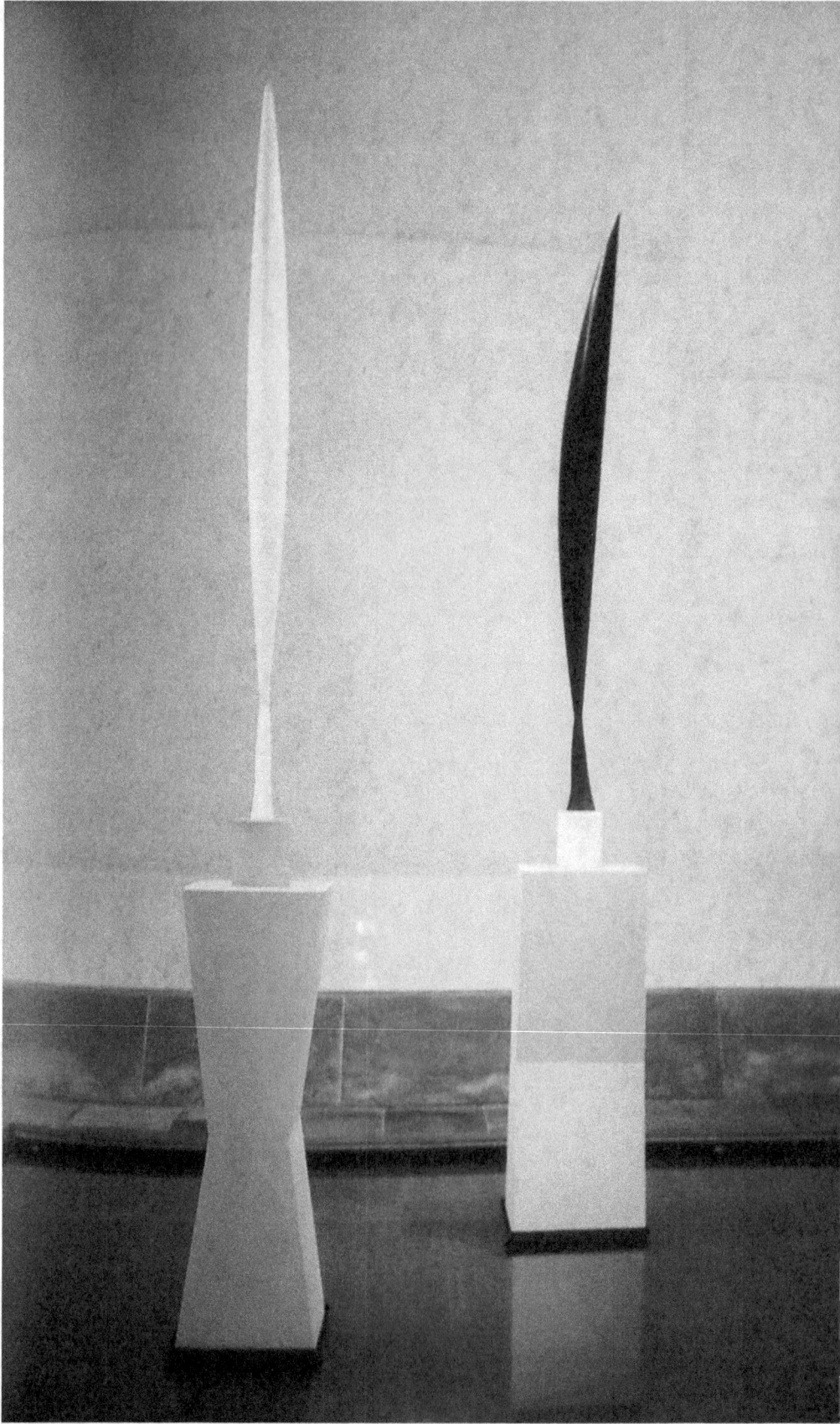

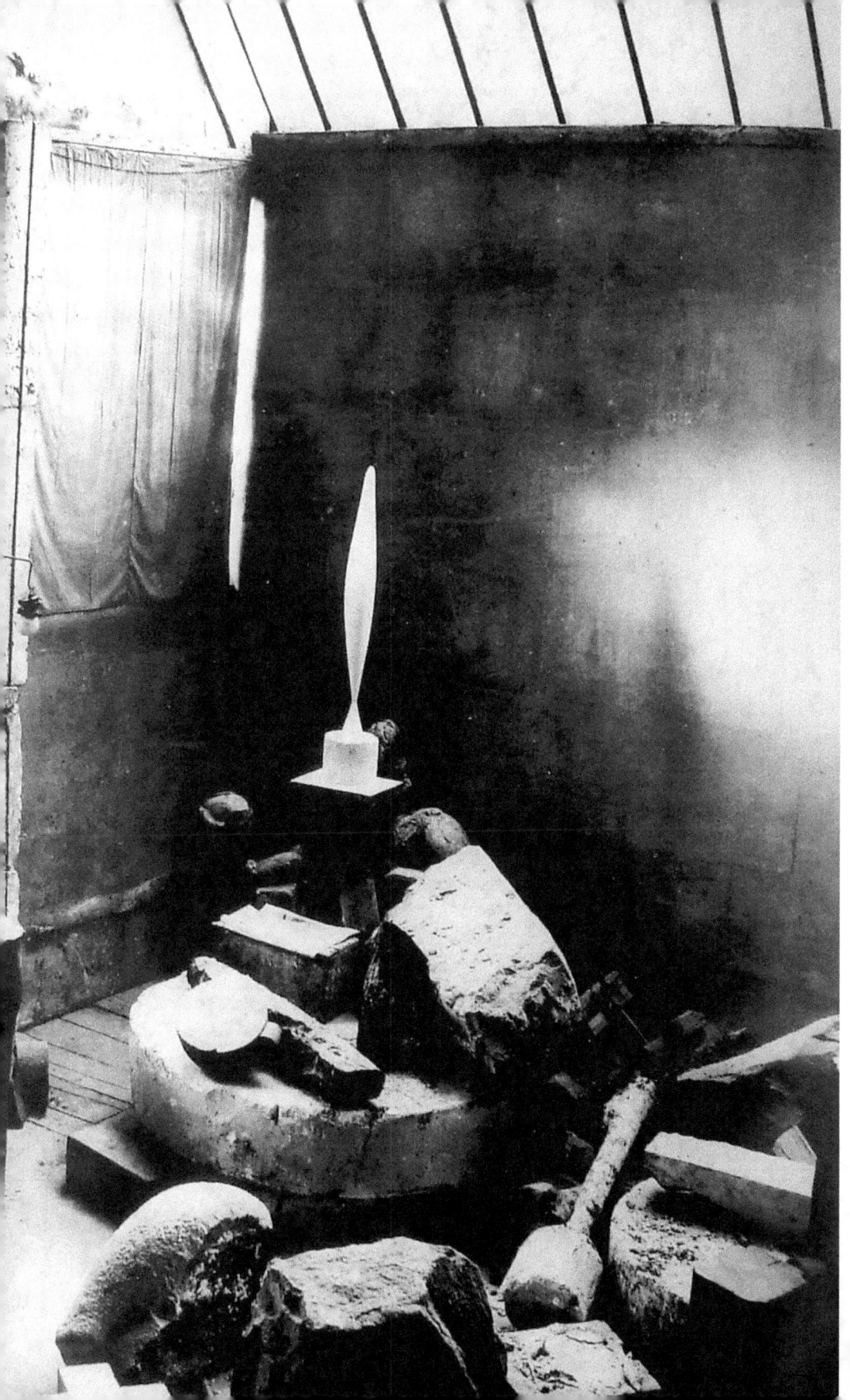

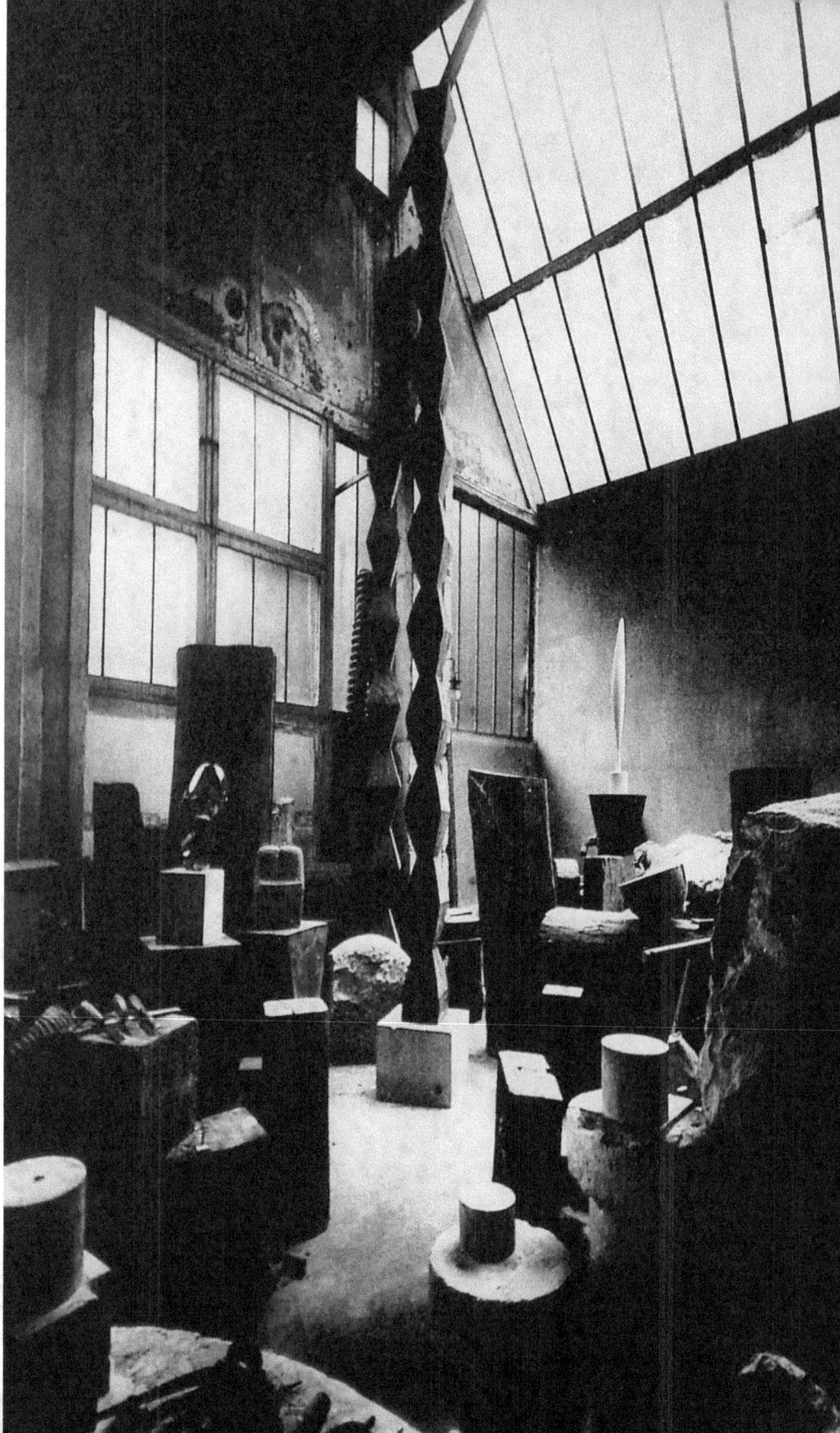

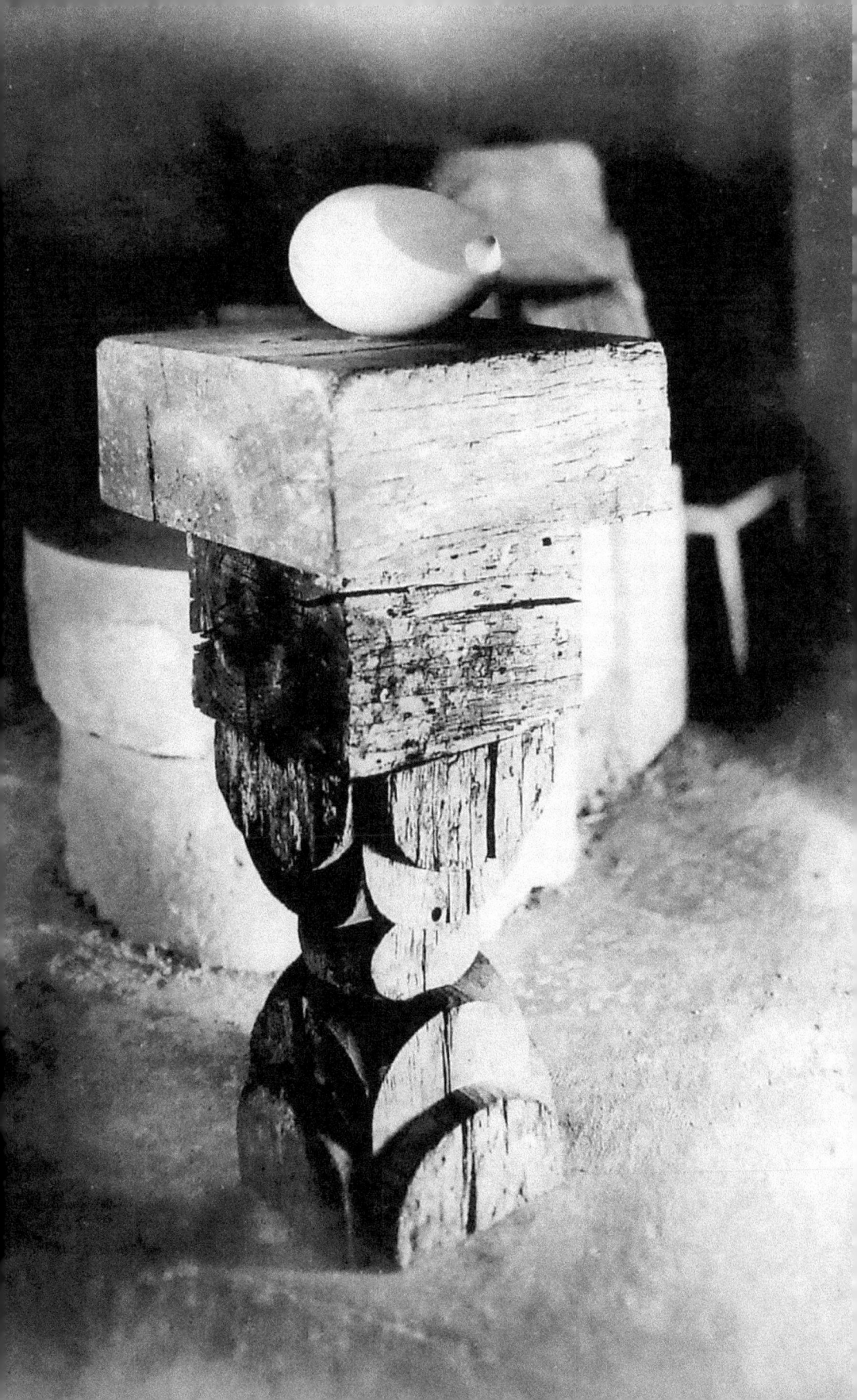

1 / Essence

My life has been a succession of miracles.

Constantin Brancusi [1]

Constantin Brancusi (1876-1957) is the key sculptor of the modern period –
not Auguste Rodin, Henry Moore, Pablo Picasso, Barbara Hepworth, Naum
Gabo, Marcel Duchamp, Alberto Giacometti, Jean Arp or other candidates.
This book will explore some of the reasons why Brancusi's art is so
important, and how his influence can be discerned in much of
contemporary art. Brancusi's art endures: it doesn't look dated at all, it can
easily hold its own when set beside contemporary sculpture, it looks as if it
were created yesterday. And it's very much apart from academy sculpture,
or the 19th century sculpture that preceded it.

Constantin Brancusi's sculpture is diametrically opposed, aesthetically,
to Auguste Rodin's, and it's quite different from the art of Naum Gabo,
Pablo Picasso or other contemporaries. Brancusi's art has some affinities
with Henri Gaudier-Brzeska – it is interesting to compare Gaudier-Brzeska's
heavy, gaunt *Standing Birds* (1914, New York) with Brancusi's slim *Birds in
Space* series (for example, *Yellow Bird*, 1923-24, yellow marble,
Philadelphia). Jean Arp's abstract, semi-organic sculpture also has affinities

with Brancusi's, as does some of the Constructivists' art. But Brancusi exists in a space all of his own in modern art – a space he carved out for himself with his sculptures and his aesthetic principles.

'Le Douanier' Henri Rousseau told Brancusi that he had 'made the ancients modern'. Edward Lucie-Smith glossed this view thus: '[n]o more perceptive remark has ever been made about Brancusi's work' (1986, 103). It's as if Brancusi took the whole history of sculpture and distilled it and reconfigured it. An alchemical transformation of old, traditional forms into something recognizably from the history of sculpture, but also indisputably 'new'. At once old and new, highly individual yet also miraculously universal.

The impact of Constantin Brancusi's sculpture stems partly from his praeternatural talent for developing forms, for reducing organic shapes to their 'essence'. Brancusi's sculptures are absolutely compelling in their form, shape, texture, colour, light, presentation and feel. Brancusi developed all of the erotic formal aspects of sculpture to their extreme. He reduced (or simplified) organic, natural forms to what he called their 'essences' or 'spirits'. Yet he maintained that his sculpture was not abstract. Wassily Kandinsky, the Russian abstract painter, said that abstraction = realism,[2] that abstraction was not separated from the natural world or reality, but was absolutely 'real', as 'real' (and valuable) as figuration. This is true of Brancusi's art. Brancusi vigorously stressed the *realism* of his works, defending his sculptures against critics who saw them as detached from the real world:

> They are imbeciles who call my work abstract; that which they call abstract is the most realist, because what is real is not the exterior form but the idea, the essence of things.[3]

A realistic copy of a horse in bronze or marble wasn't true creation, Brancusi claimed; there is more to a horse than that. It was the alivenes of the horse, its spirit.4 It is a quest for things, for things-in-themselves, as Existential philosophers such as Jean-Paul Sartre and Martin Heidegger put it, the 'thingness' (*dasein*) of German poet Rainer Maria Rilke, or the 'thereness' of Zen Buddhism.

The 'things' of Brancusi's art are organic forms, not abstract ideas or obscure conceptualizations. In fact, Brancusi's aesthetic aim is the *opposite* of mystification, or being deliberately (or self-consciously) difficult or clever or fussy. It is, rather, a gesture towards clarification, towards ensuring the forms were as clear as possible, as direct, as uncluttered by extraneous material. As Henry Moore wrote (he could be describing Brancusi): a 'sculptor is a person obsessed with the form and shape of things... the shape of anything and everything.'5 Critic Robert Hughes remarked in *The Shock of the New* that 'Brancusi's love of solidity lent itself to feelings of repose, dream, and self-absorption' (1991, 310).

Though Constantin Brancusi denied the urge towards abstraction, he did found his sculpture on the abstractions of Platonism. It was Plato's ideal philosophy that influenced much of Brancusi's sculpture (like Piet Mondrian and Wassily Kandinsky, Brancusi was a Theosophist). Plato's notion of Ideal Forms and essences excited Brancusi. Reducing his art further and further, Brancusi aimed to get as close as possible to the 'essence of the thing'. It is a process of Neoplatonic purification, as Dorothy Adlow noted when she visited the sculptor's studio in 1925:

> Brancusi has purified his sculpture of every attracting feature. He has swept out of his plan every motive that might distract him or the observer from what he considers the central idea... He has tried to make of his sculpture a working philosophy. He calls it the philosophy of Plato. (37f)

For Plato, forms (or ideas) can exist in an ideal state, but forms in the world can only approximate to or be shadows or traces of the ideal forms or ideas. (The notion that some ideal form or idea can exist at all is part of Plato's utopian project). The artist is thus always aiming to reproduce an ideal, but that always remains unattainable (which's the fundamental desire at the heart of Western philosophy and religion). It has to remain unattainable, it can never be achieved. Because desire is the foundation (and in sculpture, desire is eroticized, because sculpture is an art of forms).

As Elizabeth Grosz put it, summarizing the Lacanian psychoanalytic system: desire produces more desire. The problem is a religious, philosophical one, as well as an aesthetic, formal one (but the two are really the same: aesthetics and religion, formalism and philosophy). The challenge was one, to put it bluntly, of making spirit into flesh, of making something transcendent immanent. So Brancusi was destined to aim for ideal forms but they could never be achieved. However, part of Brancusi's achievement is that he got closer than most artists. Describing Brancusi's sculptures, Robert Hughes wrote:

> All is made clear, on the surface, in a display of perfection whose calm sign is the Apollonian reflection of light. There is no such thing as a "tragic" Brancusi; all suggestions of struggle, defeat, or even moral tension are abolished by the clarity of form and skin. (1991, 308)

There is a parallel to this radical purification and reductionism of sculpture in modern poets and novelists. French writers, such as Stendhal, Gustave Flaubert and André Gide spoke of wanting to clear away all the garbage that gets in the way of purity of expression. For instance, Samuel Beckett (an adopted Frenchman, one could say), steadily pared away his language, moving from the relatively conventional literary forms of books such as *Mercier and Camier* in the 1930s through the reduced vocabulary and syntax of *The Unnamable Trilogy* in the 1940s to the severely reduced poesie of the *Company* trilogy and *Still* in the 1970s and 1980s.

Beckett found that he could say quite a lot with minimal means (but it can take a lot of experimentation, a journey which includes mistakes and failures, to reach that kind of artistic maturity. Only a few artists, such as Arthur Rimbaud, get there when they're very young). For some artists, nothing must get in the way of the expression of the idea or emotion. As Dorothy Adlow wrote:

> It is the *idea* that should be related, that is all. Everything else is superfluous... Brancusi is not satisfied with the things of the moment, he looks out for what is true of all time.

British sculptor Henry Moore (probably the major sculptor of the 20th century in Albion), who admired Brancusi, like so many other major modern artists (Amedeo Modigliani, Frank Stella, Donald Judd, Carl Andre and Barbara Hepworth), wrote of Brancusi's search for pure, organic form:

> Since the Gothic, European sculpture has become overgrown with moss, weeds – all sorts of surface excrescences which completely concealed shape. It has been Brancusi's special mission to get rid of this overgrowth, and to make us once more shape-conscious. To do this he has had to concentrate on very simple direct shapes, to keep his sculpture, as it were, one-cylindered, to refine and polish a single shape to a degree almost too precious. Brancusi's work, apart from its individual value, has been of historical importance in the development of contemporary sculpture. (1937, 449)

Simplicity, as Brancusi and many artists have said, was the key: but it is a mystical simplicity, that arises out of the sculptor's materials: '[s]implicitly is not an objective in art, but one achieves simplicity despite oneself by entering into the real sense of things' (1925). (Of course, it's easy for Brancusi to say that – as he just happens to be an artistic genius. For other artists, simplicity is *very* difficult to achieve satisfactorily).

For Mircea Eliade, the historian of religions who was a fellow Romanian, and often wrote of Constantin Brancusi, the sculptor's talent was one of 'interiorization', a mythic descent simultaneously into himself, into his personal and national past, and into mythic forms. Eliade wrote in an important essay on Brancusi (and one of the best accounts of the sculptor):

Brancusi's encounters with the creations of the Parisian avant-garde and those of the archaic world (Africa) triggered a process of "interiorization," a journey back toward a world that was both secret and unforgettable because it was simultaneously that of childhood and that of the imagination... he set himself to "interiorizing," as it were, his own vital experience. So that he succeeded in rediscovering the "presence-in-the-world" specific to archaic man... thanks to the process of "interiorization"... and the anamnesis that followed it, Brancusi succeeded in "seeing the world" in the same way as the creators of prehistoric, ethnic, or folk-art masterpieces. He rediscovered, in a way, the presence-in-the-world that enabled those anonymous artists to create their own plastic universe within a space that had nothing whatever to do with, for example, the space of classical Greek art.[6]

The end-point of Constantin Brancusi's quest for the 'essence of things' was what one could term a mystical sculpture. Although Brancusi declined to talk in religious terms of his art, it is distinctly mystical. Some of Brancusi's statements admit to a mystical solidarity with materials and sculptures:

I am no longer of this world. I am far from myself, I am no longer a part of my own person. I am within the essence of things themselves.[7]

The quote is one of Brancusi's instantly memorable phrases (I used it as the sub-title of this book back in 1993, so I was a bit miffed when it was stolen by some writers for a 2004 book on Brancusi).

The German poet Rainer Maria Rilke (who worked in the early 1900s with Auguste Rodin, widely regarded as the 'father' of 20th century sculpture), wrote illuminatingly in his poetry of surfaces and essences. Of the transformation of his art in his *Neue Gedichte* (*New Poems*), which was a breakthrough for the poet, Rilke wrote that 'it had to arrive at the essence.'[8] And in a fragment of his greatest work, the groups of poems entitled *Duino Elegies* (1922), Rilke wrote of 'the *infinite thereness* of statues',[9] a concept that many artists, from Michelangelo Buonaroti to Brancusi, or philosophers from Plotinus to Friedrich Nietzsche, would agree with.

'Infinite thereness' describes an aspect of sculpture that was emerging in the early 20th century, in the art of Brancusi, Rodin, Arp and Gaudier-Brzeska (but it was also Rilke's way of trying to get at the presence of an object and rendering it in poetic language).

Rainer Maria Rilke's notion of 'Kunst-Ding' or 'innerness' or 'thingness' (also called *innigkeit*), has much in common with Constantin Brancusi's idea of 'the essence of things'. The poet's task, Rilke said, was to capture the 'thingness' of an object, without ornamentation or rhetoric, rather in the manner that Paul Cézanne did with his still life paintings (one shouldn't forget that Cézanne was a huge influence in modern art in the first quarter of the 20th century, even more than Edouard Manet, or Paul Gauguin, or the then not so well-known Vincent van Gogh. Cézanne's approach to rendering objects in paint is an important comparison to make with Brancusi's sculpture. D.H. Lawrence wrote perceptively of the way Cézanne painted apples that also throws light on the new approaches to form that were emerging in the early 1900s. For Lawrence, Cézanne gave us the actual essence of an apple (1950, 339-240). Cezanne captures the 'mysterious shiftiness of the scene', Lawrence reckoned (ib, 342).)

Constantin Brancusi's aim is also that of Rainer Maria Rilke; the poet wrote:

> When I attempt to visualize my task, it becomes clear to me that it is not people about whom I have to speak, but things. Things. When I say the word (do you hear?) there is a silence; the silence which surrounds things. All movement subsides and becomes contour. And out of past and future time something permanent is formed: space, the great calm of objects which knows no urge.[10]

Rilke's spatial mysticism is a poetic, lingual equivalent of Brancusi's sense of a spatial, Platonic essence. For Rilke, expressing a sense of space meant the poem could expand the Within outwards, towards what Rilke termed the 'Open' (a kind of void that surrounds all things. As Rilke put it, death was one of the ways in which the 'Open' could be apprehended).

Constantin Brancusi too spoke of mystical openness, though he called it 'infinity' (so did Rilke on occasion). Brancusi's *Endless Column* series of sculptures explored a Rilkean 'openness'. Like a sculptor, Rilke spoke of a sense of space being deep and alive, and in the poet's 'song' (the poem) setting alive space, like, Rilke said, fruit filling your mouth, where the song, and breathing, is equated, in Orphic fashion, with life itself ('if one could create as one breathes. That would be true happiness. One should arrive at that', Brancusi said).[11] Modern and contemporary sculpture has been as concerned with the space around the sculpture or the space in which the sculpture is displayed, as the sculpture itself.

In poems such as 'The Panther', 'Archaic Torso of Apollo' and 'Blue Hydrangeas', Rainer Maria Rilke tried to present things (objects) as they really were. This extract from 'The Bowl of Roses' demonstrates Rilke's poetic goals:

> Living in silence, endless opening out,
> space being used, but without space being taken
> from that space which the things around diminish;
> absence of outline, like untinted groundwork
> and mere Within; so much so strangely tender
> and self-illumined – to the very verge: –
> where do we know anything like this?[12]

One of the great poems about sculpture is the famous sonnet 'Archaic Torso of Apollo' by Rilke, where the statue comes alive (though not in the manner of Pygmalion and his statue, or Hermione at the end of William Shakespeare's *The Winter's Tale*, where Leontes takes the reborn Hermione's hand and gasps 'o, she's warm! | If this be magic, let it be an art | Lawful as eating').

Rainer Maria Rilke's quest for mystical innerness and Constantin Brancusi's goal of mythic interiorization have affinities with philosopher Martin Heidegger's notion of Being and presence, with James Joyce's idea of the aesthetic 'epiphany' of authentic art, with Lawrence Durrell's poetic concept of the heraldic 'sigil' or signature of a thing, and with the *sammadassana* of Zen Buddhism. D.T. Suzuki, one of the chief commentators on Zen Buddhism in recent times, wrote:

> Seeing is experiencing, seeing things in their states of suchness (*tathata*) or is-ness. Buddha's whole philosophy comes from this "seeing", this experiencing.[13]

Constantin Brancusi spoke of a similar mystical 'seeing', where the viewer of his sculptures sees not simply beautiful surfaces, but essences. He wrote:

> What is real is not the external form, but the essence of things. Starting from this truth it is impossible for anyone to express anything luscious and real by imitating its exterior surface.[114]

(This is the opposite of film director Jean-Luc Godard, who remarked once: how do you get inside? By staying resolutely outside).

Brancusi starts with the essence, and ends up with those severely reduced but open forms – the birds, heads, fish, eggs, lovers and columns. Searching for the essence, Brancusi nevertheless bases his art on natural forms, on elemental forms (the world – or the experience of being-in-the-world – is always the initial inspiration. One has to start somewhere, and Brancusi usually took natural forms as his starting-point).

Constantin Brancusi was a devotee of the materiality of sculpture (he always made objects, not ideas, as later Conceptual artists did). The material that makes the sculpture itself helps the artist in the quest for the essence of things. The final form of the sculpture was, Brancusi believed, somehow buried in the material, whether it is stone, marble, wood or bronze (again, the notion of an ideal Platonic essence recurs – that there is some animistic 'Something' buried in the material). That idea is still around today, and is still applied to the great sculptors in history, such as Antonio Canova or Michelangelo Buonaroti or Gianlorenzo Bernini.

Constantin Brancusi had a *participation mystique* (to use Mircea Eliade's term) with his artistic materials, much as archaic or prehistoric societies had a *participation mystique* with nature and the earth. Each material had its own feel, tensions, problems (and cost). Somehow, the material 'renders up' the final form. 'Each material has its own life,' Brancusi wrote (in D. Dudley, 124). The 'essence' must be brought out by the artist, as Brancusi said:

> The natural element in sculpture means allegorical thinking, symbol, sacredness or the search for essences hidden in the material and not the photographic reproduction of external appearances.[15]

Brancusi's sculptures bear out how successful he was in pursuing the Holy Grail of Platonic purity and mystical essence. His career was one long quest for the essence of form. 'Everything I do is a seeking after form', he said in 1949.[16]

Constantin Brancusi celebrated the *touch of* sculpture (he produced sculptures for blind people to touch. How wonderful). A sculpture, Brancusi asserted, must be 'lovely to touch, friendly to live with'. It must be part of the celebration of being alive. 'What is so glorious as the privilege that man enjoys of being alive, and being able to see and discover the beauty all around him?' Brancusi remarked. [17]

Constantin Brancusi's works seem to be so *right,* so spot on in their depiction of their subject. Those sculptures based on fishes, birds, heads, cocks and seals capture the 'essence' of their subject so lyrically, so (apparently) effortlessly. For example, *The Cock* (1935, polished bronze, Brancusi Studio, Paris), or *Golden Bird* (1919, polished bronze, Arts Club of Chicago), or *The Seal* (1943, blue-grey marble, Paris), or *Head of a Woman* (1910-c. 1925, white marble, private collection).

Constantin Brancusi wanted to keep all his sculptures in his studio. The studio, Brancusi said, must become a museum, with his work exhibited as he wished. Brancusi lovingly photographed his sculptures, again and again, sometimes varying the lighting and arrangements.

British artist Barbara Hepworth, one of many sculptors who found Brancusi an inspiration, wrote of her 1932 visit to Brancusi's Paris studio:

> In Brancusi's studio I encountered the miraculous feeling of eternity mixed with beloved stone and stone dust... The simplicity and dignity of the artist; the inspiration of the dedicated workshop with great millstones used as bases for classical forms; inches of accumulated dust and chips on the floor; the whole great studio filled with soaring forms and still, quiet forms, all in a state of perfection in purpose and loving execution, whether they were in marble, brass or wood – all this filled me with a sense of humility hitherto unknown to me. (1952)

Brancusi's studio is one of the most celebrated of modern artists' studios (others would include Gustave Moreau's completely remarkable house in Paris – if you haven't been, you **must** go, the Musée Rodin in Paris, and Barbara Hepworth's beautiful home and studio in St Ives, Cornwall). Brancusi used his Montparnasse studio from 1928 to 1957. He bequeathed its contents to the French nation, asking that a reconstruction be made: the studio itself was regarded as a work of art. It has been recreated in a special building next to the Pompidou Centre in Paris: this is one of the global centres of Brancusi's art.

Sidney Geist wrote:

> It made an impression which, as many writers have attested, was over-whelming, with its white walls and the light falling on precious objects gleaming among rough blocks of wood and stone. It seemed at once a temple and laboratory of art, the site of a confrontation of man-made order and natural chaos. (1968, 167-8)

Another impression is of hard work. Brancusi was a sculptor, like Michelangelo, who enjoyed the physical labour of making sculpture

(Michelangelo, according to Giorgio Vasari, told visitors that he continued to carve in his old age partly because it kept him healthy). In his early life in Paris, Brancusi put up encouragements in red letters around his studio:

'don't be afraid, you'll make it!',

'don't be discouraged',

'create like a God, order like a King, work like a Slave!'

2 / Fish

Constantin Brancusi's sculptures of fish (usually entitled *Fish*), in marble or bronze, are mesmeric objects, with their sleek bodies. They are supremely erotic sculptures, not least because of their connection with animals that swim in the sea (the fecund ocean being, quite literally, the womb of life on this particular planet). Brancusi in his *Fish* sculptures aimed to capture what it was that was special about fish. He said:

> When you see a fish, you do not think of its scales, do you? You think of its speed, its floating, flashing body seen through water... I've tried to express just that... I want just the flash of its spirit.[1]

The *Fish* sculptures of Brancusi, such as *Fish* (1932, white marble, 5.3 x 16.8 x 1.1 inches, base, a mirror, diameter 17 in, on oak, 24 in high, Philadelphia), or *Fish* (1924, polished bronze, Museum of Fine Arts, Boston), are often set on mirrors, perhaps to hint at water, the alien realm in which they swim. The circular mirrors, like all circular forms in Brancusi's art, hint at cosmological levels of interpretation, representing the Great Round of existence, the cycles of life, the cosmos itself, and those spherical forms from which all life comes: the circular ocean, pools, cells, wombs, seeds, hearts, planets, stars.

The 1926 *Fish* (polish bronze, private collection) is placed upon an elaborate base. The importance of the base upon which sculpture rests is crucial for Brancusi. His bases are very distinctive, setting him instantly apart from all other sculptors. The Brancusi base is – and is not – part of the sculpture. British sculptor William Tucker described the Brancusi base:

> The base is at once physical, in terms of support; visual, in terms of presenting the object at proper level; and symbolic, in terms of the objects' relation with the world. The bases are not works of art, but are as worthy consideration as many works of art in view of the way they perform an exact ancillary function. Most of Brancusi's sculpture is modest in size, physically unobtrusive. Yet its presence is enormous even from a considerable distance, and where surrounded by the work of other artists. The Brancusi is marked off by its carved and constructed base as being not only different from other things in general, but as being different from all other sculpture, *a completely new order of object.* (57)

Tucker is absolutely right here, noting how Brancusi's forms leap out at the spectator, how they make their presence felt immediately when surrounded by all manner of other works (look at the way that Brancusi's sculptures work in a museum setting). Brancusi's pedestals have become one of the chief inspirations for subsequent sculptors. Many artists have commented on the significance that Brancusi's supports have had for them, as well as the sculptures themselves. The pedestals were made for each individual sculpture. Although they might have appeared similar, they were crafted to match particular pieces.

Constantin Brancusi's art is, as William Tucker remarked, 'the antithesis of Rodin's – private, silent, withdrawn, morally neutral' (131). Despite being 'private, silent, withdrawn, morally neutral', Brancusi's sculptures have immense authority and presence. As Tucker argued, it is precisely this intimacy ('interiority', as Mircea Eliade called it) that makes Brancusi's works so powerful (131-2).

3 / Gender

There are inherent paradoxes in Constantin Brancusi's aesthetics. For example, philosophic Platonism emphasizes the 'idea' or 'essence'. Yet these 'essences' or 'ideas' must be manifested in flesh-and-blood bodies and organic forms. Platonism could not reconcile these two things – spirit and flesh – successfully, and neither could Christianity (and still can't, even after two thousand years of hacking away at the problem).

For, while Constantin Brancusi emphasizes 'essence', what you see in his sculptures are highly polished, highly worked surfaces, an emphasis on beautiful surfaces, on smoothness and sleekness. Robert Hughes wrote that no modern sculptor 'had a more rapturous feeling for surfaces than Brancusi' (1991, 308). Absolutely.

Brancusi's sculptures, like those of the American Minimal artists Donald Judd, Sol LeWitt or Carl Andre, are smooth and slick. Roughness, where it appears, as in the stone bases and pedestals, is similarly worked and carved, integrated stylishly into the design. Even as they exalt idealism and essence, then, Brancusi's sculptures are caught up in all kinds of problems to do with expression, manifestation, formalism, material and intention.

There is, for instance, an intrinsic sexism in Brancusi's treatment of male and female types, masculine and feminine forms. His *Torso of a Young Woman III* (1925, onyx, Paris) is, typically, a softly rounded volume, like a vase, recalling the eternal and mythical association of women with vessels, of women as something to be filled, or as containers (nurturers) of life. Brancusi's *Torso of a Young Woman* is supremely stereotypical and sexist, from a (second wave) feminist viewpoint.

The male *Torso of a Young Man* (after 1924, bronze, Cleveland Museum of Art), on the other hand, is, as you might expect, phallically upright. Indeed, it looks like a phallus. Interestingly, however, Brancusi claimed that '[n]ude men in sculpture are not as beautiful as toads'.[1] Maybe. But the entire corpus of ancient Greek sculpture, not to mention al of the Italian Renaissance up to the crowning achievement of Michelangelo Buonaroti, would counter that odd statement.

Further sexism occurs in Mr Brancusi's *Adam and Eve* (1916-21, chestnut and oak, 89 in high, base of limestone, 5.2 in, Guggenheim Museum, New York), where people are reduced to genitals, once again. So Eve is a mouth and vagina, and Adam is a phallus and testicles. Brancusi described *Adam and Eve* thus:

> Eve is above, Adam is below. Eve's part is to continue life. She is charming and innocent. She is fertility, a bud opening, a flower germinating. Adam below tills the earth, he toils and sweats.[2]

The problem is reducing cultures of people to 'essences', which can lead to right-wing philosophies. Second wave and third wave feminists have been highly critical of 'essentialist' or 'biologist' philosophies, those ideologies which are based on or in the body. Brancusi's aesthetics are very much of his time, of course, but essentialism and biologism have been taken apart from feminists and cultural critics, who see in them a reductionist, essentializing ideology.

Constantin Brancusi's sculptures of women turn out to be as sexist as any portraits of depictions of the female body in the history of art – by artists such as Henri Matisse, Peter Paul Rubens, Jean-Auguste-Dominique Ingres, or Pablo Picasso. Brancusi's *Madame Pogany (Madame Pogany III*, 1939, white marble) and *Princess X* (1916, polished bronze, both Philadelphia) are the usual rounded, 'feminine' forms, while works such as *The White Negress* (1923, white marble, Philadelphia) and *Blond Negress* (1933, polished bronze, 15.8 in high, base of marble and limestone and two wood sections, 55.5 in high, New York), can be seen as racist (in these works, Brancusi is dealing with feminine and ethnic issues).

4 / Phallus

When Constantin Brancusi exhibited the curved bronze *Princess X* in 1920, Pablo Picasso – or was it Henri Matisse – said 'Voici, le phallus!' Indeed, *Princess X* does look phallic, and it is featured on the cover of a survey of 'erotic' art.[1] But the art object, sculpted, painted or otherwise, is for psychoanalytic theorists a kind of displaced phallus, a fetish object turned into high culture. The art object is a thing made to provide pleasure. Most of sculpture is designed and crafted as a *beautiful* object, to use that key word – *beauty* – of Platonic philosophy. Sculptures embody 'The Beautiful'... they *are* 'The Beautiful'. Sculptures are beauty concretized, eroticism made into bronze, marble and stone.

Constantin Brancusi was involved in some scandals. One concerned his sculpture *Princess X*, which some thought was phallic; the police were called to remove the work from the Salon des Indépendants show. Two admirers, Fernand Léger and Blaise Cendrars, took it back to the exhibition. 'My statue is of Woman, all women rolled into one, Goethe's Eternal Feminine reduced to its essence.' Thus Brancusi defended his sculpture *Princess X*.[2]

Another scandal concerned Constantin Brancusi's sculpture *Bird in Space*: when Brancusi arrived in the U.S.A. for a show at the Brummer

Gallery, the Customs Office wouldn't let the sculpture into the country. After Brancusi had to pay duty in order to release the sculpture, he sued the Customs Office and won.

The history of sculpture is the history of anal/ oral/ genital touches of pleasure, self-reflexive gestures where artists touch objects physically and, later, viewers drink them up visually, forbidden by the ropes of museums and guards to touch the sculpture itself (Brancusi provided a *Sculpture For the Blind* in 1917 which was encased in a bag, with sleeves so the viewer could touch the piece). The sculpted object is indeed the erotic object *par excellence* in art. It is the phallus endlessly caressed by the eyes, in Lacanian, scopic, scopophillic, voyeuristic pleasure. As Julia Kristeva says, 'isn't art the fetish *par excellence*, one that badly camouflages its archeology?'[3]

Maybe Constantin Brancusi's art is so successful, and so popular among art lovers, because it actualizes or embodies those barely repressed erotic desires? Maybe Brancusi's sculptures are the three-dimensional equivalents of erotic forms that go back to archaic forms, pre-œdipal forms which evoke the maternal *chora* (Julia Kristeva's term for the archaic maternal realm). They are like womb-spaces, eruptions into this world of primæval forms that speak to archaic desires. Beyond or before language, prior to the symbolic order, forms or fetishes that hint at the primal oneness experienced in the womb.

5 / Egg

Constantin Brancusi produced a number of sculptures that are pure phalluses or fetishes, seen from one, religious viewpoint. In Hindu culture, there is a holy object called Savayambhu, meaning the 'self-originated', a phallic emblem of cosmic energy. They are egg-shaped stones which are worshipped in Indian religion. They are the cosmic phallus, the *lingam*, and are associated with the World Egg or Cosmic Egg.[1] The Eggs of Brahman or Savayambhu *lingams* are phallic energy associated with elemental religious forces solidified into stone. Typically seven inches long, these Hindu phallic stones are very much like the human penis. Indeed, as Philip Rawsom noted, the cosmic egg-stones have 'surface-divisions' that imitate those 'on the actual male penis'.[2]

Constantin Brancusi's own 'cosmic 'eggs are given a clearly mytho-religious dimension, apparent not only in their supremely beautiful and sensual forms, but also in their titles: *Beginning of the World* (c. 1920, marble, polished metal disc, Dallas Museum of Art), *The First Cry* (1917, polished bronze, Art Gallery of Ontario) and *The Newborn* (1915, white marble, Philadelphia).

Sculptures such as *The First Cry* and *The Newborn* connect human birth with the birth of the cosmos, in a mythic, sensual volume. For the egg shape is obvious, as, like *The Kiss*, it looks towards a fundamental sense of life, where life begins, in the biology of cells and eggs. Indeed, Brancusi painted a version of his *The Kiss* on a real egg (date unknown, paint on an egg, the Lydia & Harry L. Winston Collection). The lovers embracing on the egg pulls together any number of erotic and cosmic dimensions, from the egg-shape of genitals (womb, clitoris, testes, glans) to the Platonic two-in-oneness symbolized by two yokes in one egg, to the womb of the universe, the cells at the heart of organic life.

Constantin Brancusi's phallic stones also recall wombs, pregnant bellies and other 'feminine' forms. Somehow, a softly curved stone seems an apposite embodiment of 'the beginning of the world'. Stones are of course highly prized in some cultures, having all sorts of associations. Children also like to collect stones, and there is always a child-like component in Brancusi's art. 'When we are no longer children, we are already dead', he said.[3]

6 / Birds

Constantin Brancusi's most famous sculpture is probably the *Birds in Space* series. It is described by Peter Selz in *Art in Our Times*:

> Much like certain mechanical objects, Brancusi's *Bird in Space* is polished to a mirrorlike smoothness. The high polish, although applied painstakingly by the artist, actually denies any handcrafted quality to this sculpture. In fact, this work was the object of lengthy litigation with U.S. customs officials, who, perceiving similarities to airplane propellers, claimed that it was a manufactured object rather than art. (272)

The many – 28 or so – *Birds in Space* sculptures are the manifestations of an artistic, spiritual quest for the essence of flight. Various *Birds in Space* include *Bird in Space* (1941, polished bronze, Paris), *Bird in Space* (1925, white marble, National Gallery of Art, Washington, DC), and *Bird in Space* (1931-36, black marble, Australian National Gallery, Canberra).

'All my life I've been looking for one thing, the essence of flight... What a marvellous thing flight is', Brancusi commented.[1] Each *Bird in Space* is a slender, upright form, a mythic striving for the sky, for ascension, for space. Ionel Jianou said that the sculptor has succeeded in

> transforming his amorphous material into an ellipse with translucent surface, of a purity so dazzling that it irradiates the light around it and embodies, in its irresistible upward impulse, the very essence of flight. (1963)

Constantin Brancusi's success of embodying the essence of flight in sculpture is all the more startling, Mircea Eliade said, because he used 'the very archetype of *heaviness,* that ultimate form of "matter" – stone' (1984, 201). The *Birds in Space* are shamanic sculptures, echoing so clearly the spiritual flight of the shaman, which is the central act of shamanism. The shaman travels to other worlds by drumming her/ himself up into a magical, ecstatic state, and by climbing up the 'World Tree', which is the *axis mundi.*[2] The Cosmic Tree or Column or mountain is the connection between the three realms of Heaven, Earth and Hell. Brancusi's *Birds in Space* are shamanic emblems of transcendence, the yearning for a 'magical flight' to other worlds, other states, other modes of being. They are sculptures of ecstasy, formed from the ecstasy of the shaman who rises up, spiritually, into the sky.

Archaic shamans dress in feathers, like birds, to emulate and take on the magic of birds, while souls are everywhere in religion associated with birds, and the soul was thought of as covered in feathers. As Mircea Eliade explained in his classic book on shamanism: *Shamanism: Archaic Techniques of Ecstasy:*

> Birds are psychopomps. Becoming a bird oneself or being accompanied by a bird indicates the capacity, while still alive, to undertake the ecstatic journey to the sky and the beyond. (1972, 98)

Constantin Brancusi's *Birds in Space* sculptures dispense with feathers and wings and tails and beaks and eyes and heads, and, typically for Brancusi, go for the essence of flight, symbolized and actualized by that slender, curving shape. The *Birds in Space* sculptures are a stretching-up to the infinite. Brancusi spoke of a desire to extend the surfaces of his sculptures to infinity:

> In bad form... the surfaces and planes all come to an end. They finished them-

selves within the mass. I think the true form ought to suggest infinity. The surfaces ought to look as though they went on forever, as though they proceeded out from the mass into some perfect and complete existence.3

The *Birds in Space* aim to be infinity-reaching sculpture, works that arch out into the 'open', into the 'beyond'. Mircea Eliade wrote of the *Birds In Space*:

> ...it is not the ascension to heaven of the archaic and primitive cosmologies that obsesses Brancusi but the sensation of flight out into infinite space. He calls his column "endless" not only because such a column could never reach a structural conclusion but above all because it hurls itself out into space that must always remain without limits, since it is based on the ecstatic experience of absolute freedom. It is the same in which his *Birds* fly. Brancusi has discarded everything from the old symbolism of the sky pillar except its central element: ascension as a transcendence of the human condition. But he successfully revealed to his contemporaries that what concerned him was an ecstatic ascension stripped of all mysticism. (1984, 199)

Illustrations

On the following pages, images of Constantin Brancusi's art, including self-portraits by the artist.

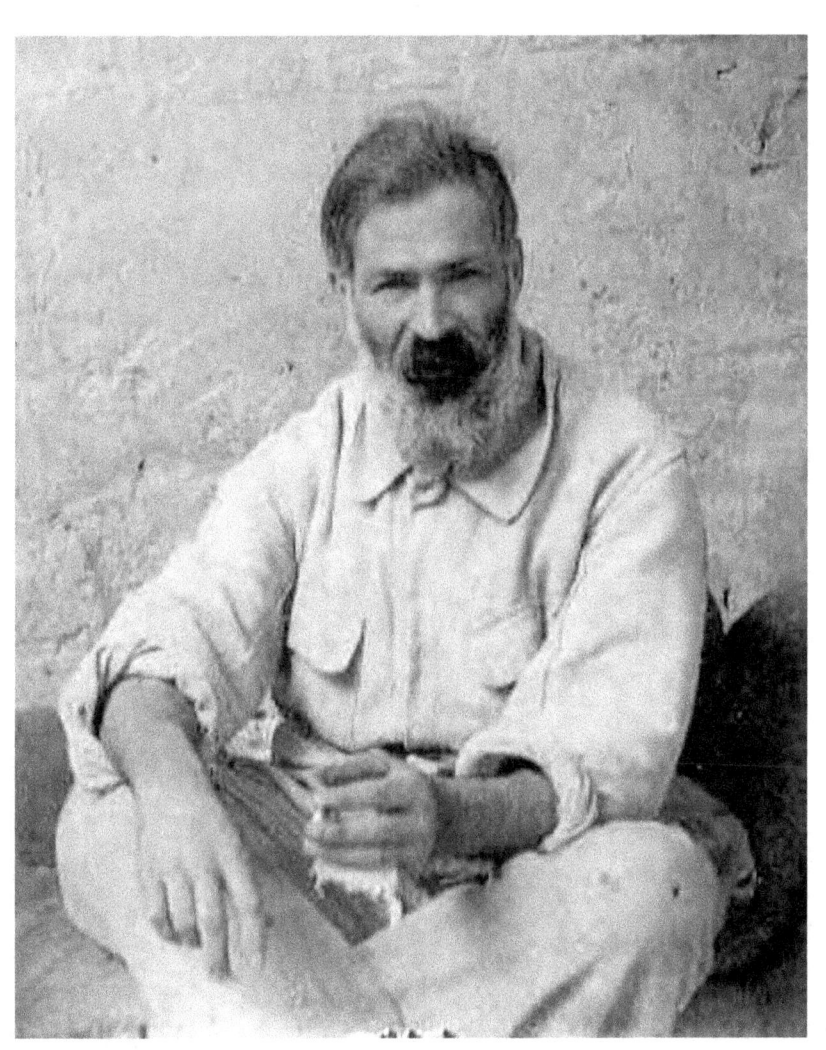

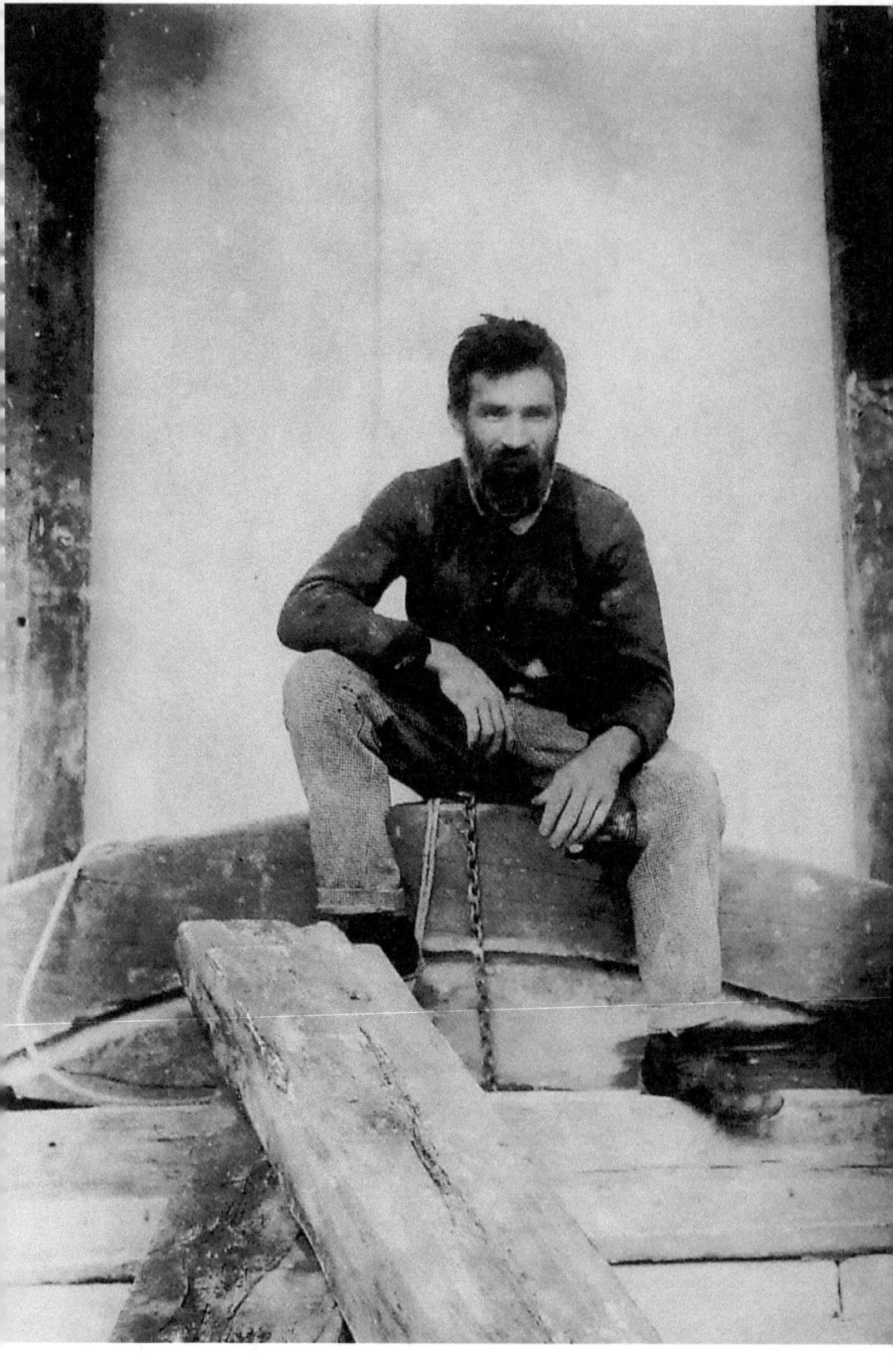

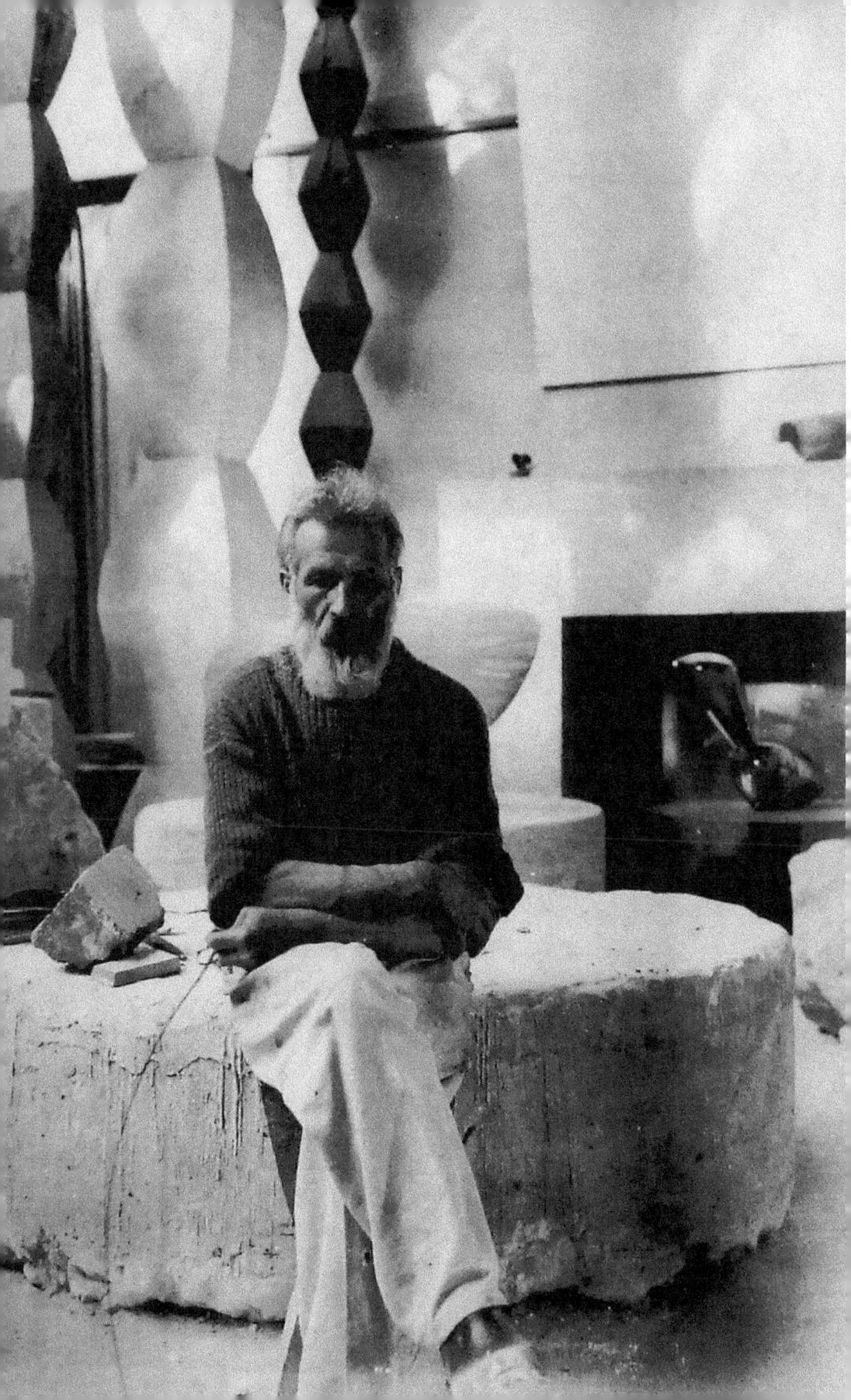

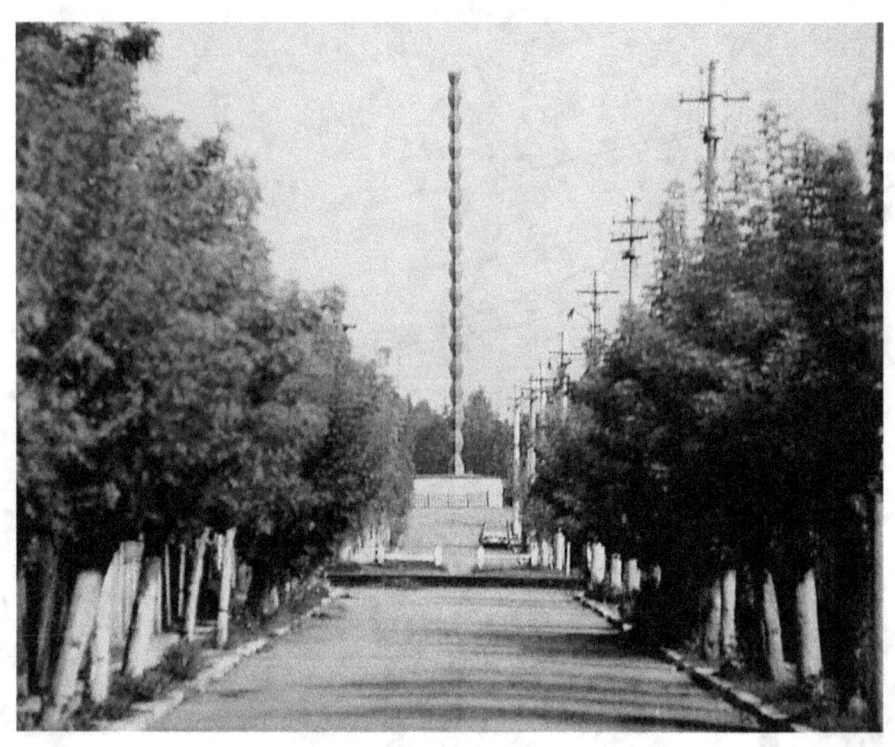

Constantin Brancusi, Endless Column

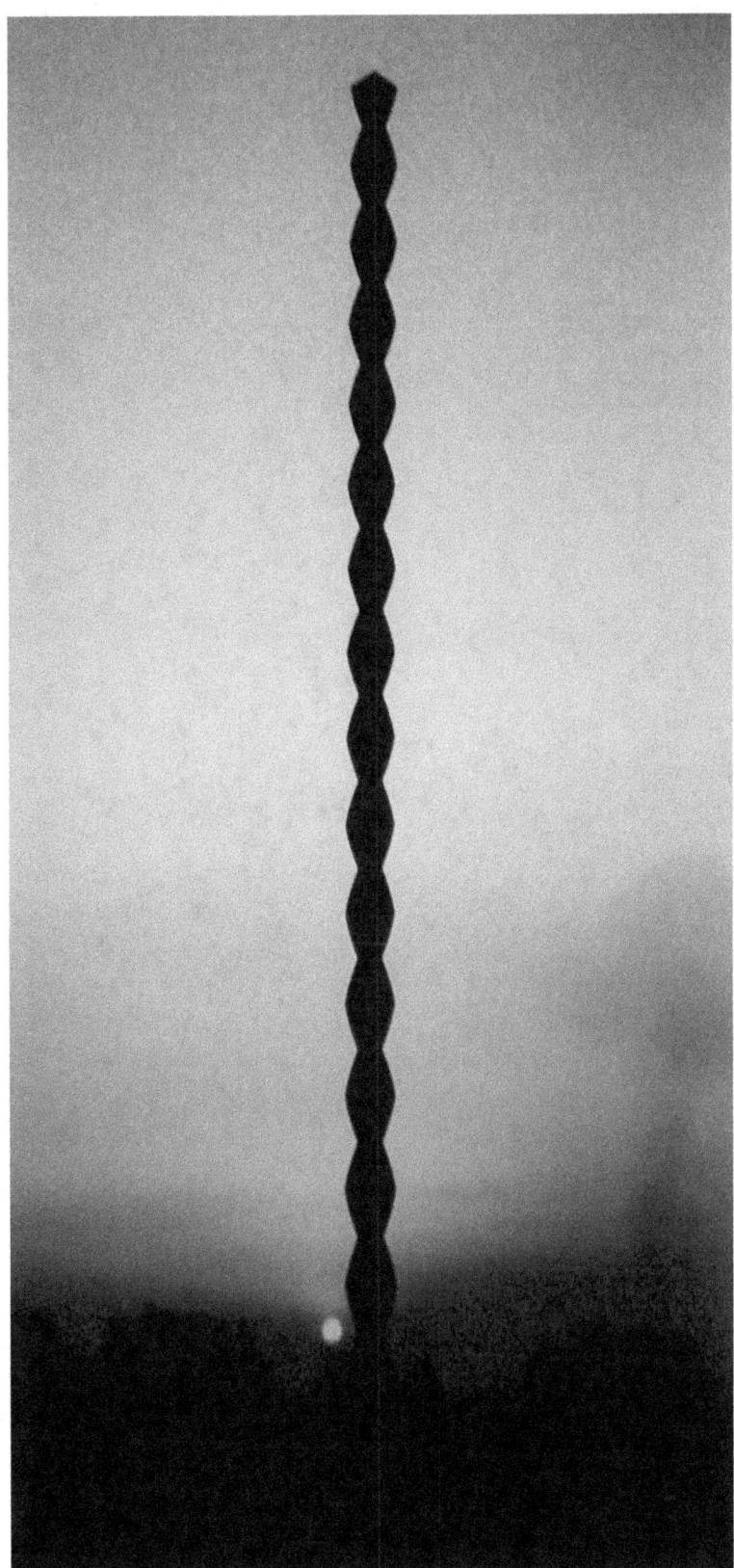

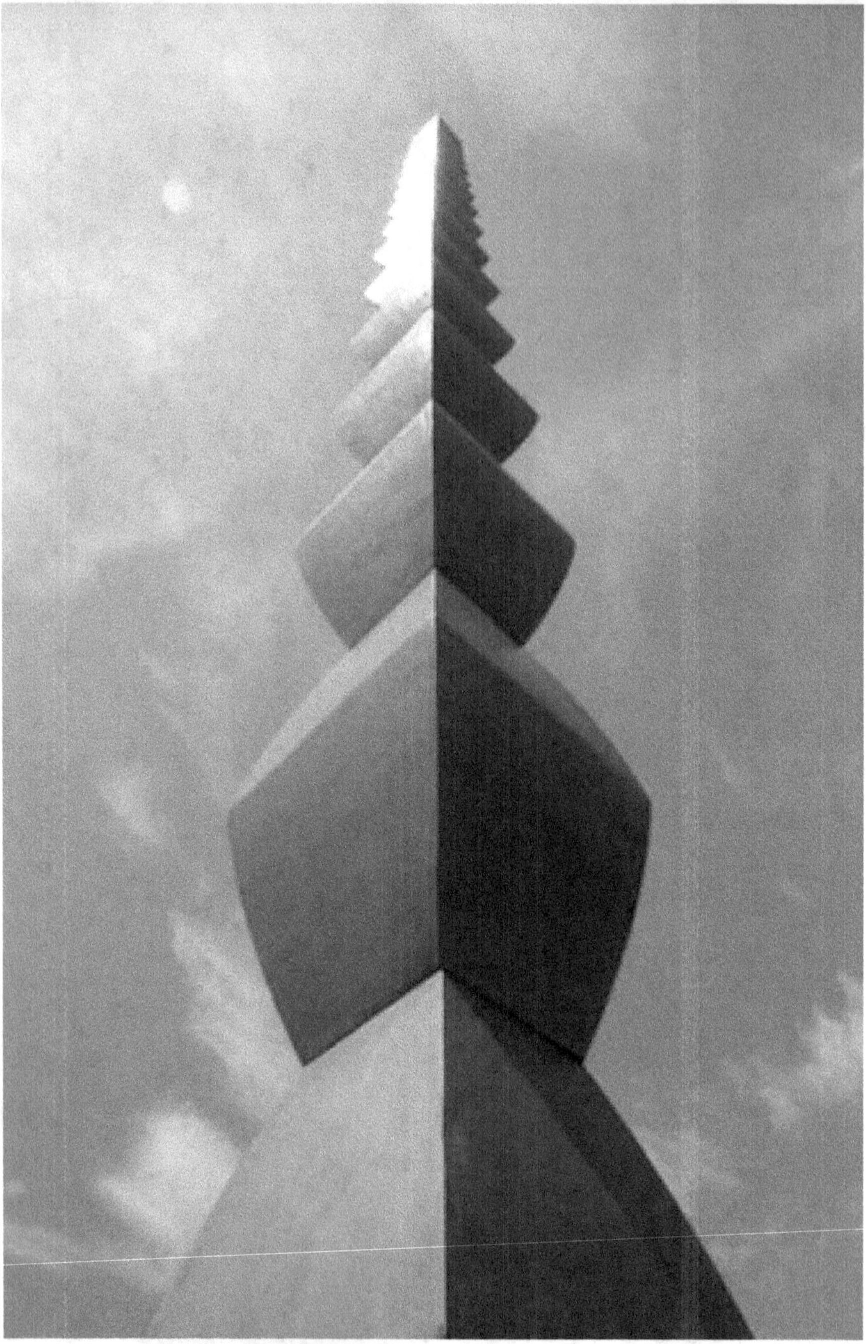

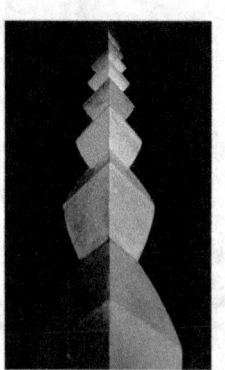

Constantin Brancusi,
Endless Column

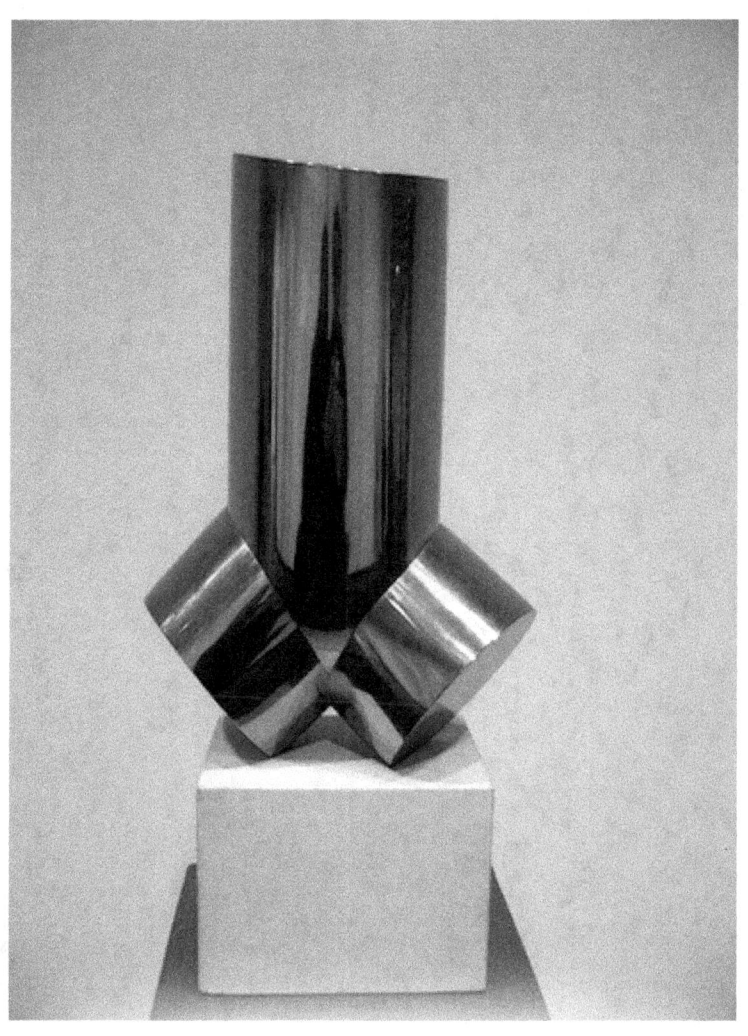

Constantin Brancusi, Torso of a Young Man, after 1924,
Cleveland Museum of Art

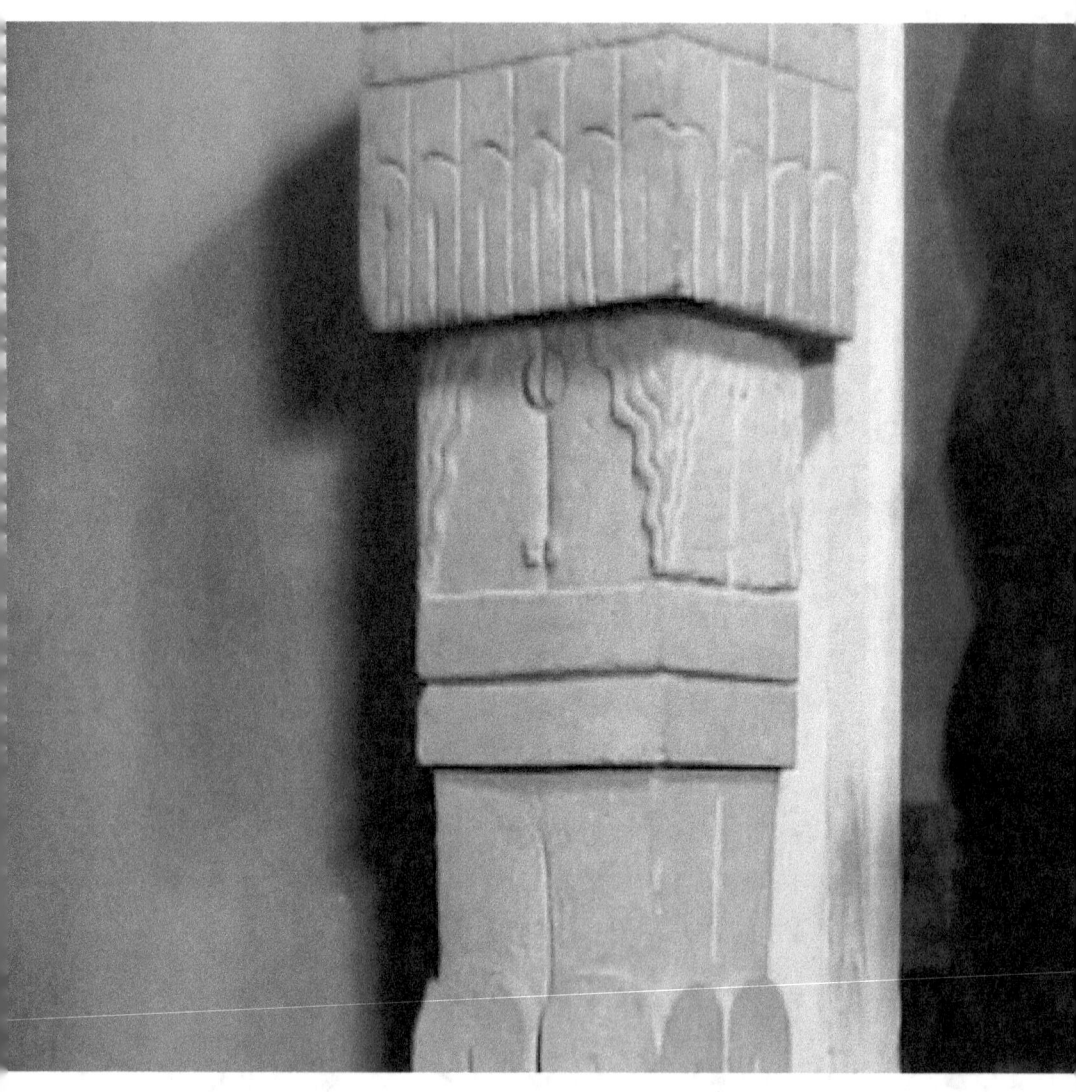

Constantin Brancusi, Boundary Marker, 1945

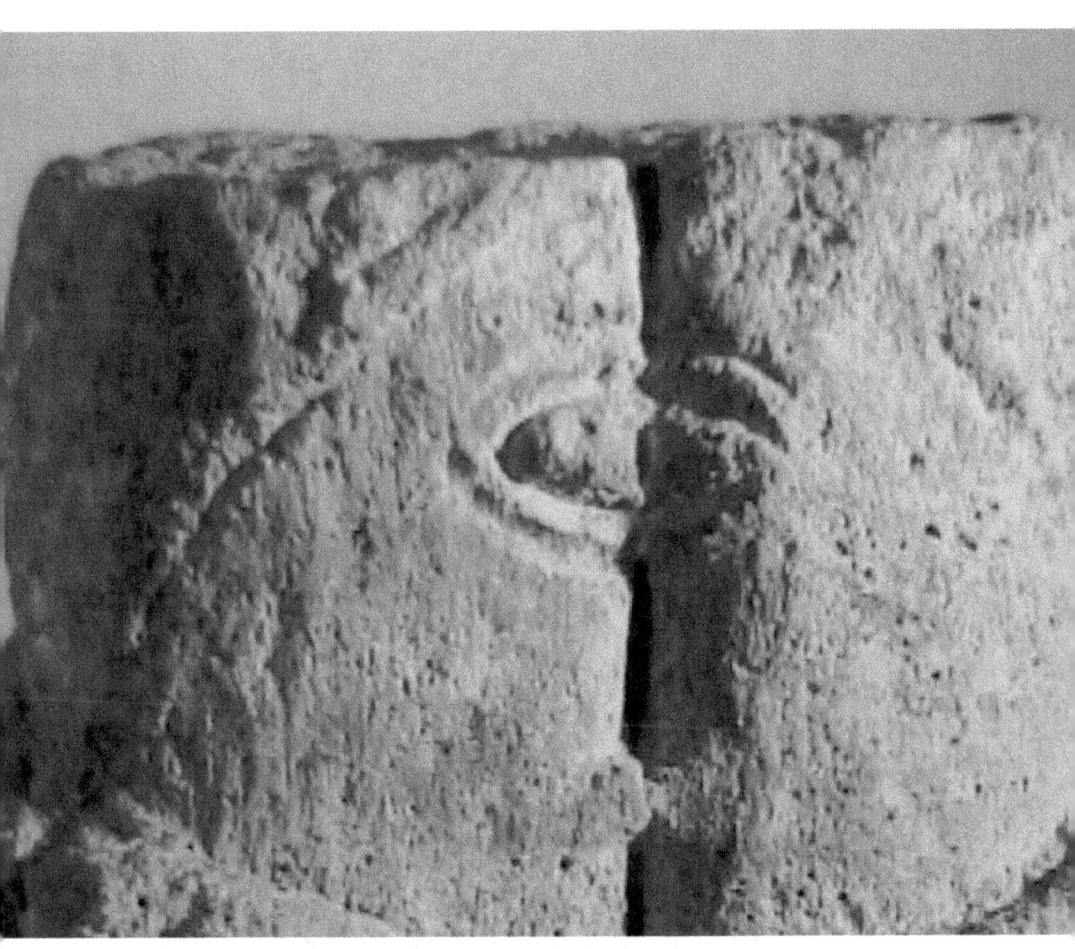

Constantin Brancusi, The Kiss 2, 1908, private collection

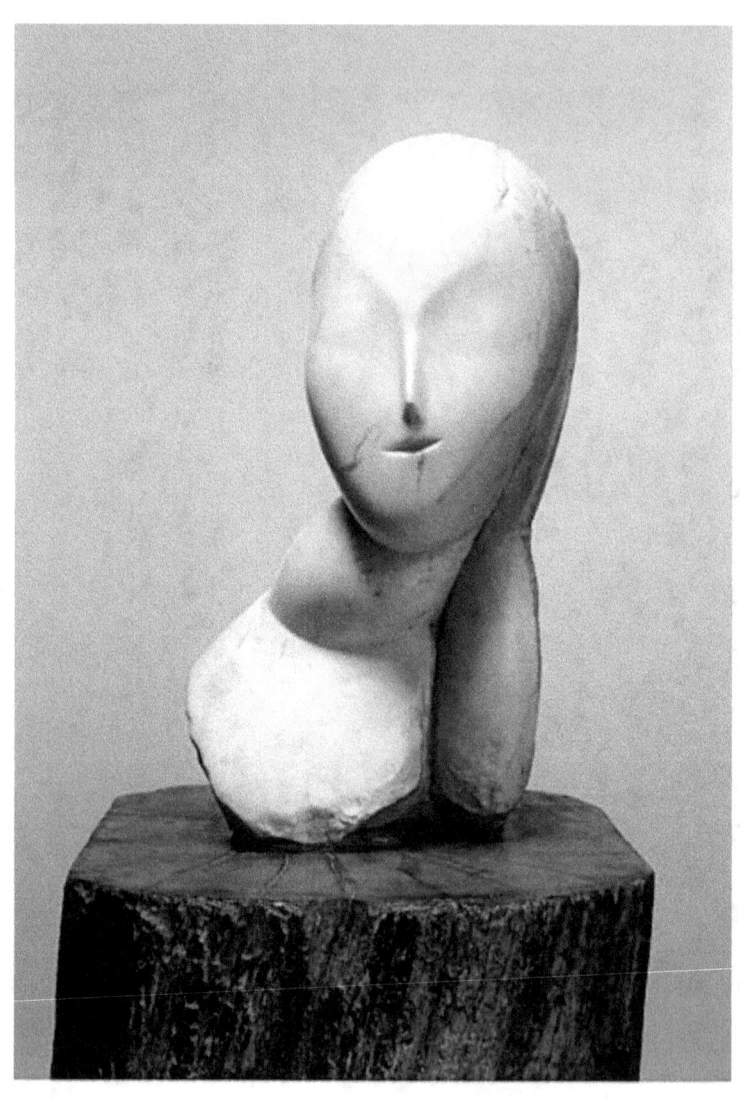

Constantin Brancusi, The Muse, 1912

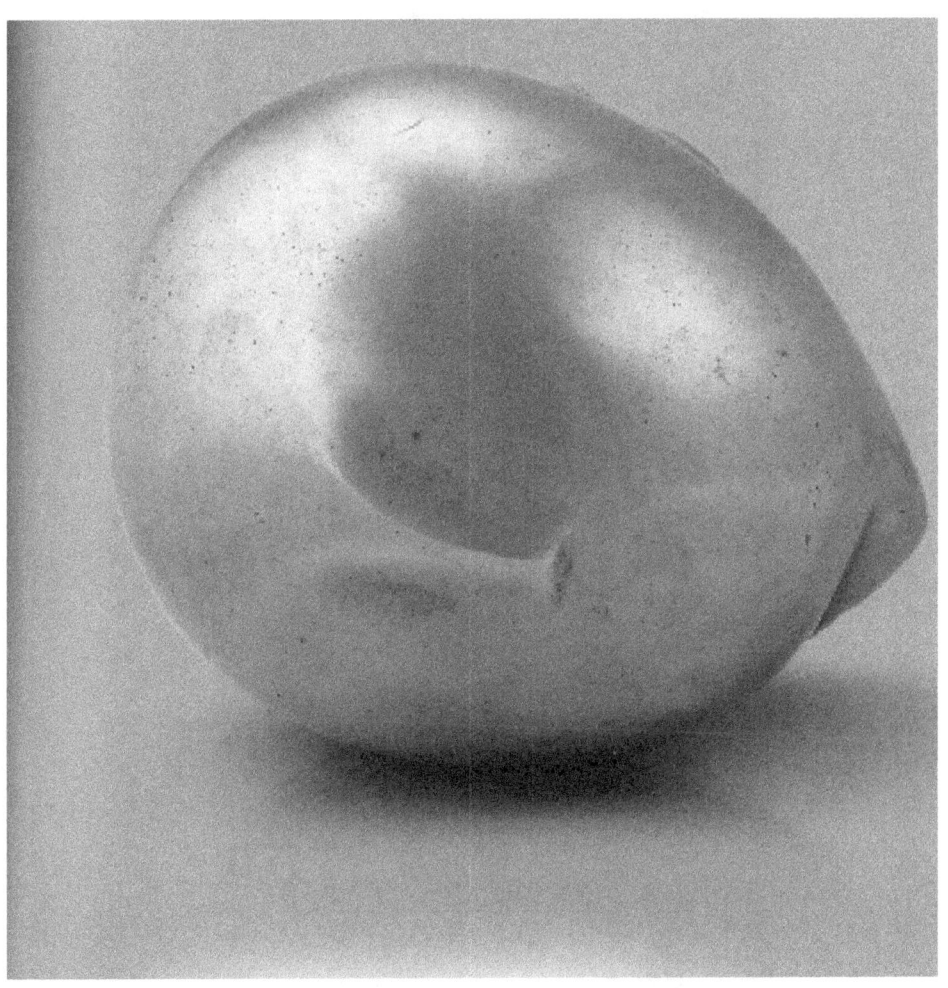

Constantin Brancusi, Prometheus, 1911

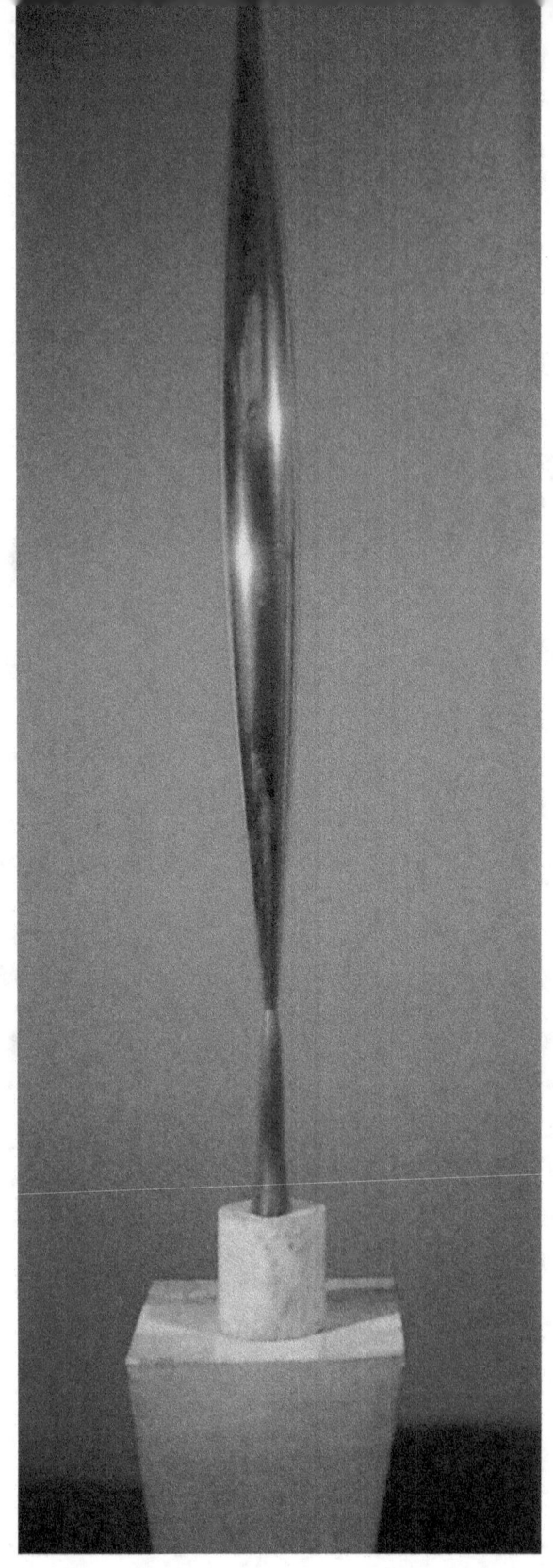

Constantin Brancusi, Bird In Space, 1941,
Paris

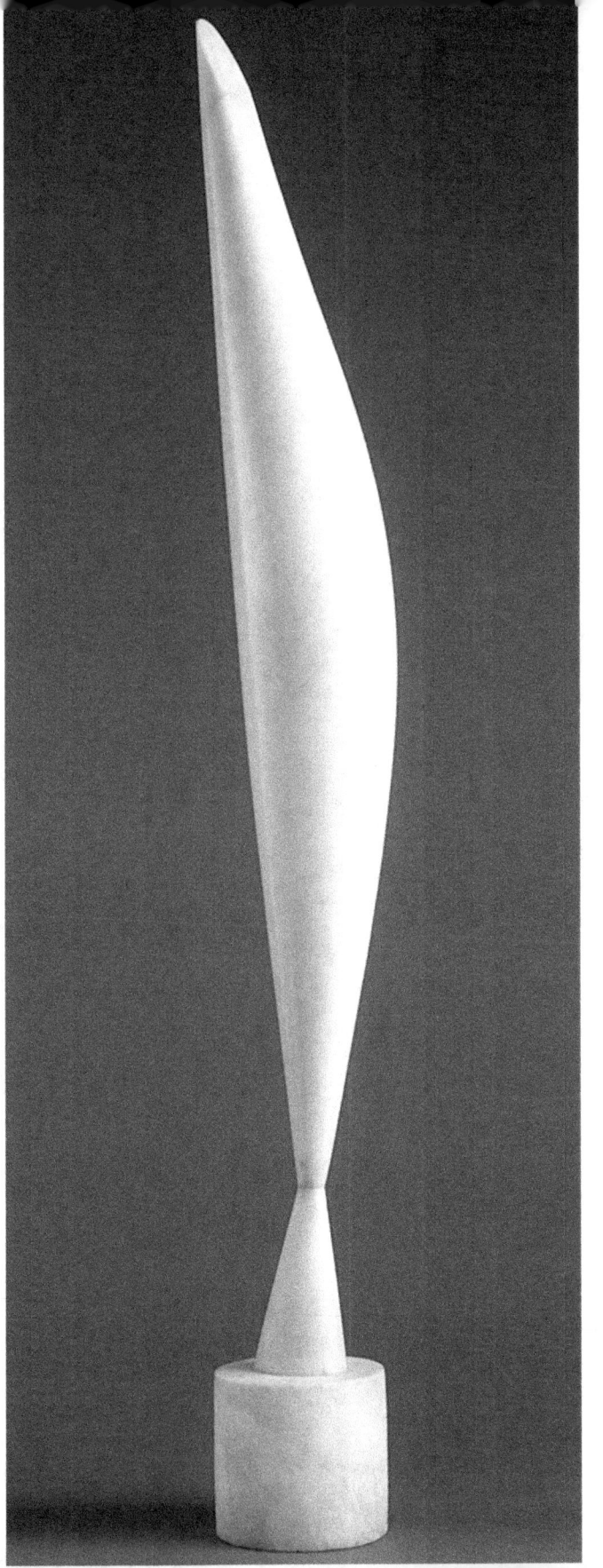

Constantin Brancusi,
Bird In Space, 1923

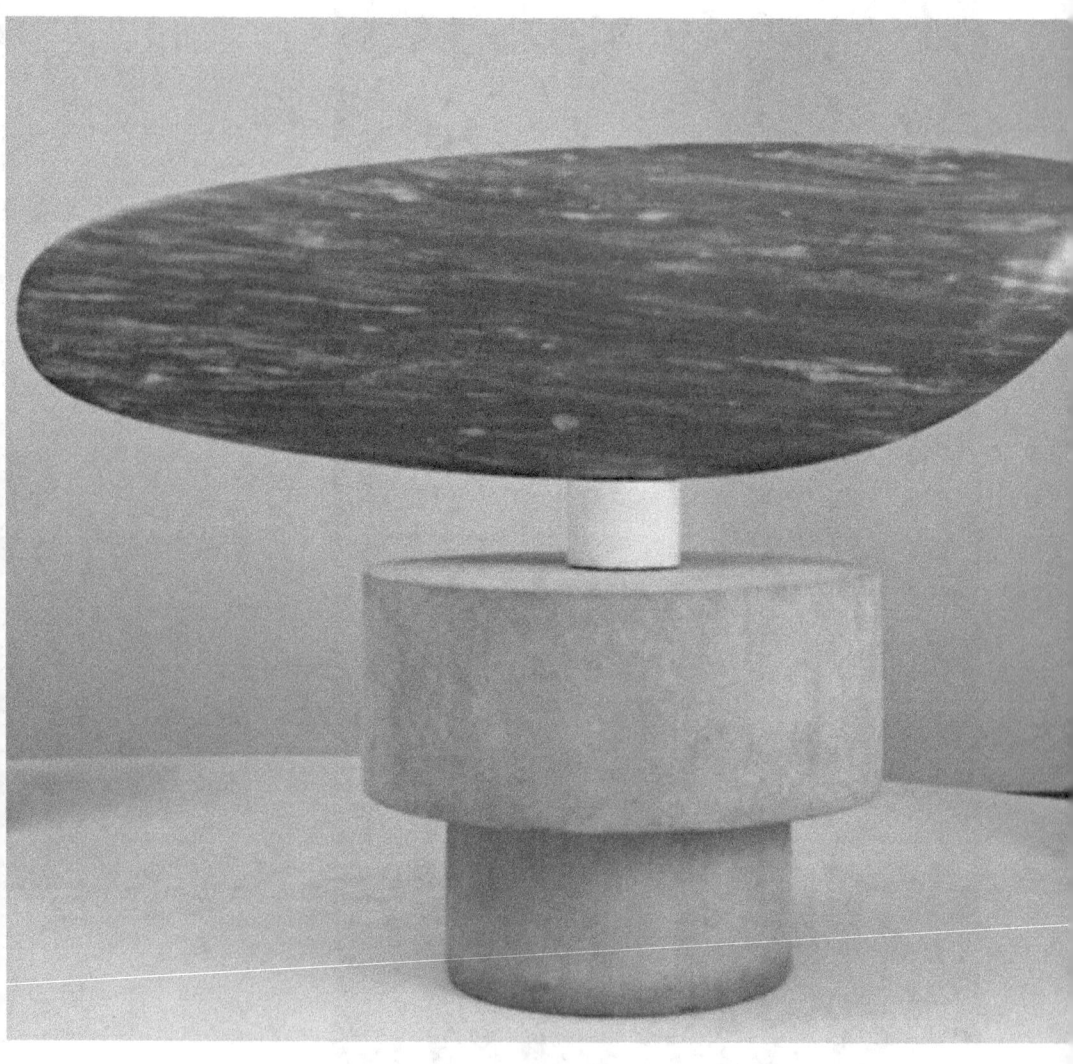

Constantin Brancusi, Fish, 1930, Museum of Modern Art, New York

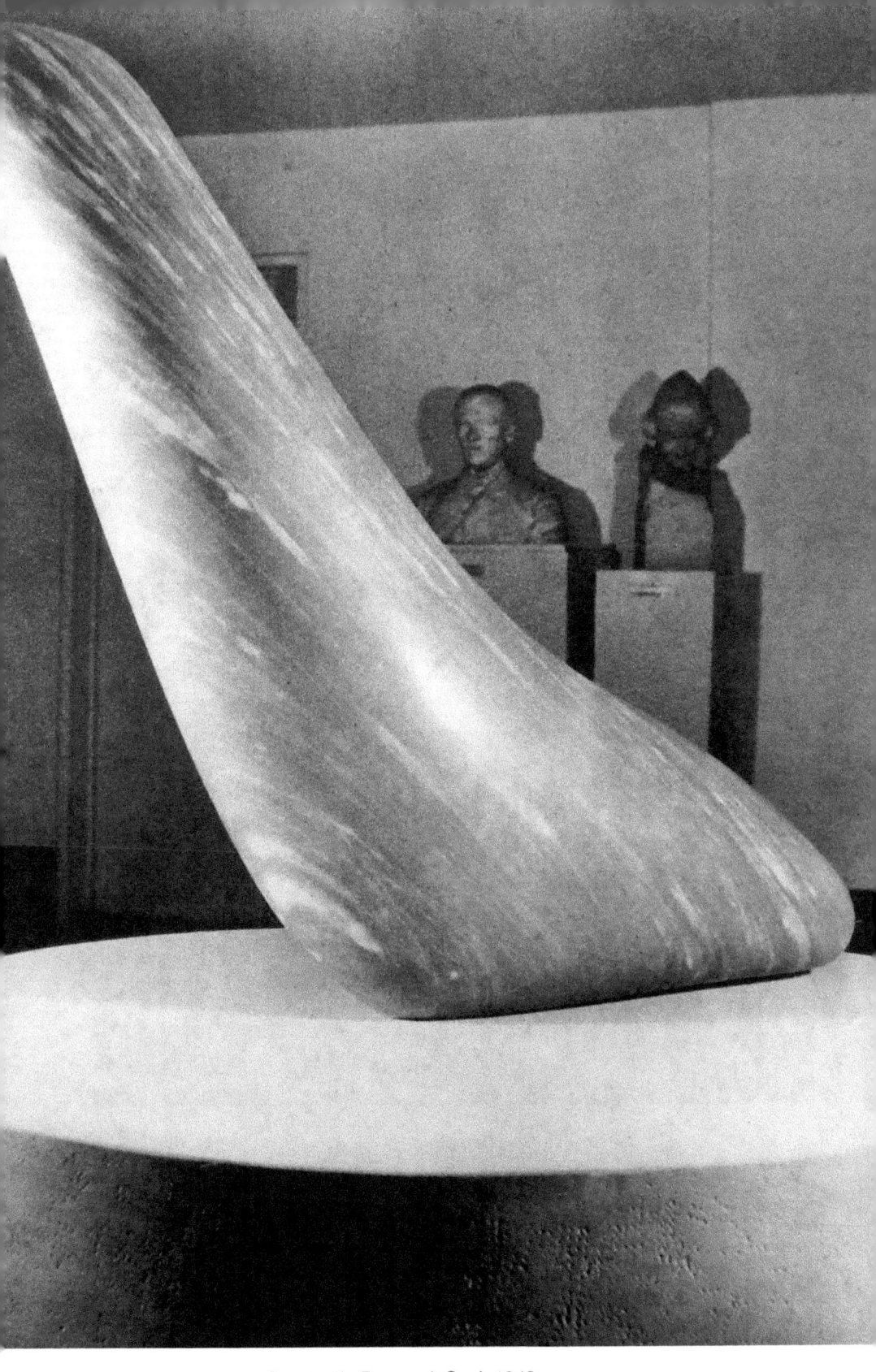

Constantin Brancusi, Seal, 1943

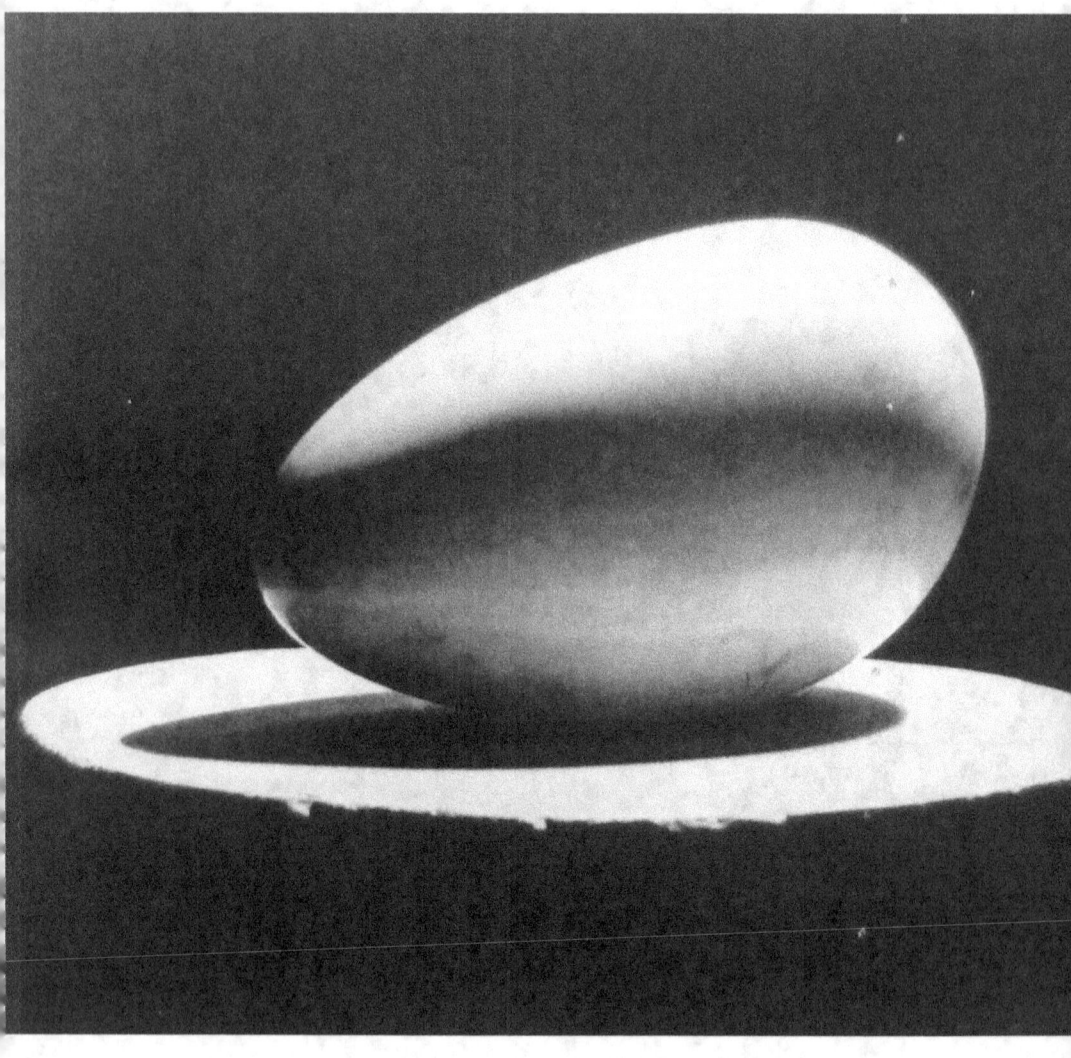

Constantin Brancusi, Sculpture For the Blind, 1916, Philadelphia
Museum of Art

On the following pages, some photos I took
at the Museum of Modern Art in New York City, in Fall, 2008

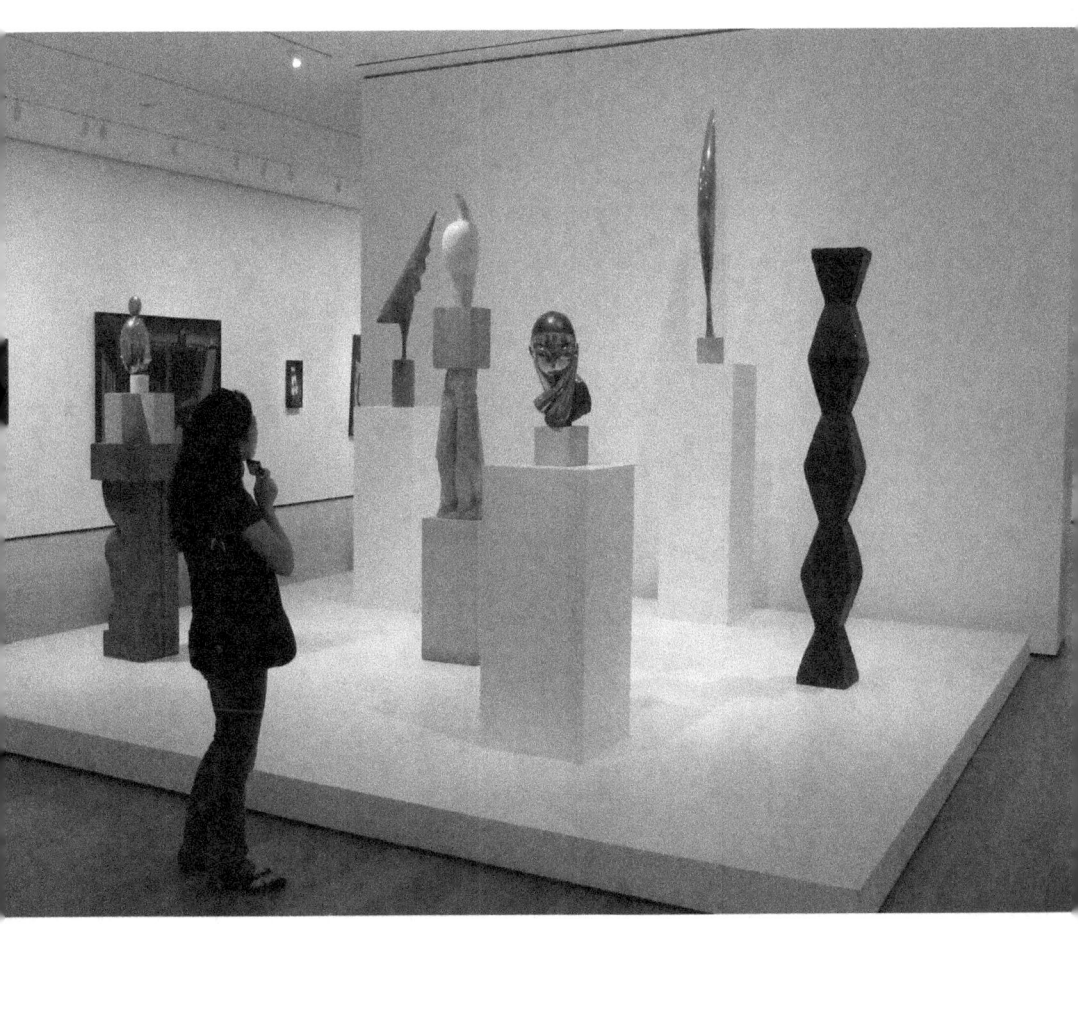

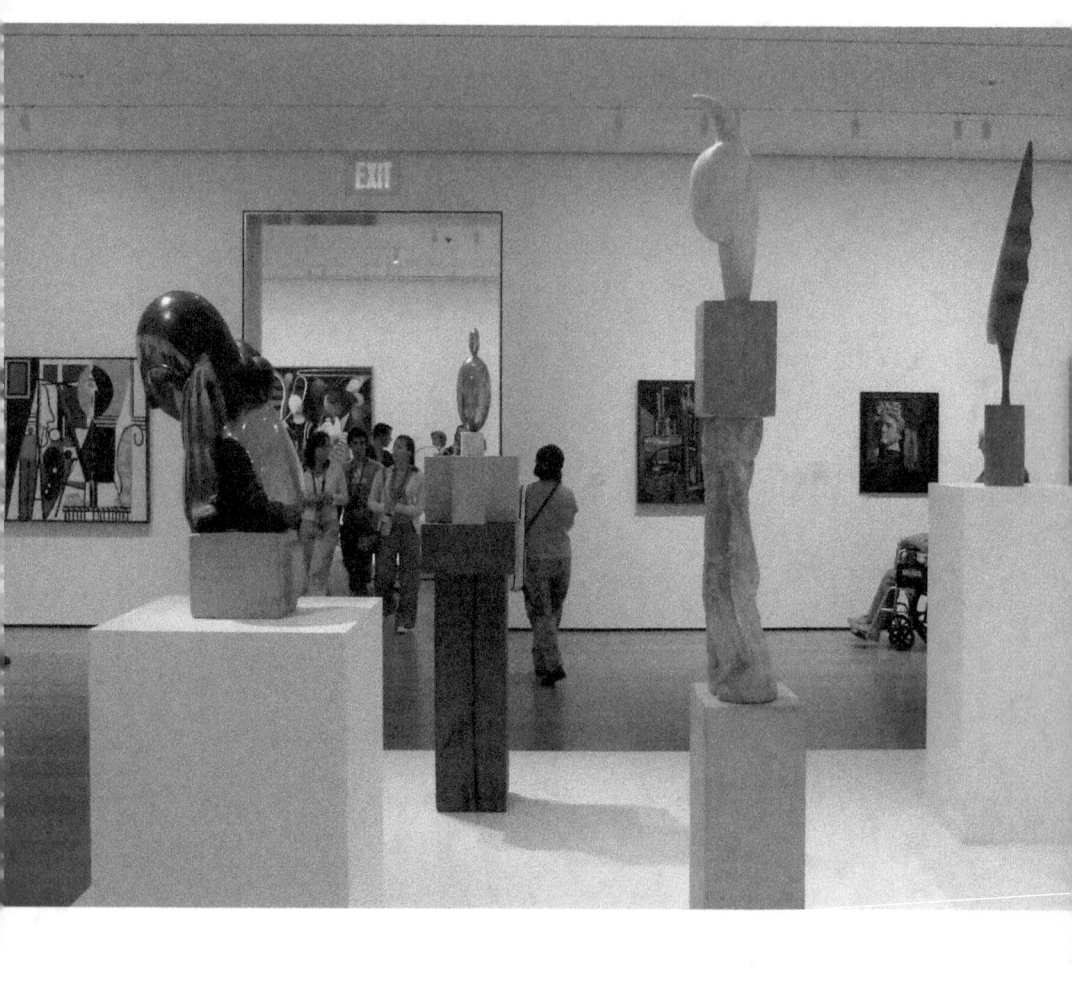

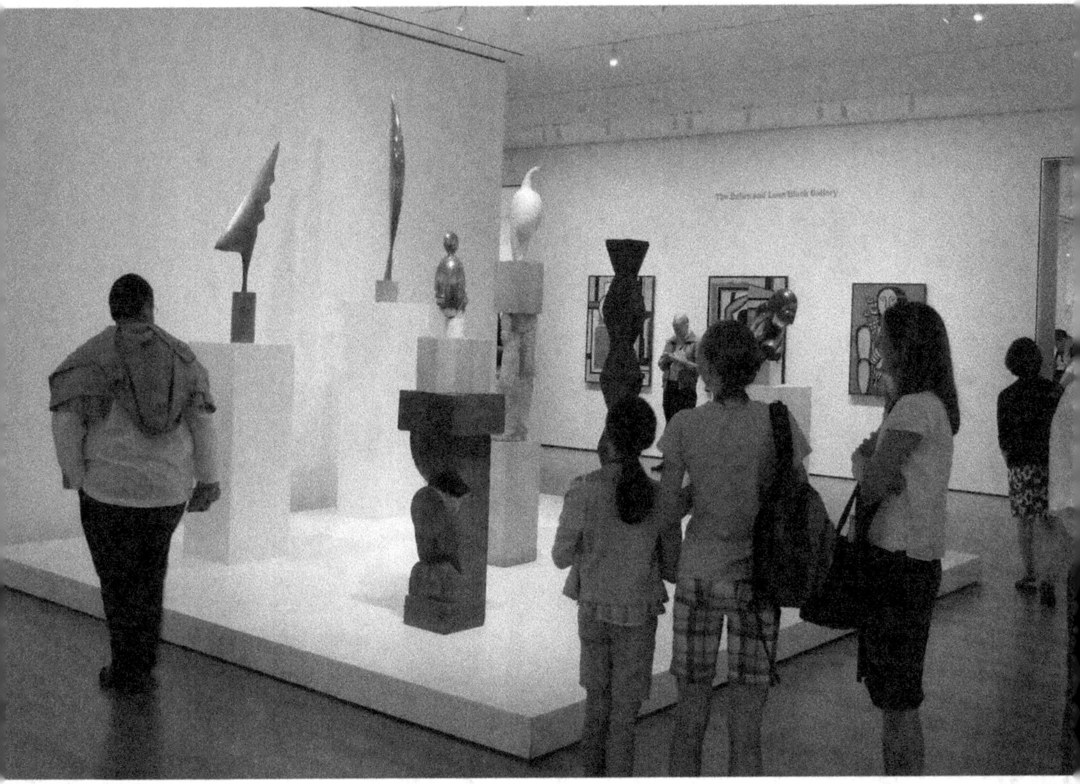

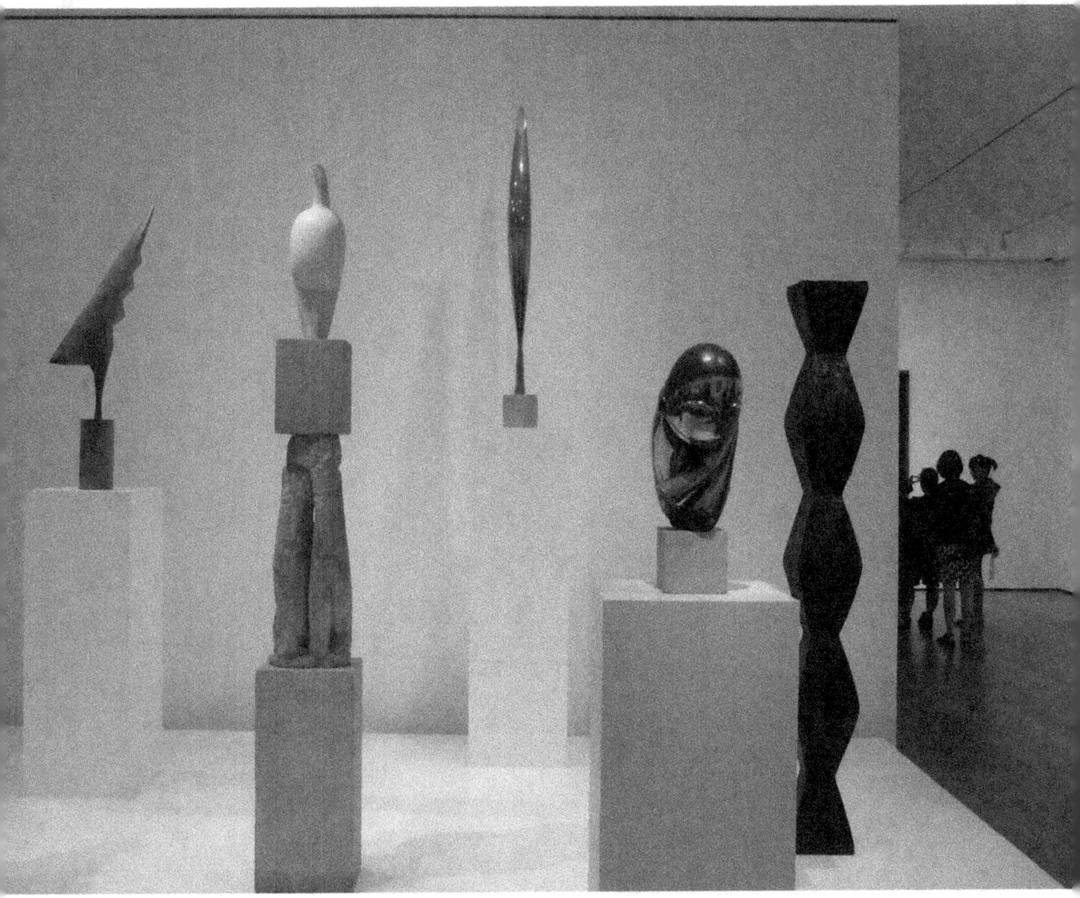

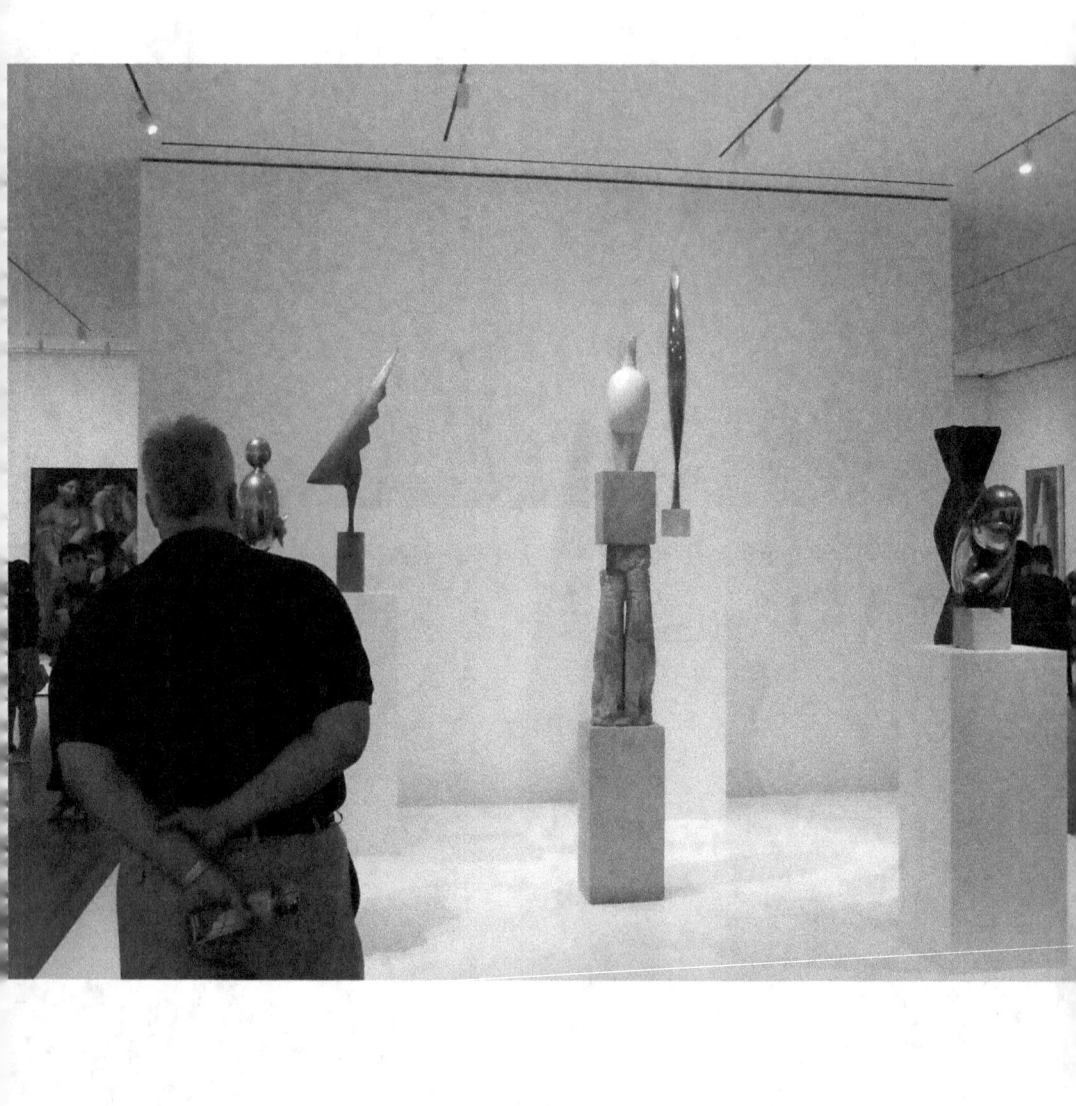

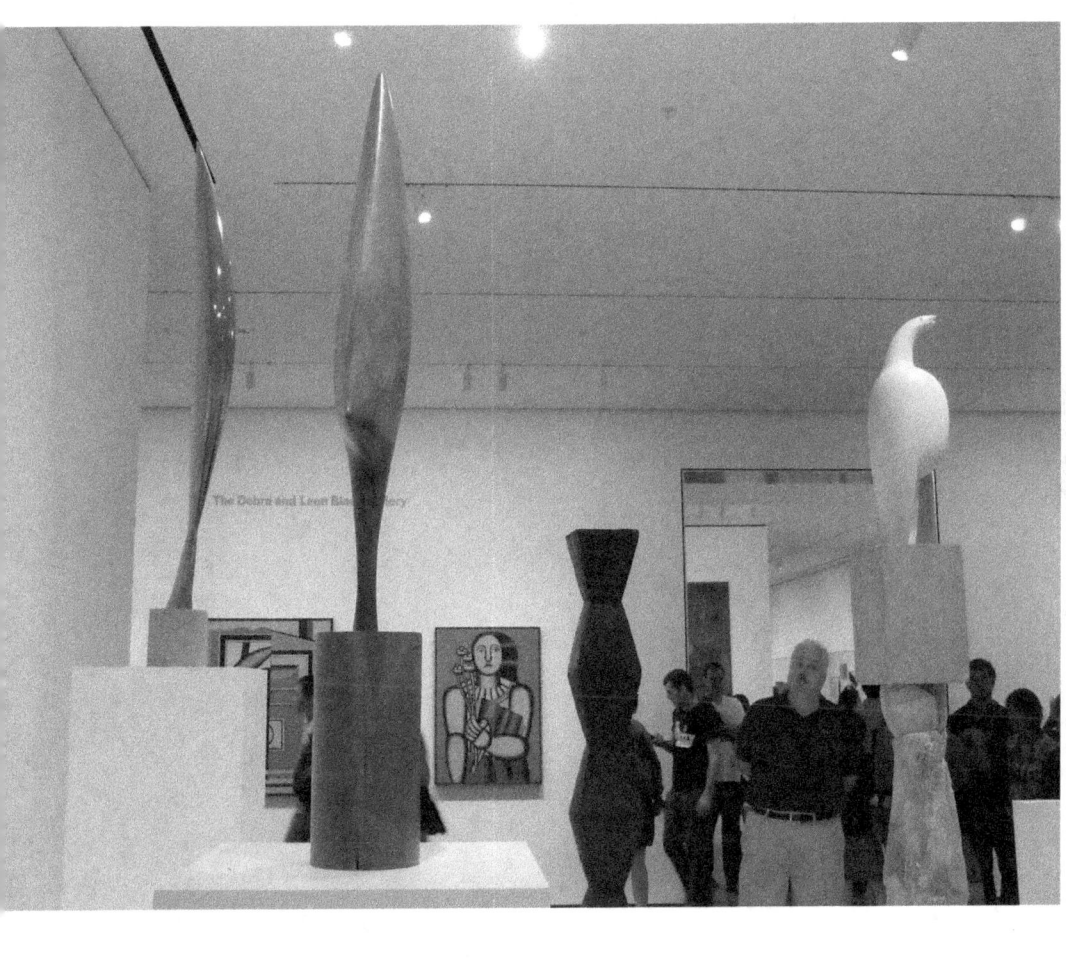

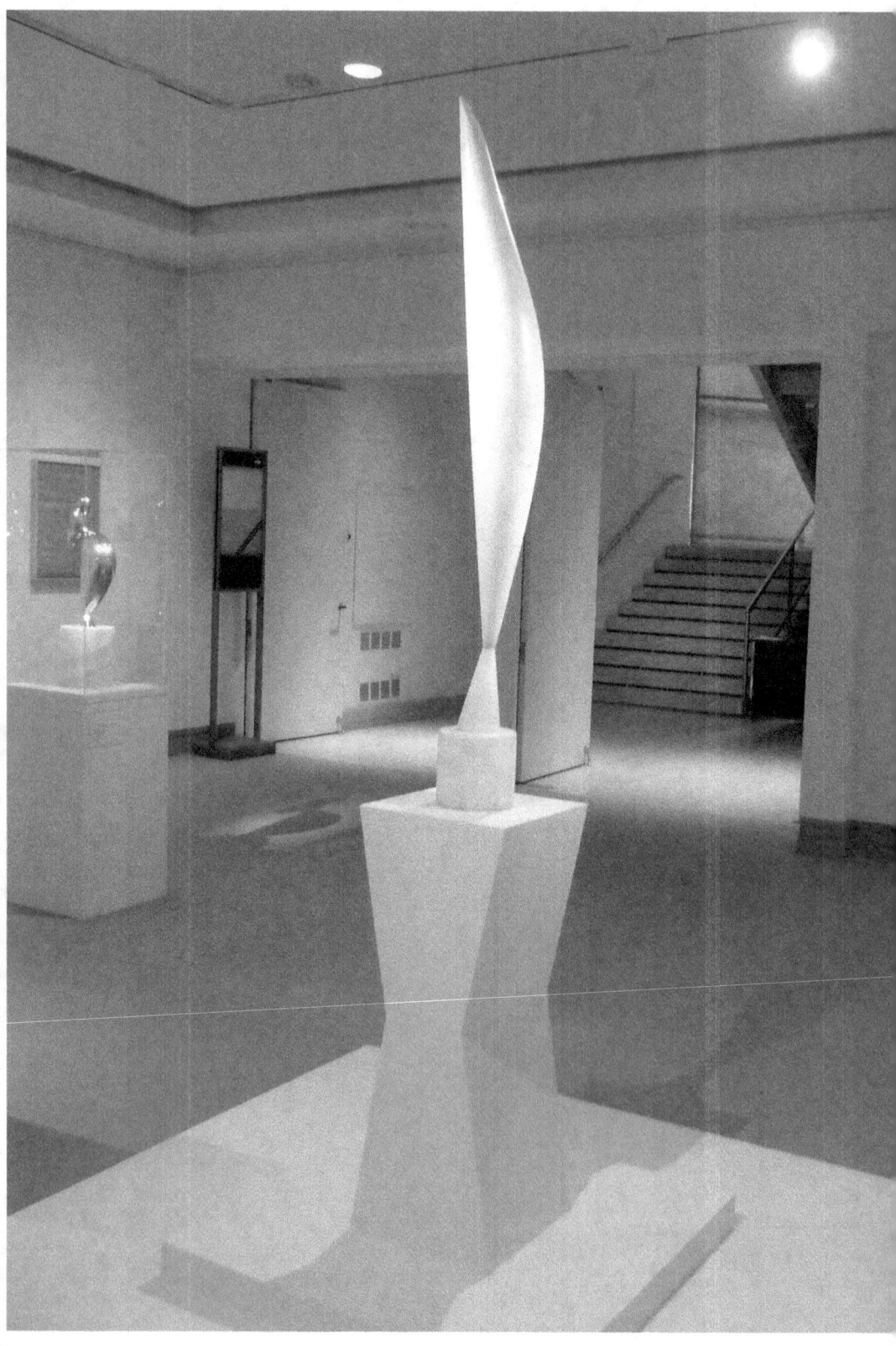

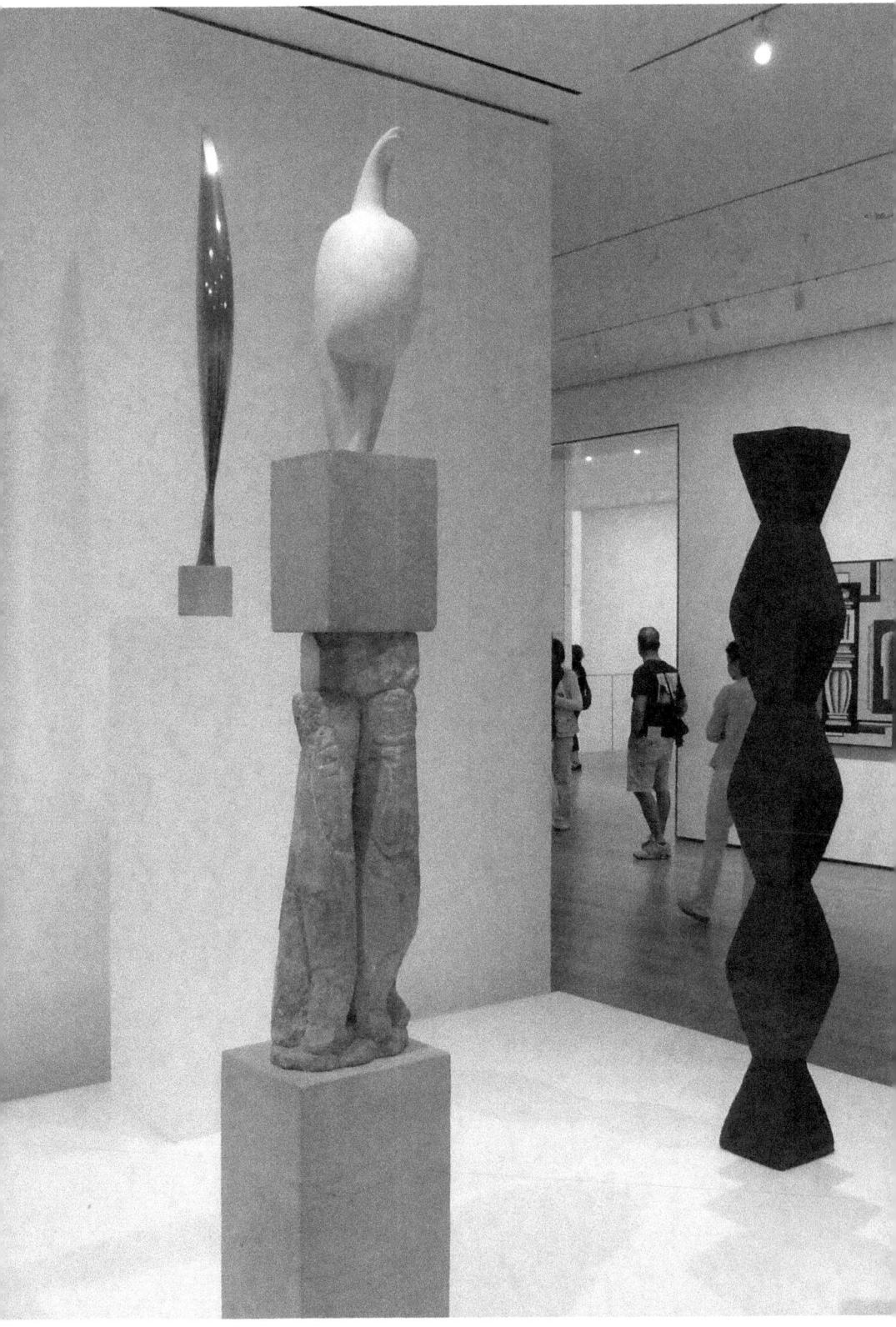

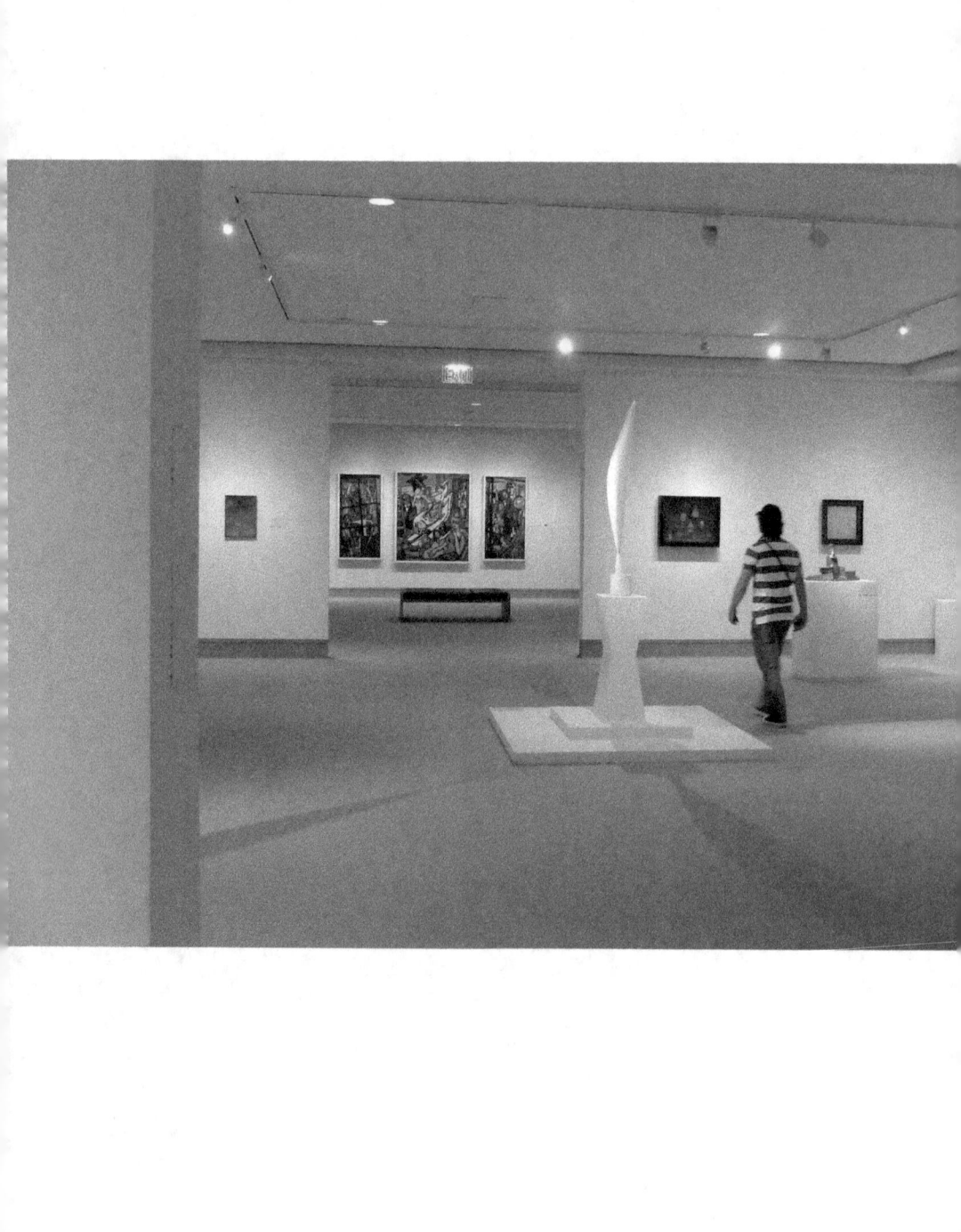

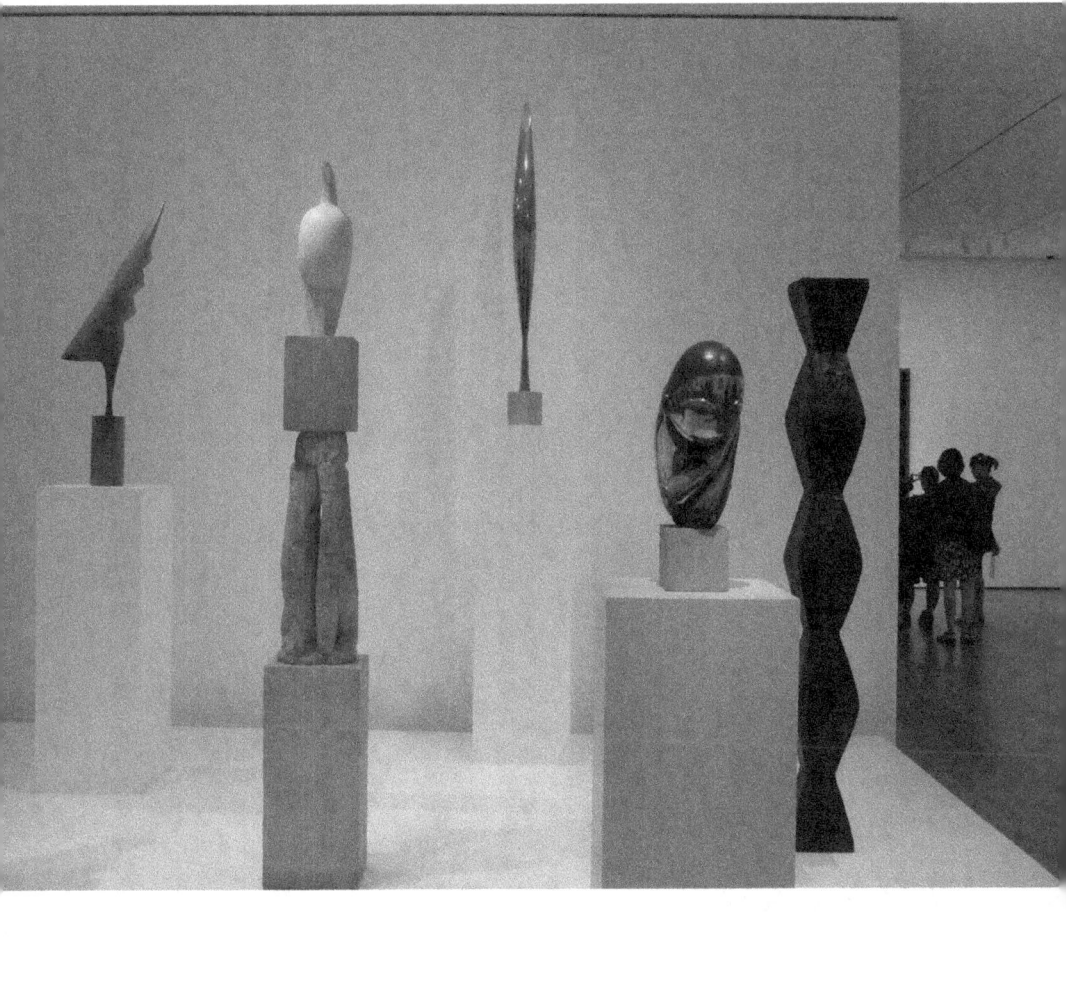

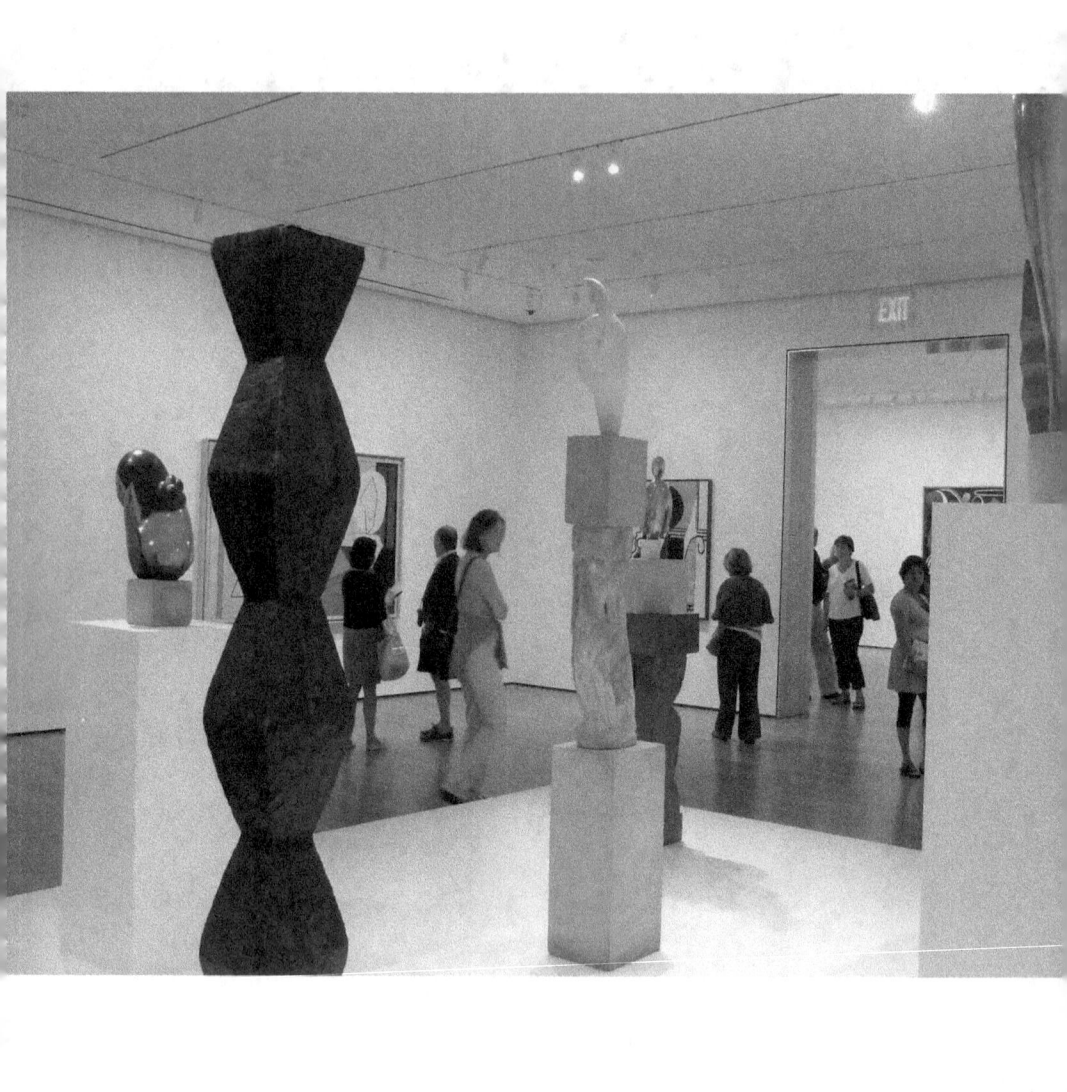

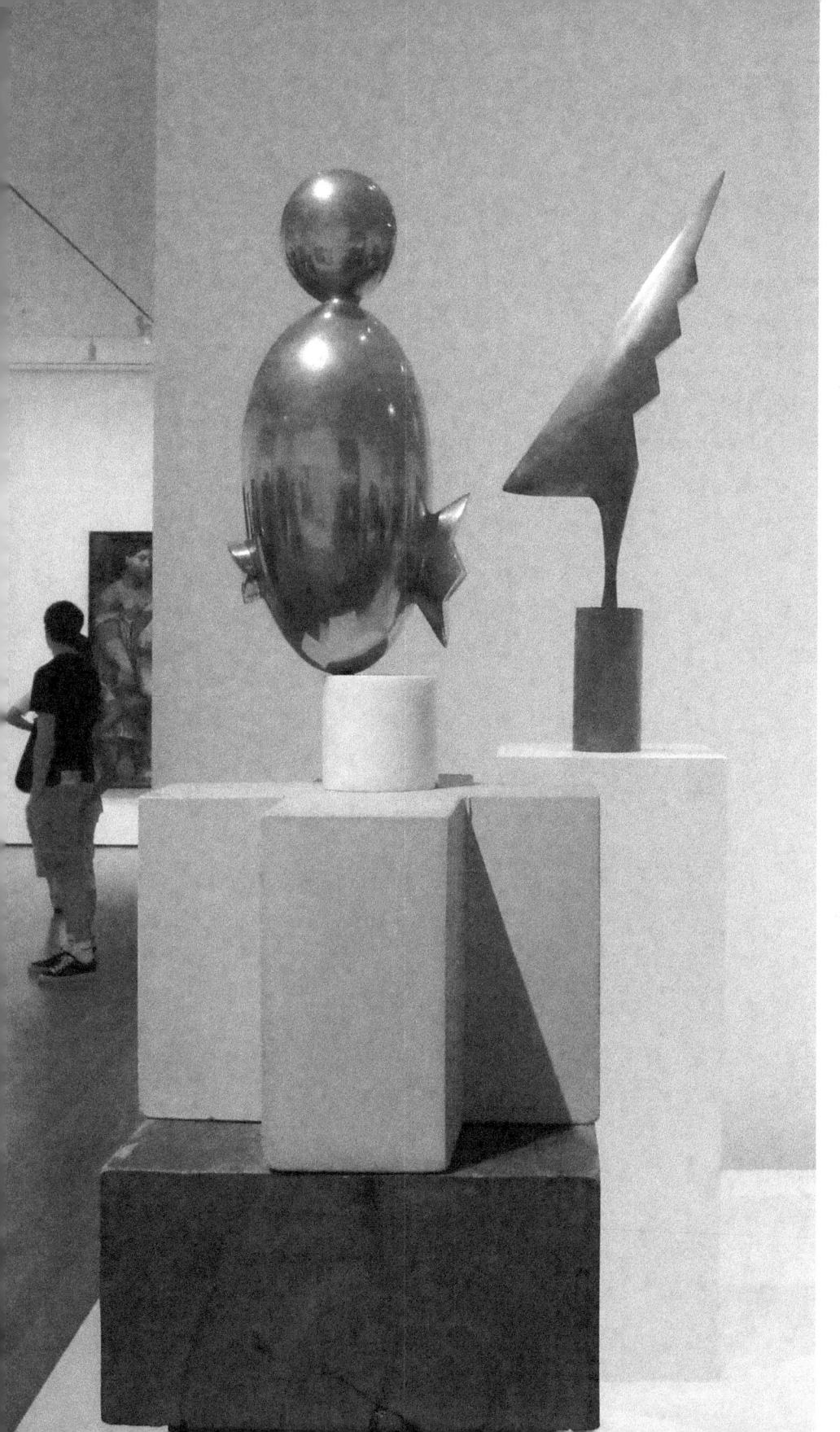

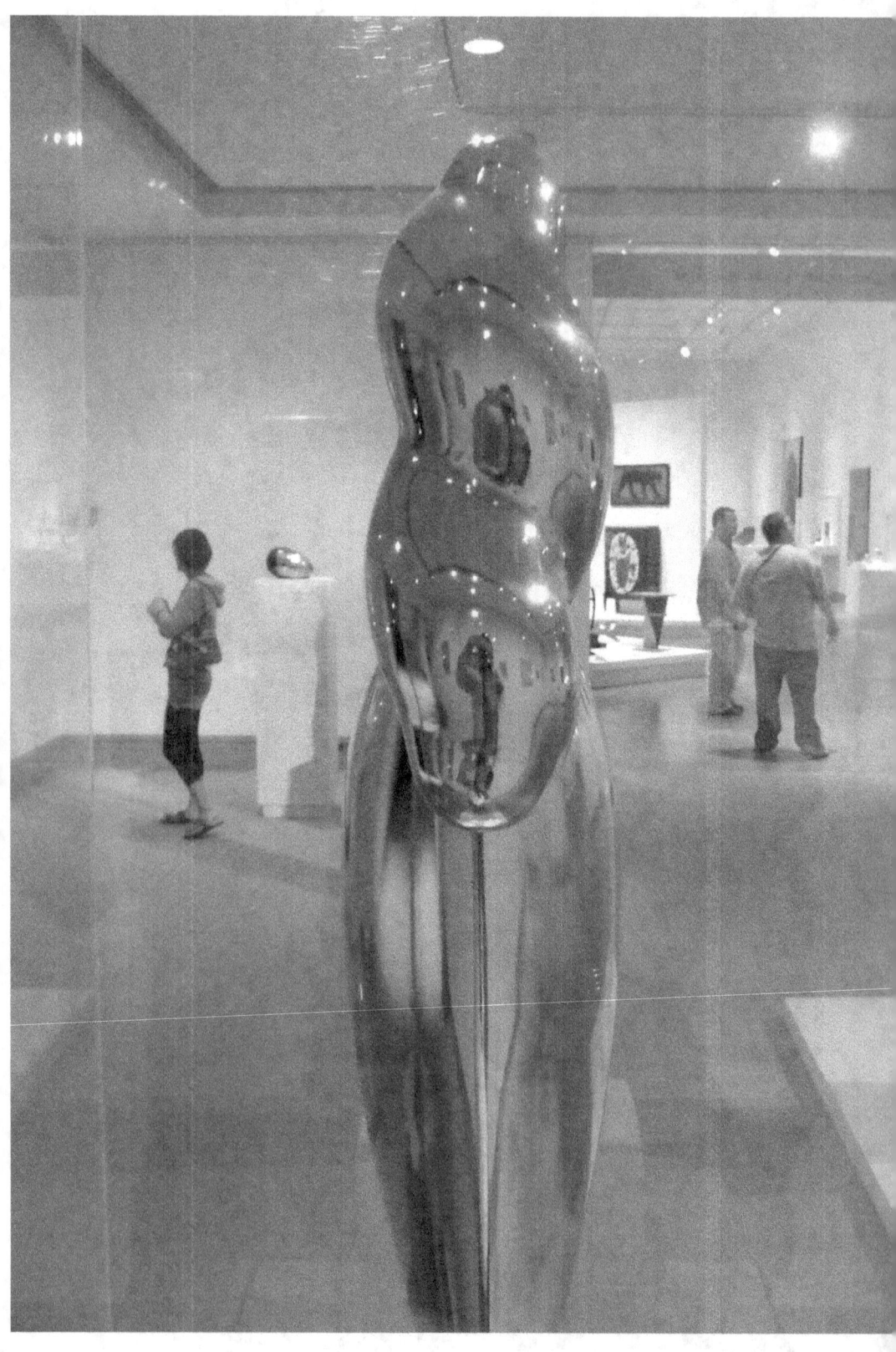

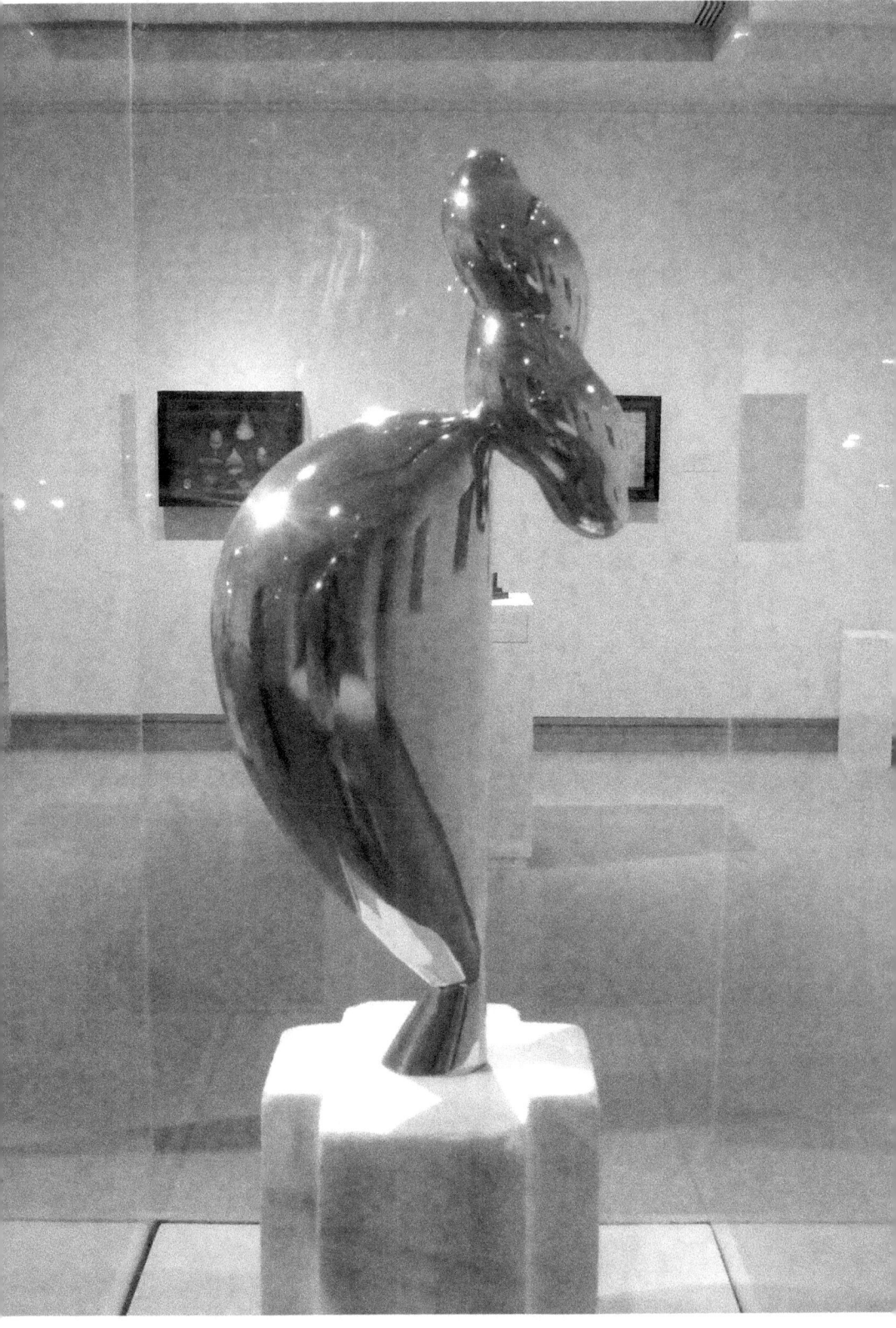

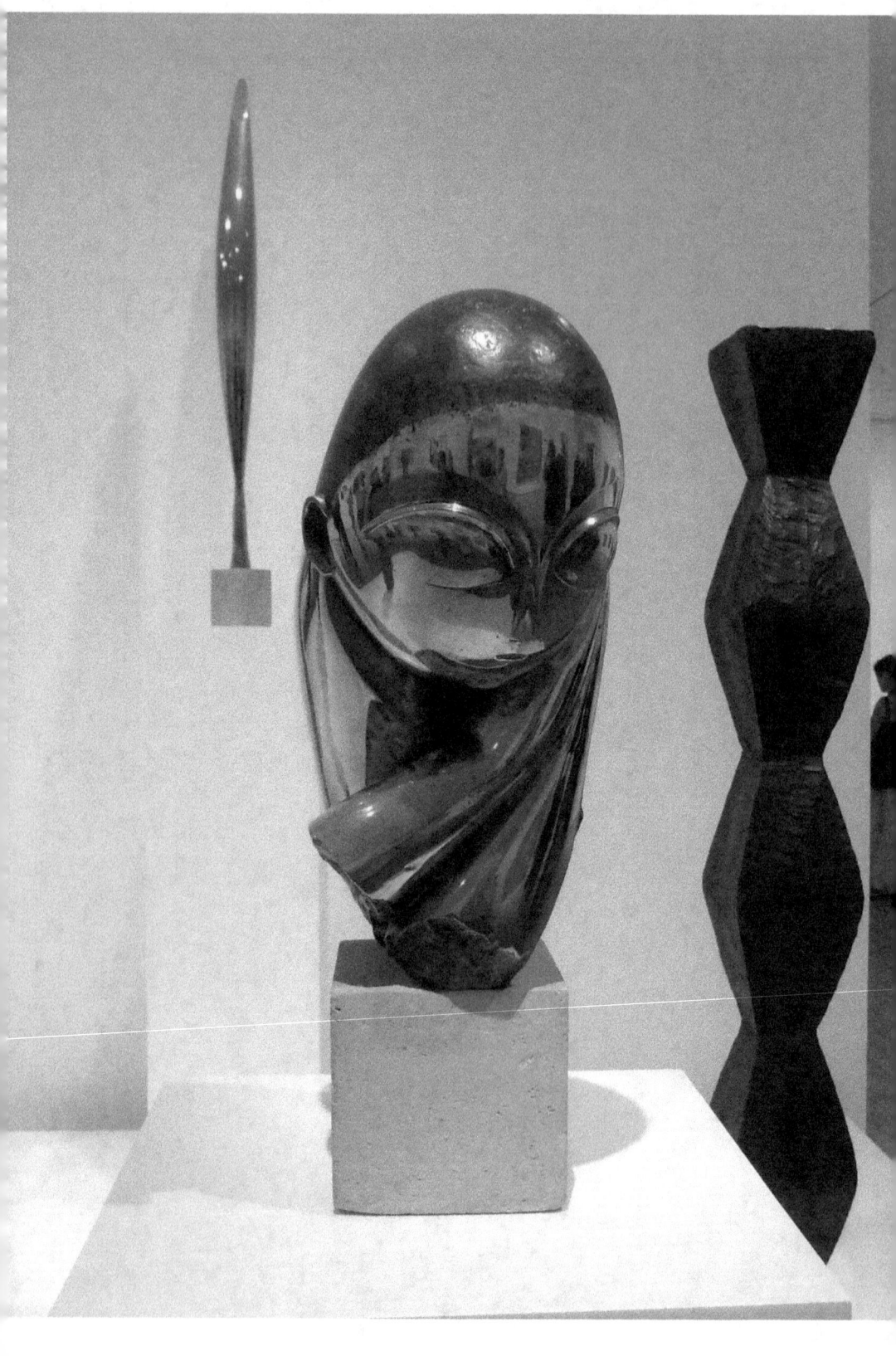

On the following pages, some photos I took
at the Centre Pompidou in Paris, at Christmas, 2008,
including many of the Brancusi Studio.

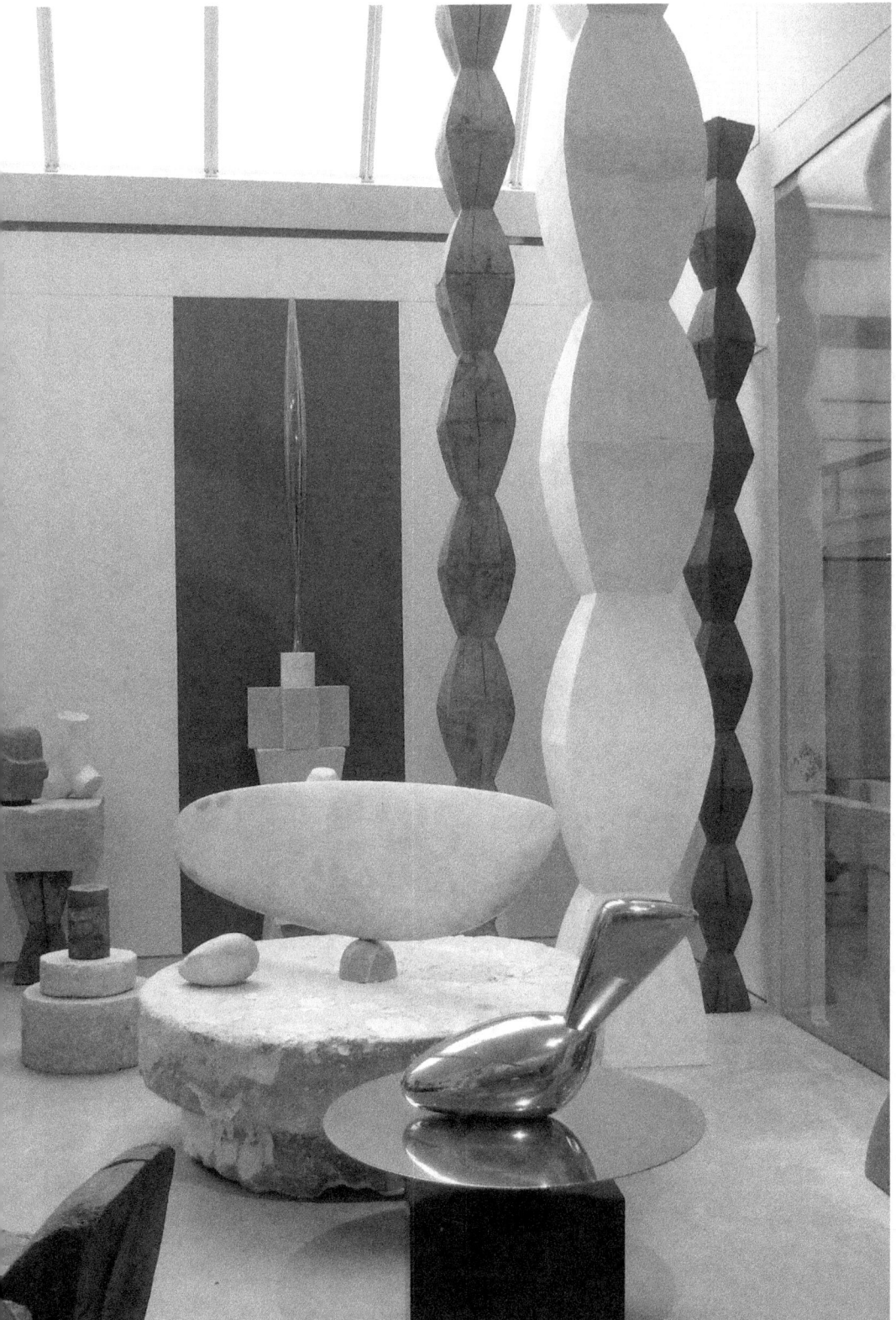

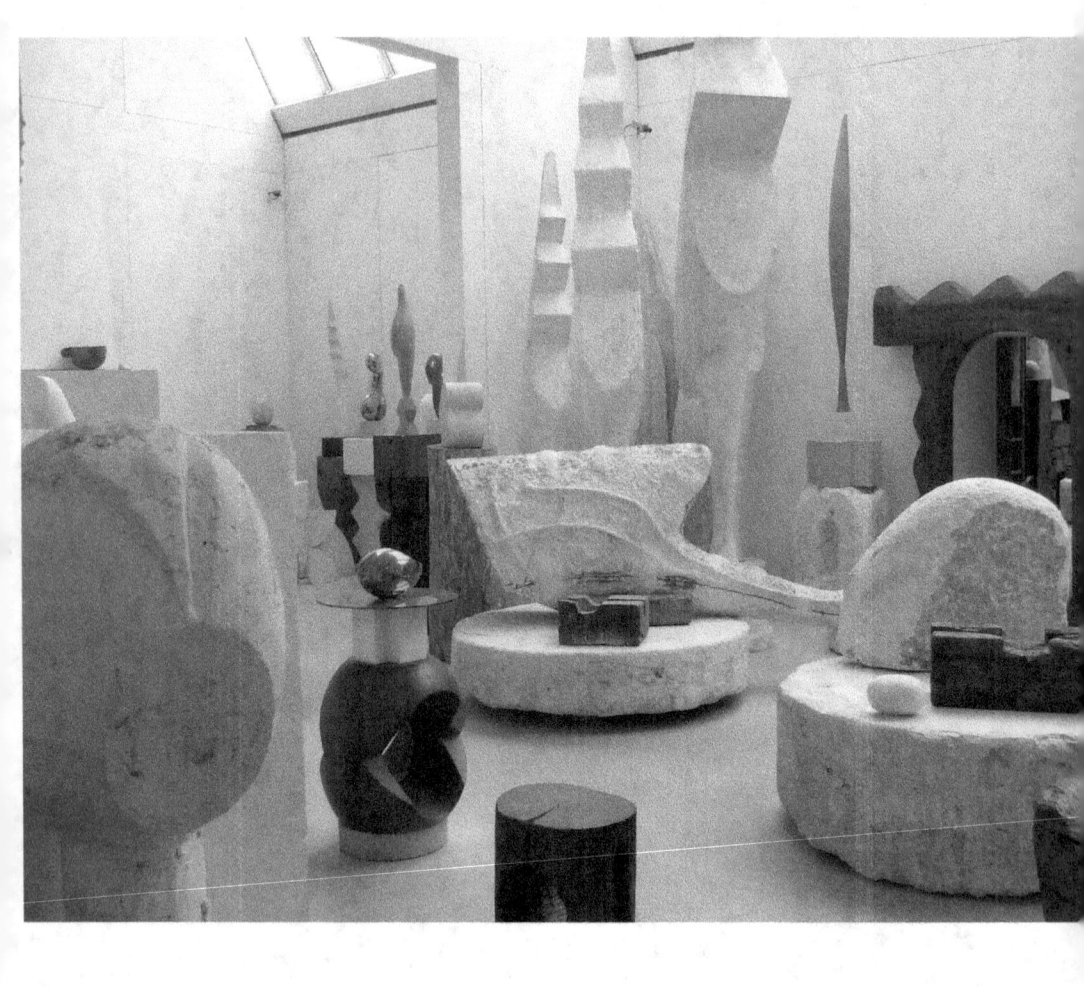

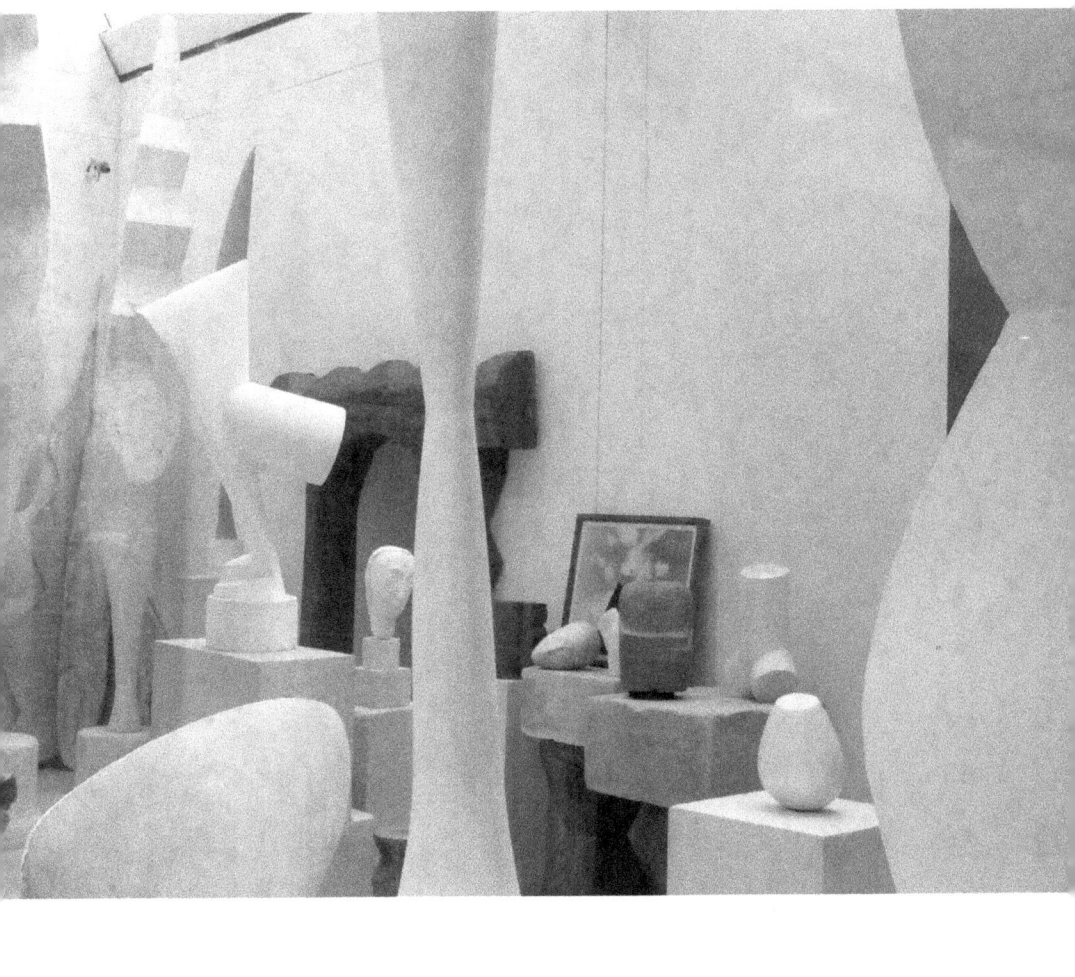

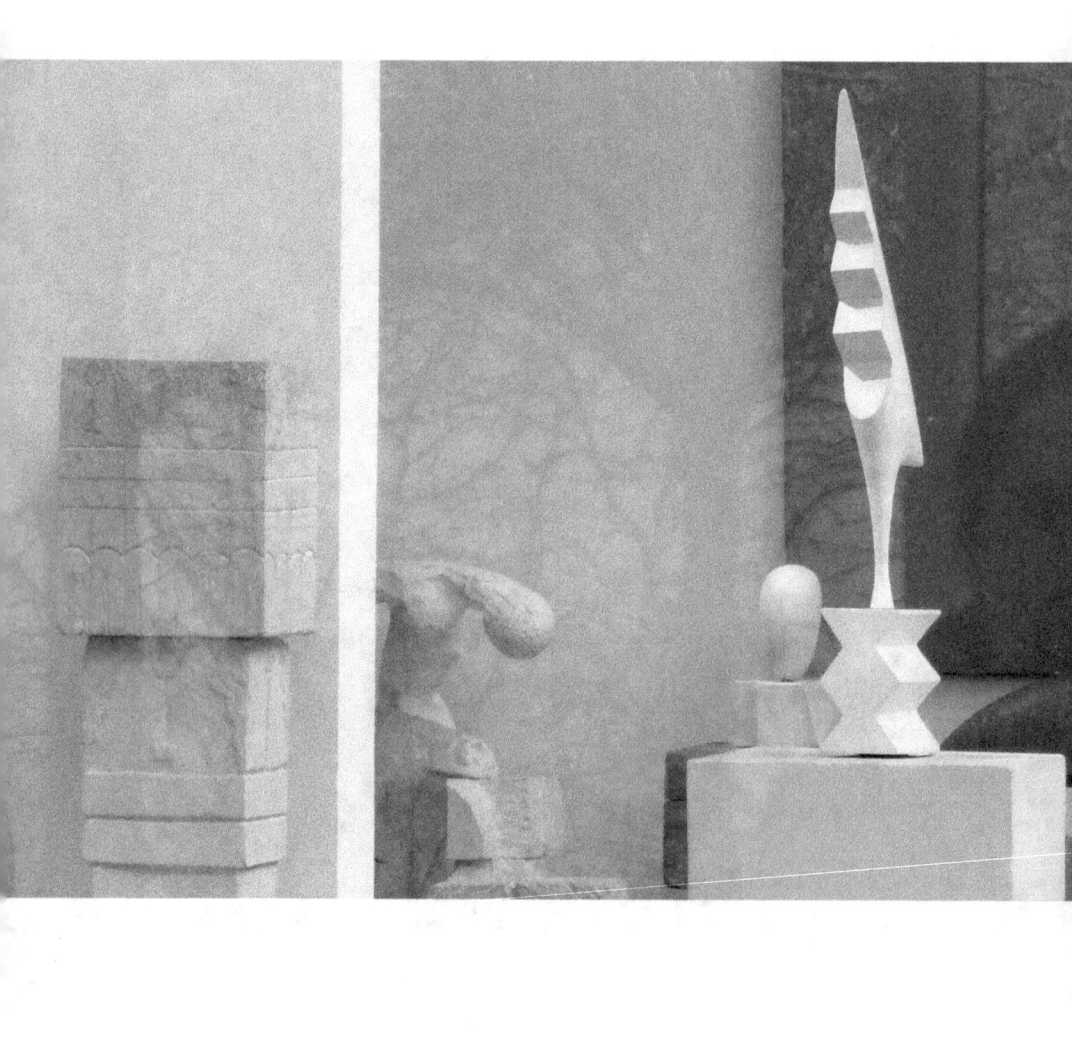

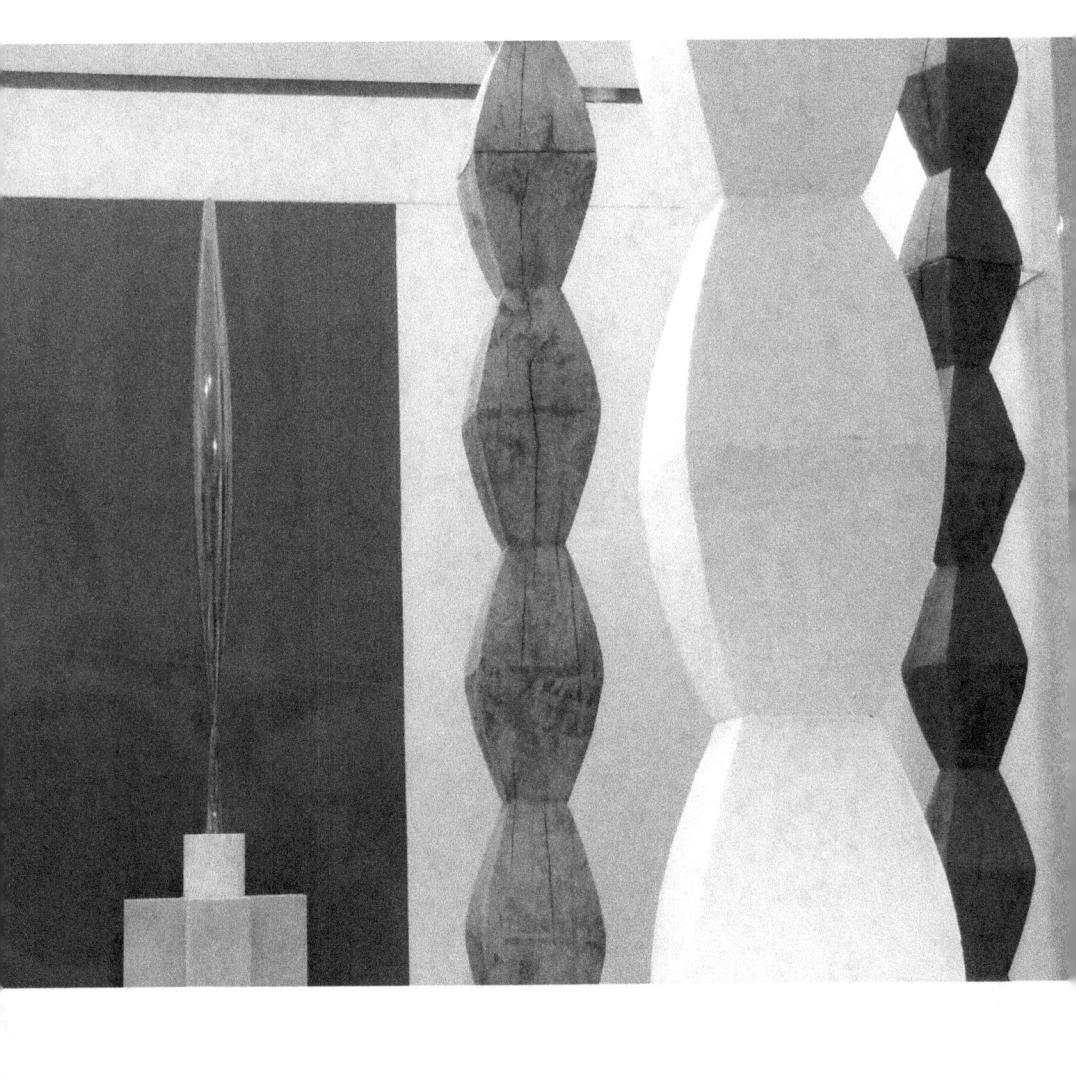

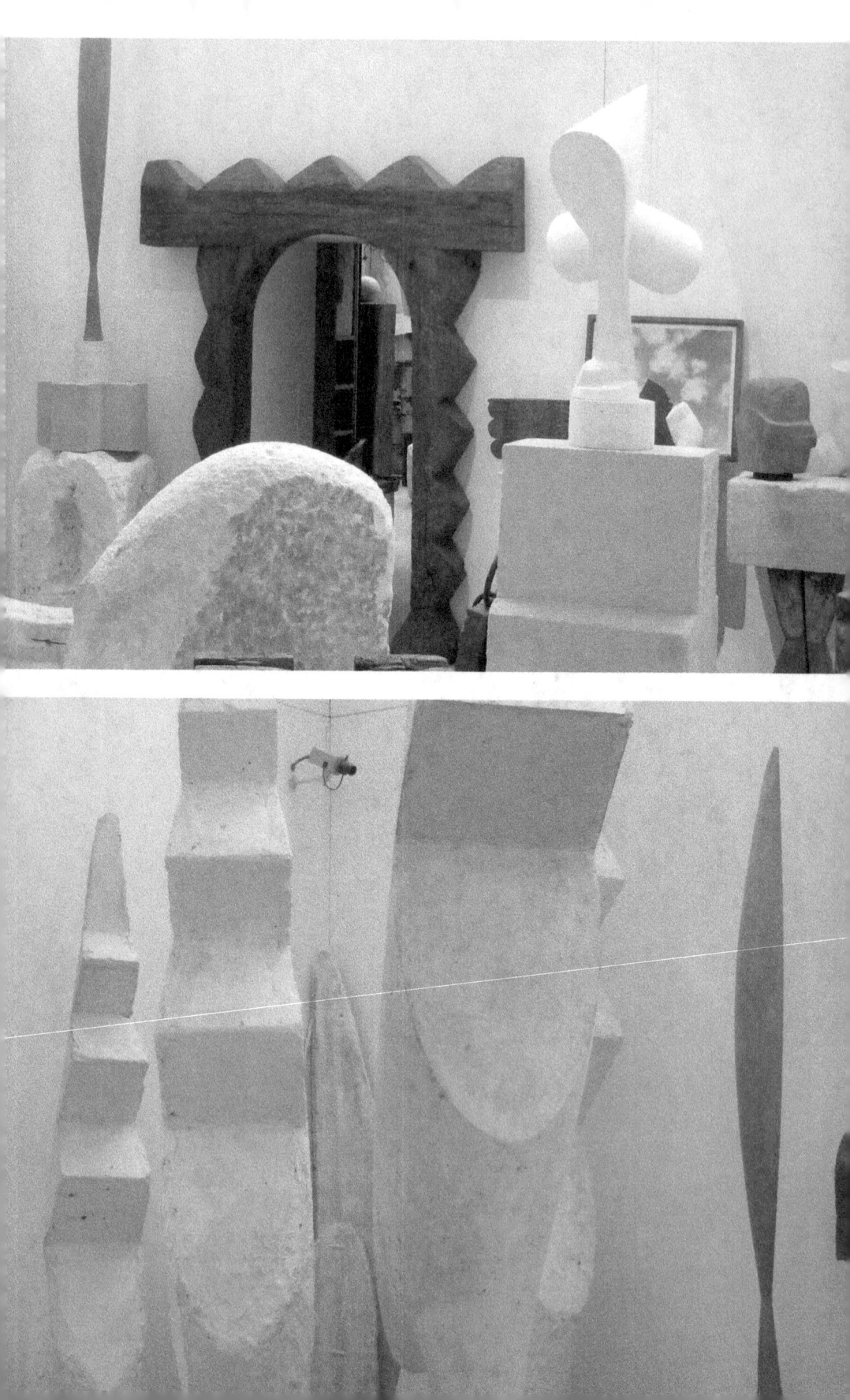

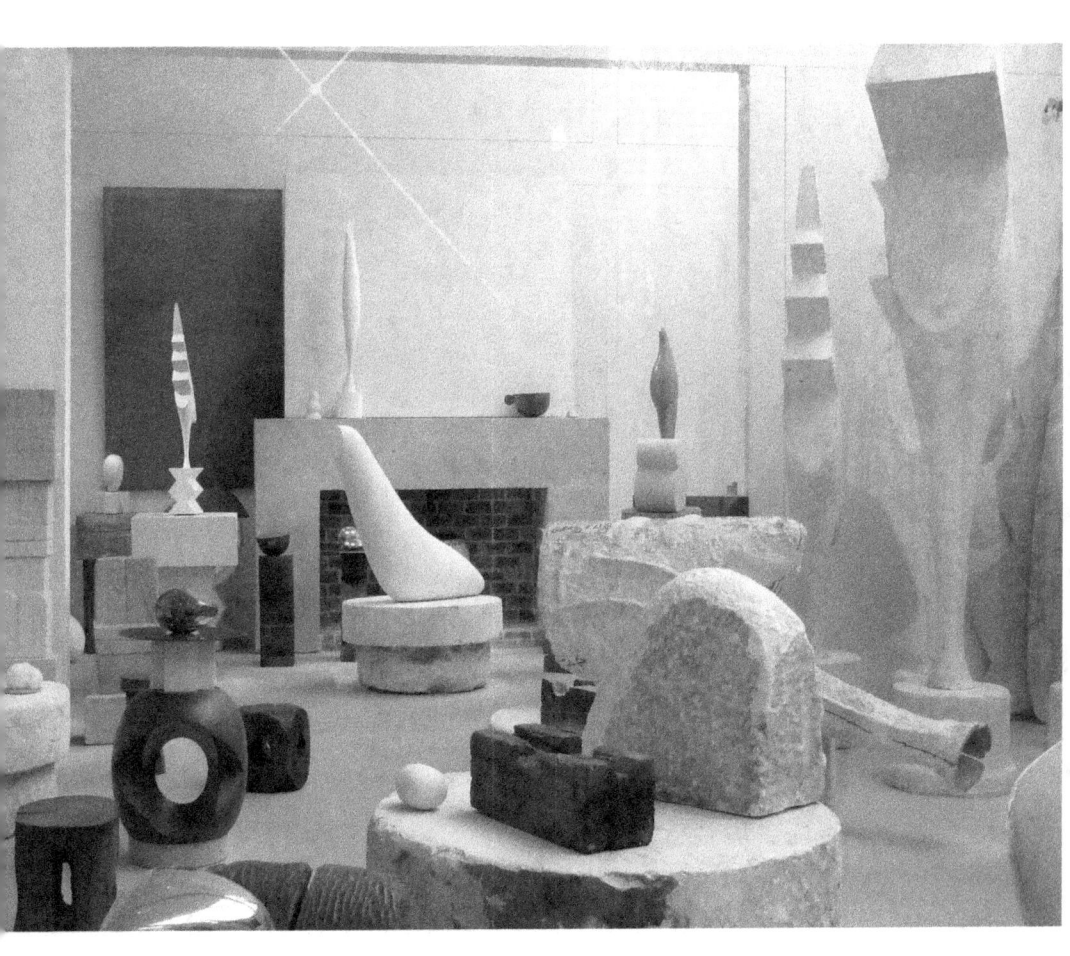

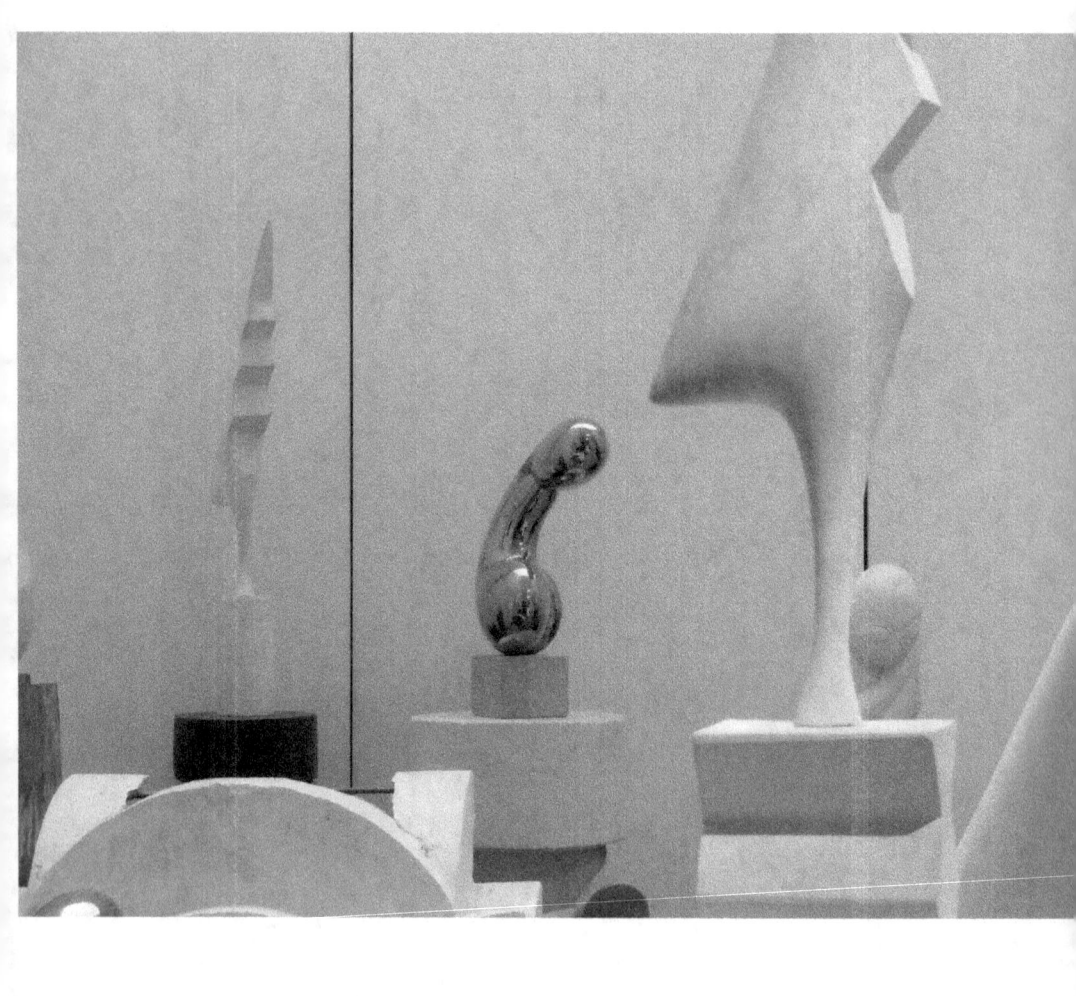

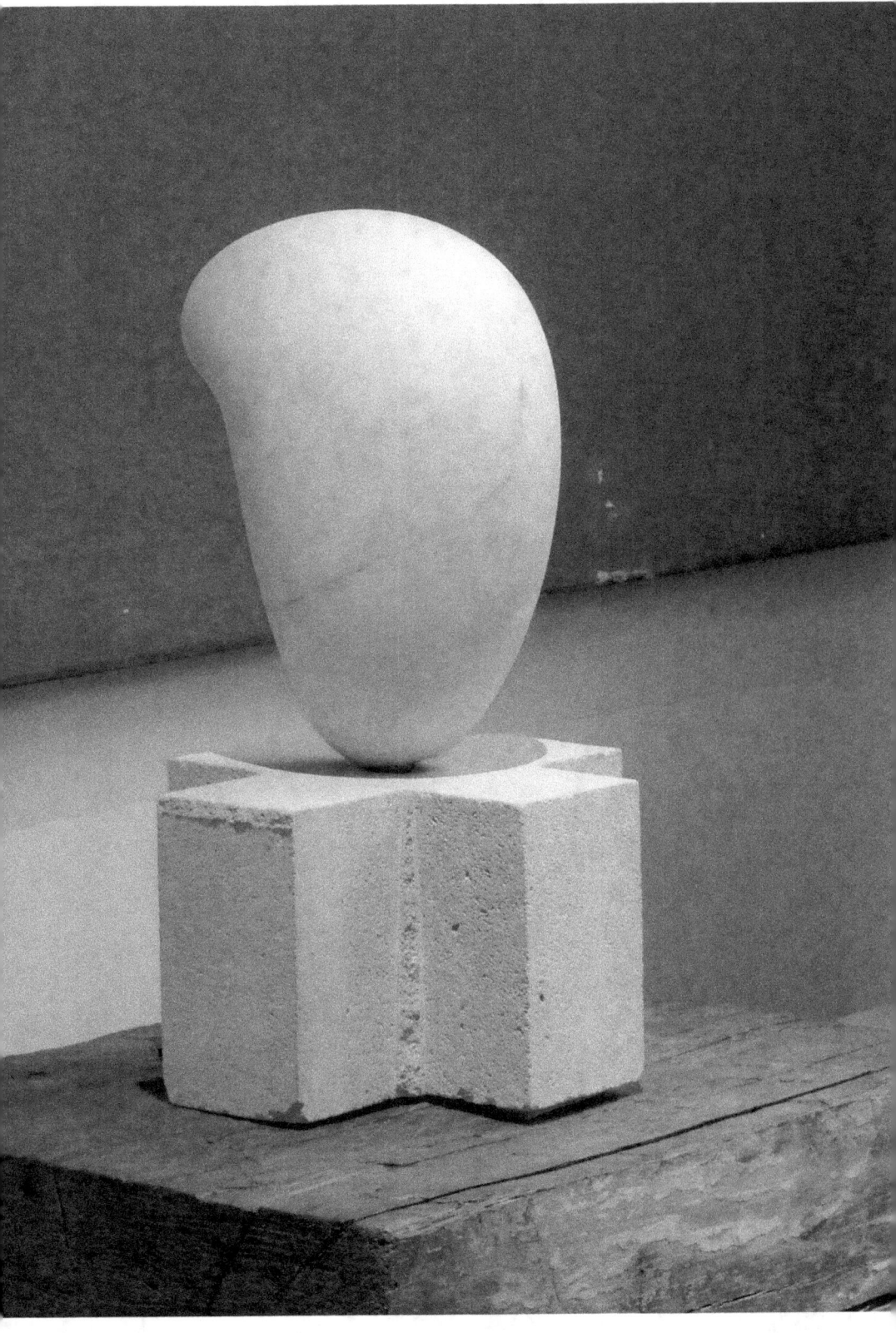

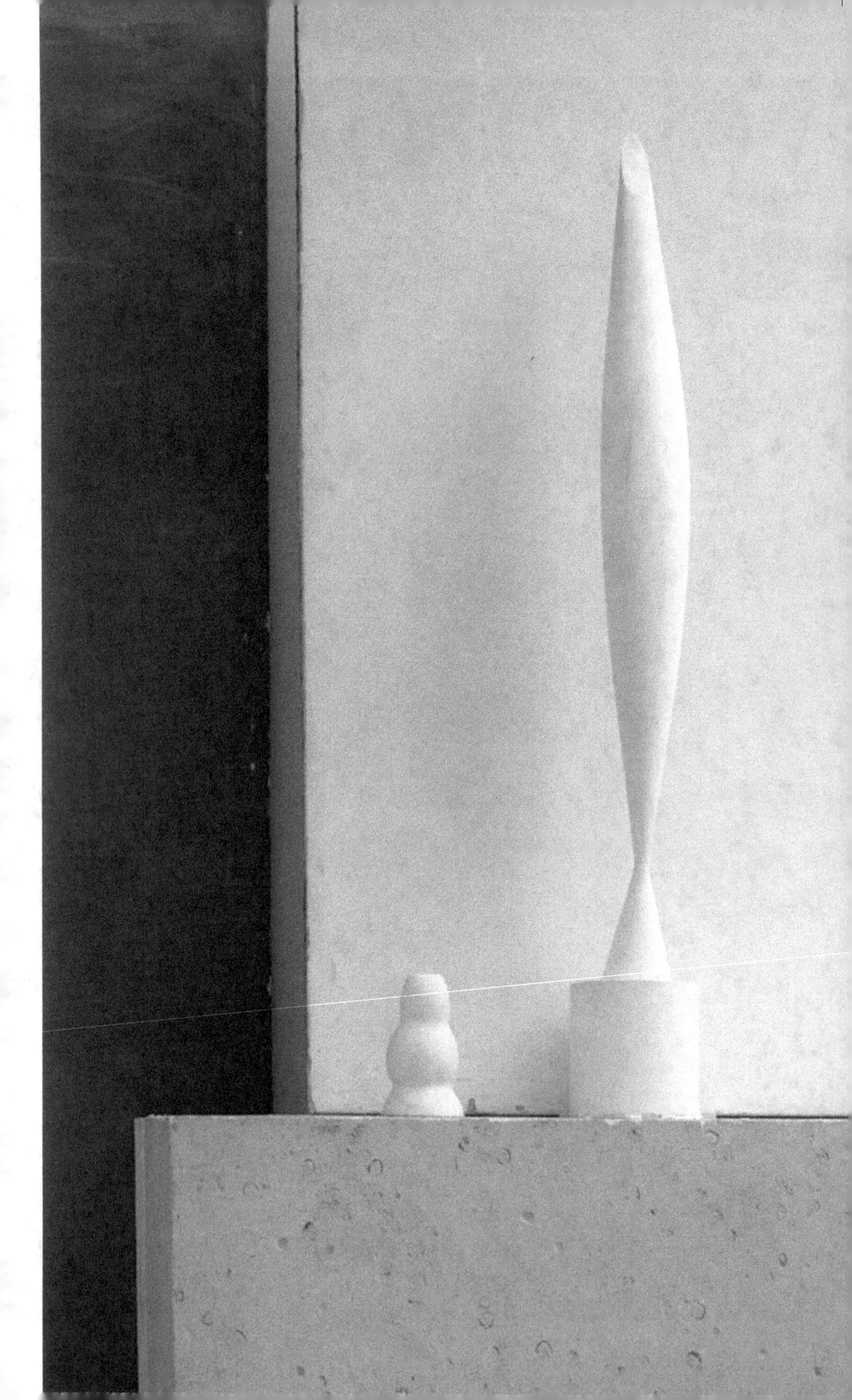

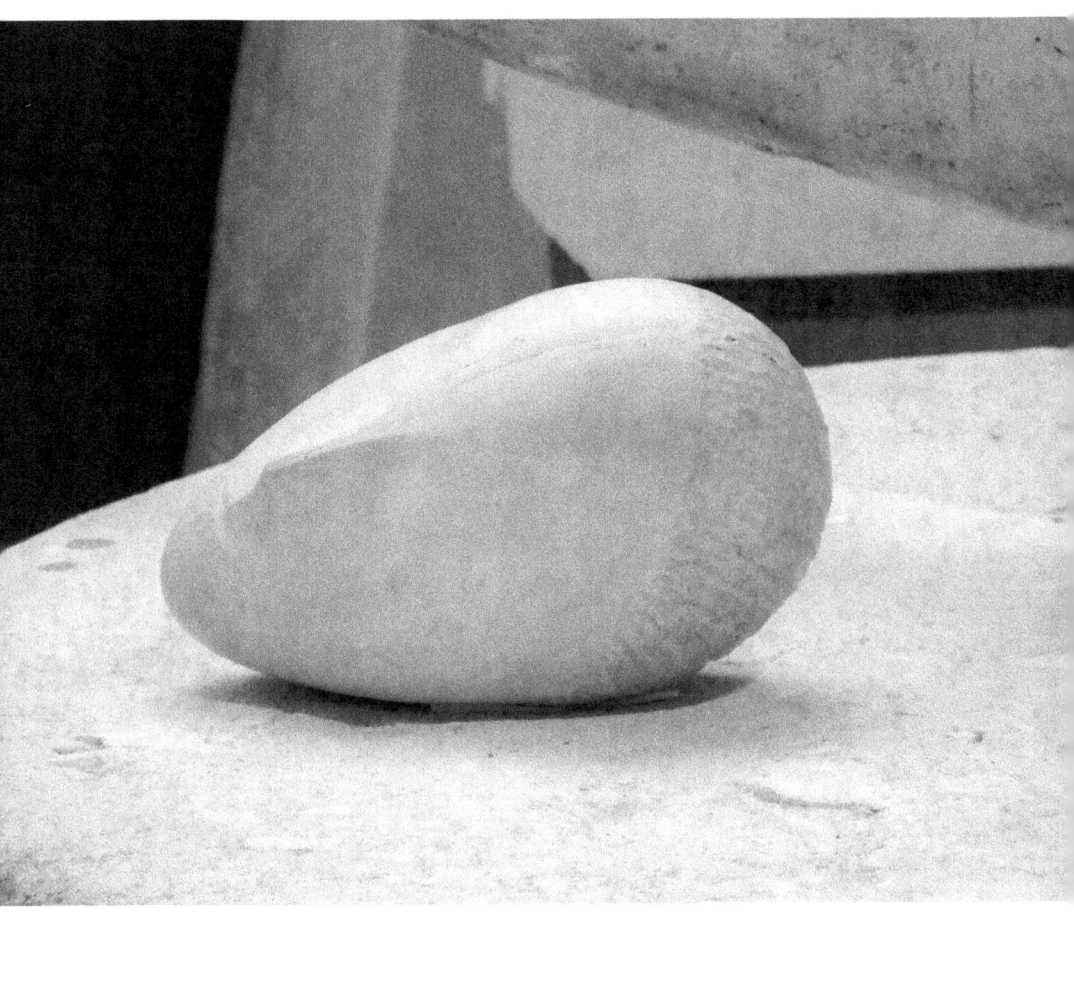

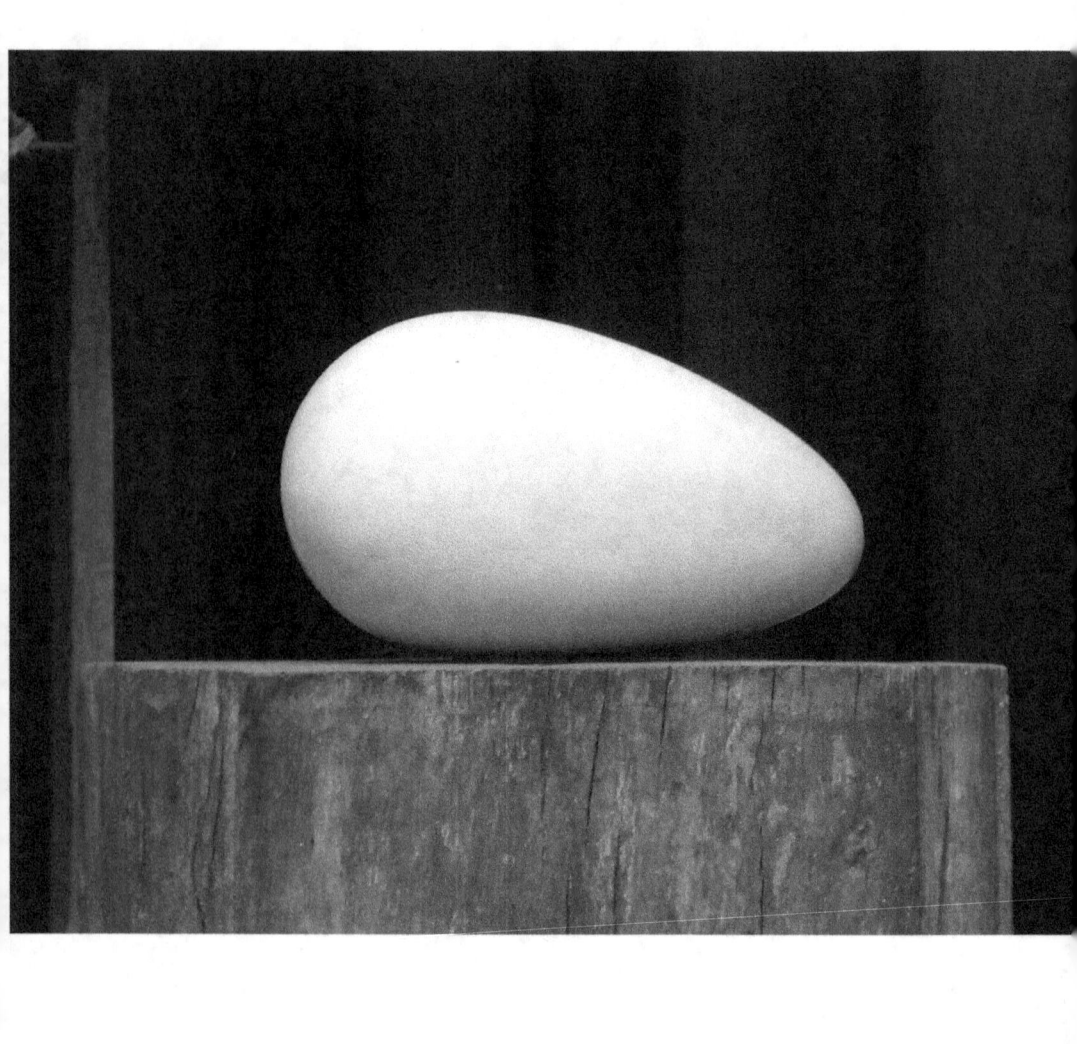

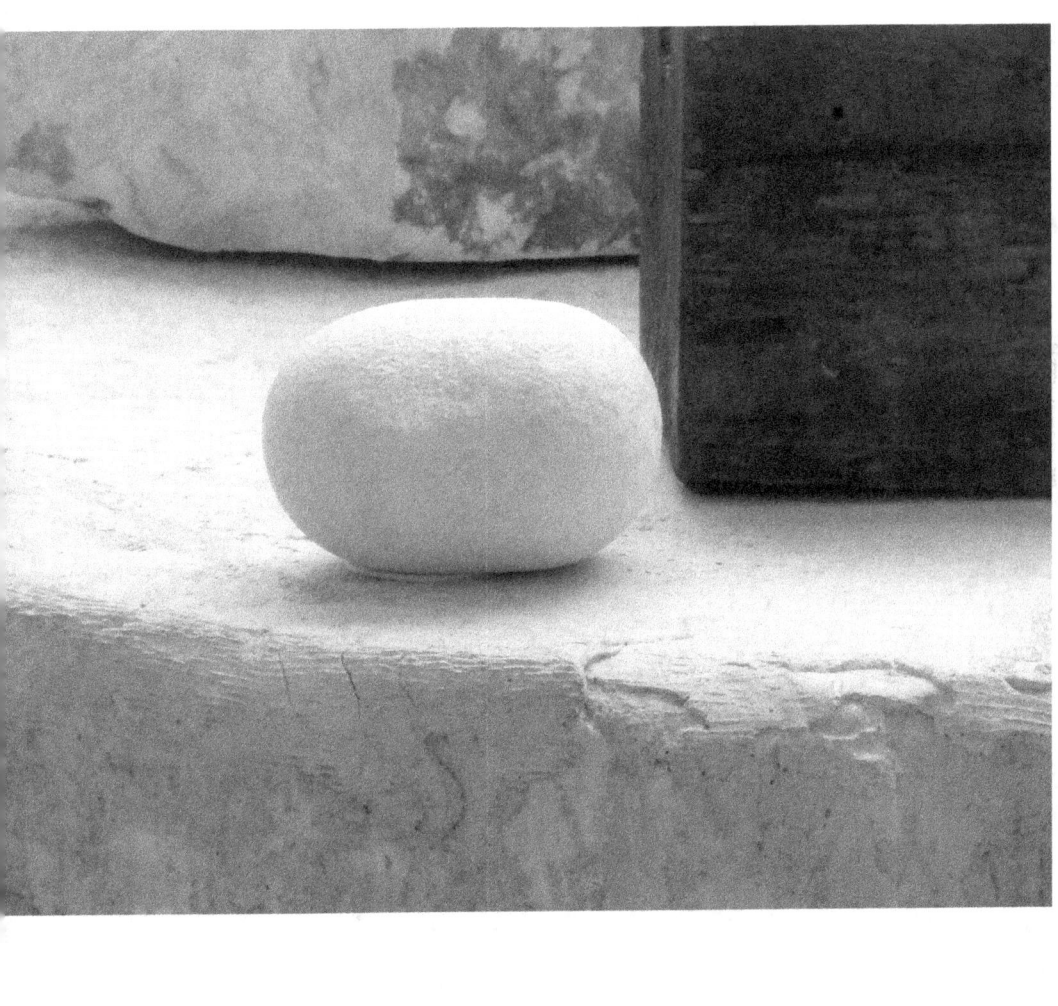

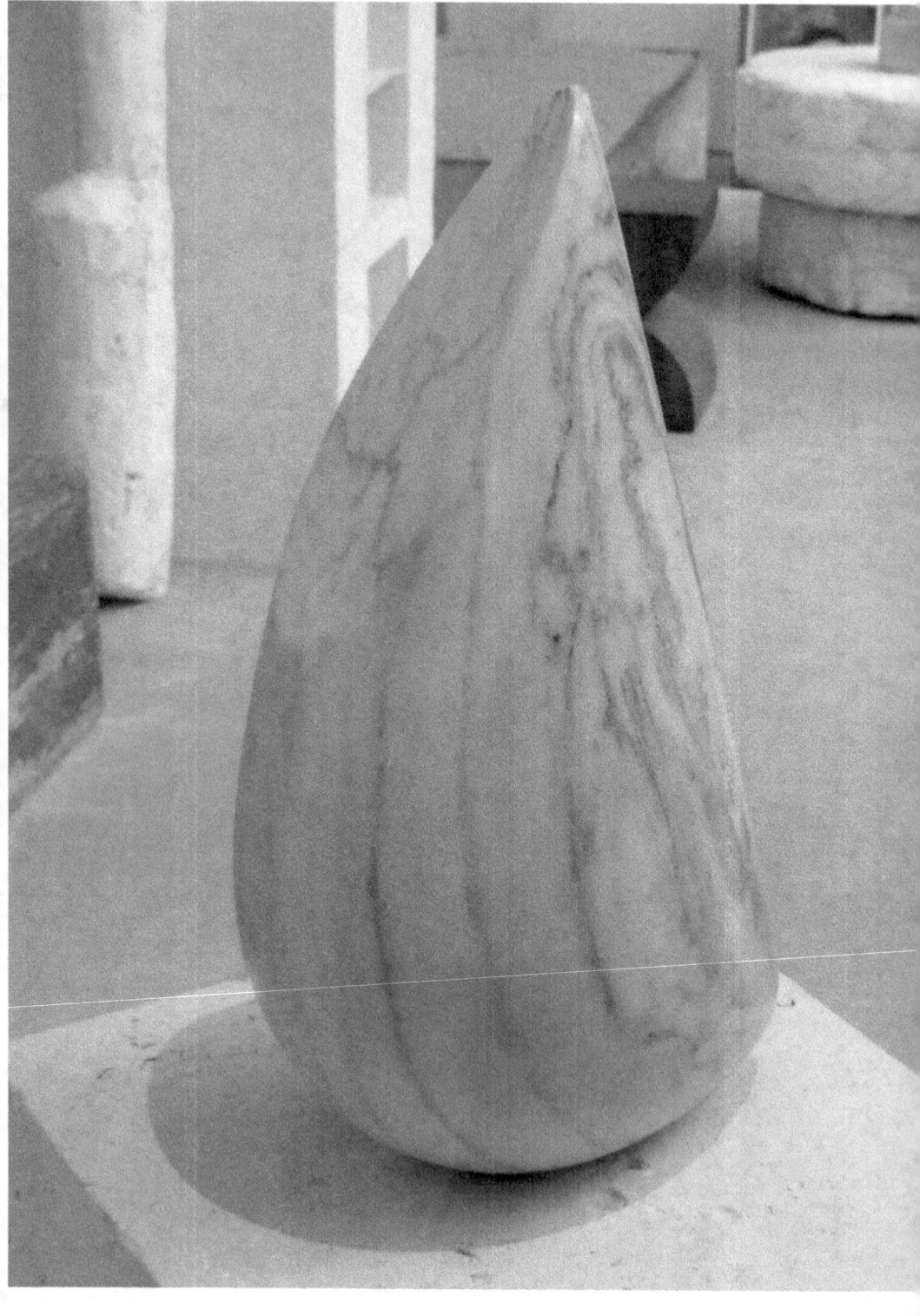

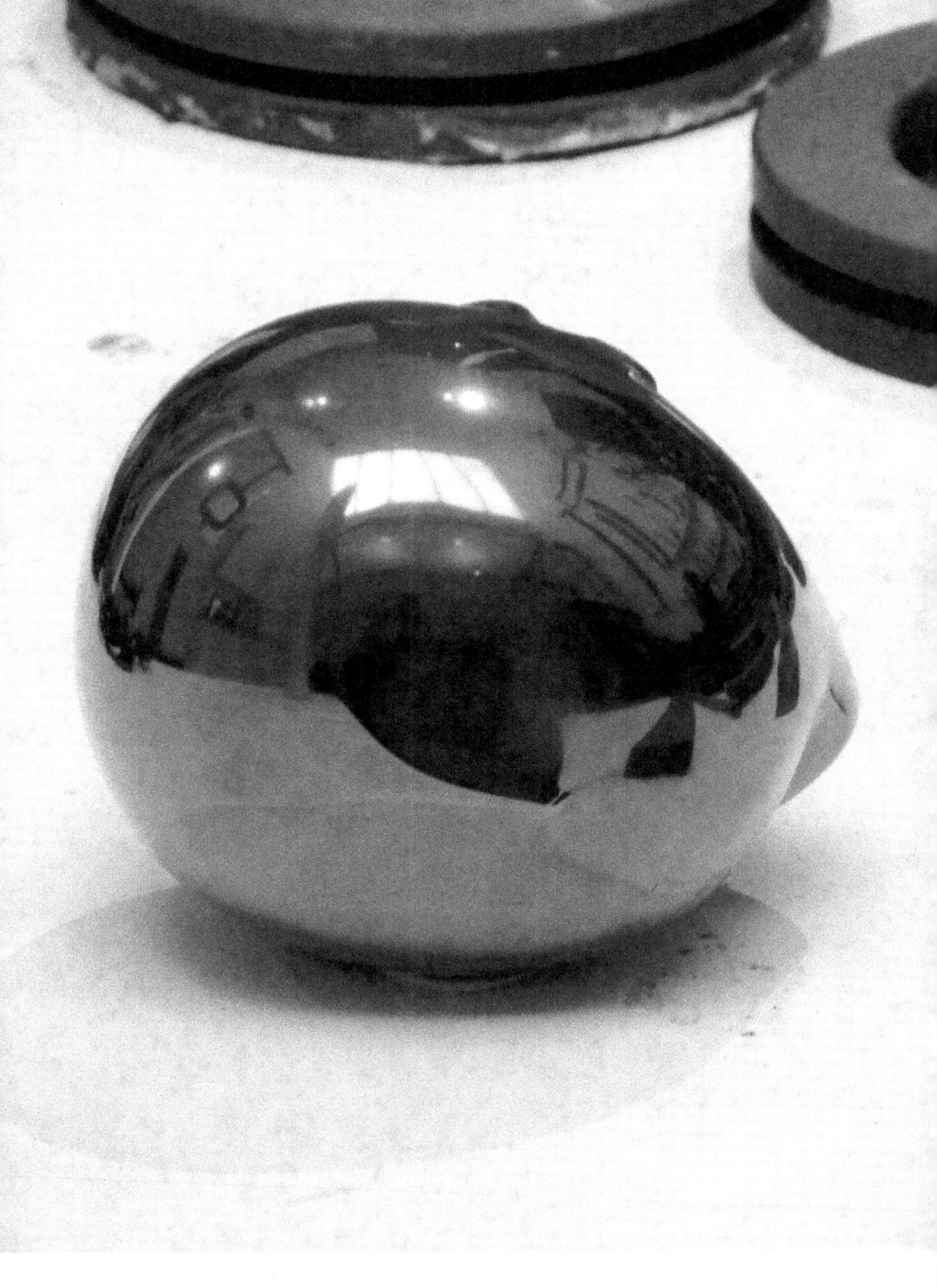

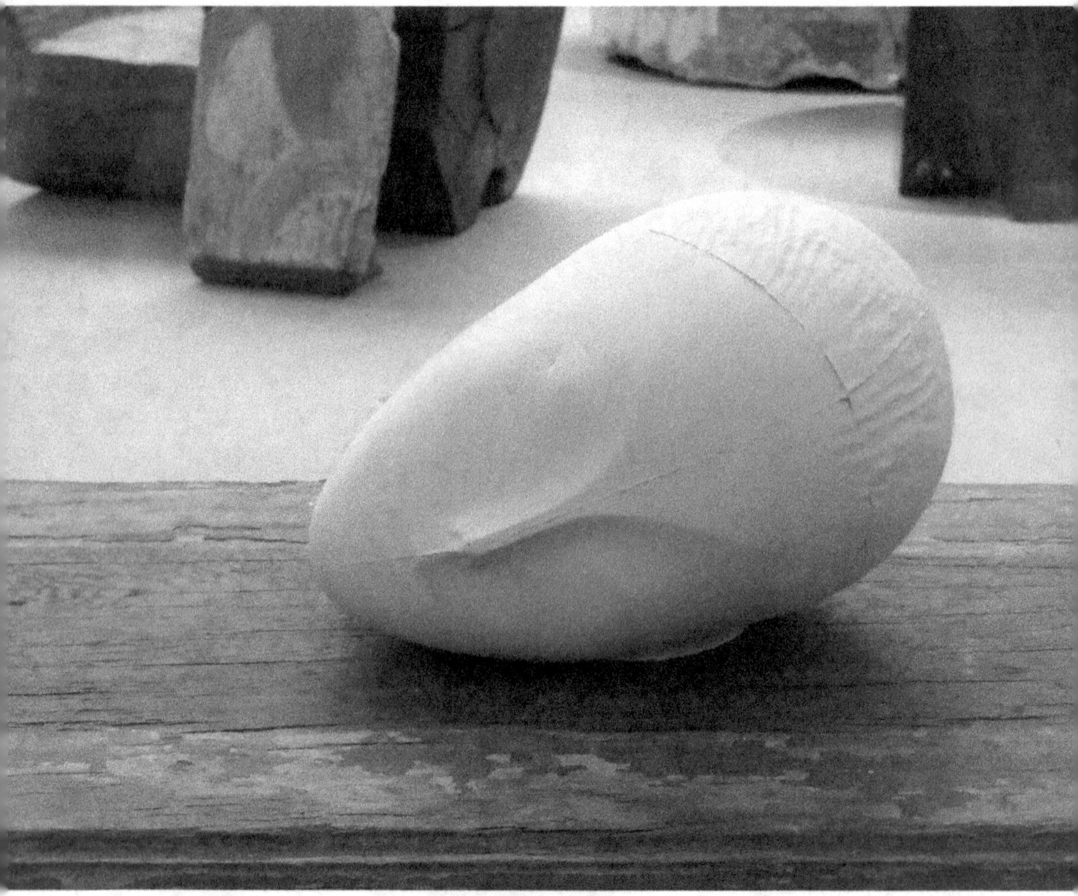

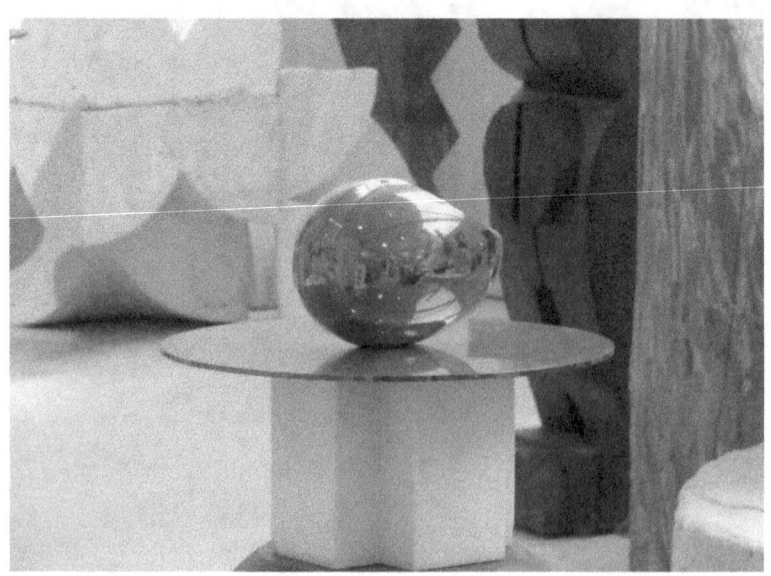

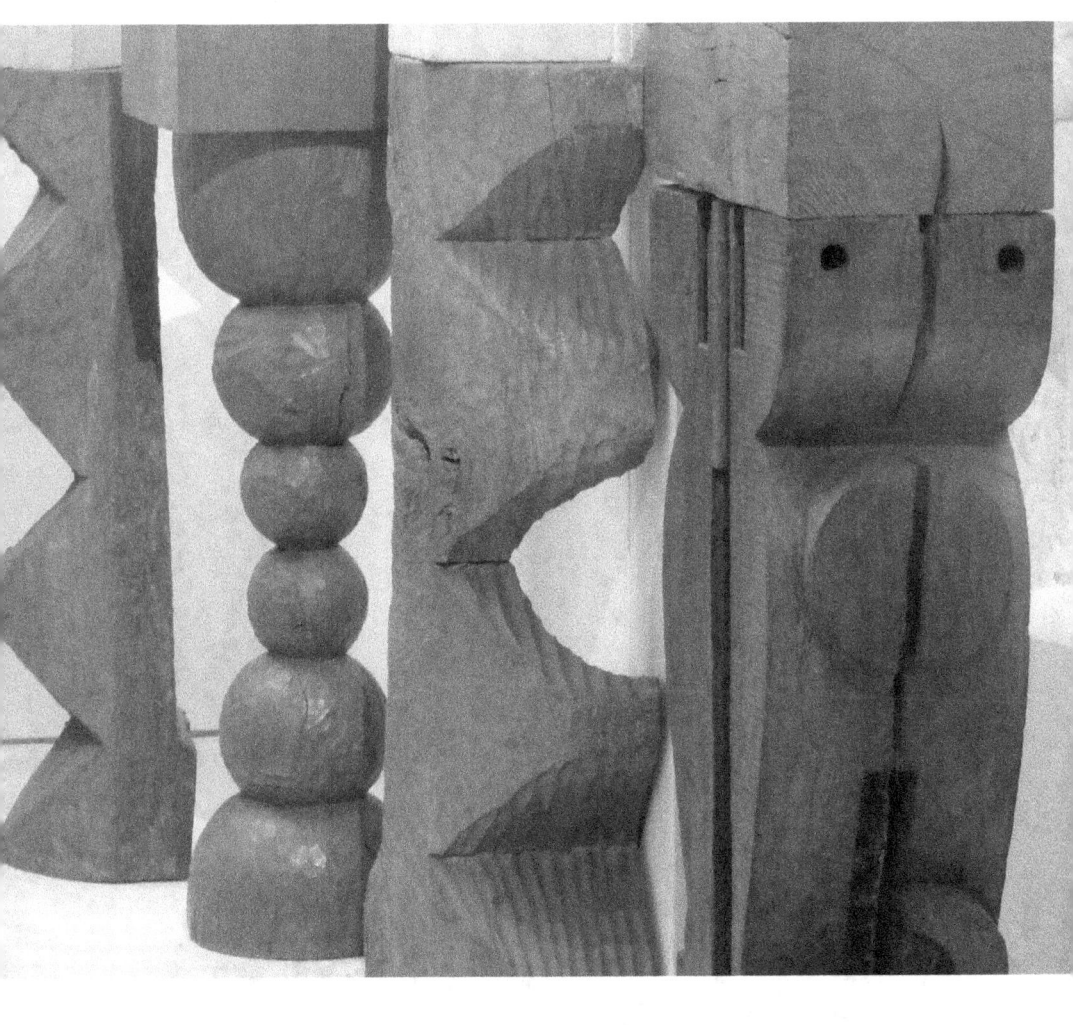

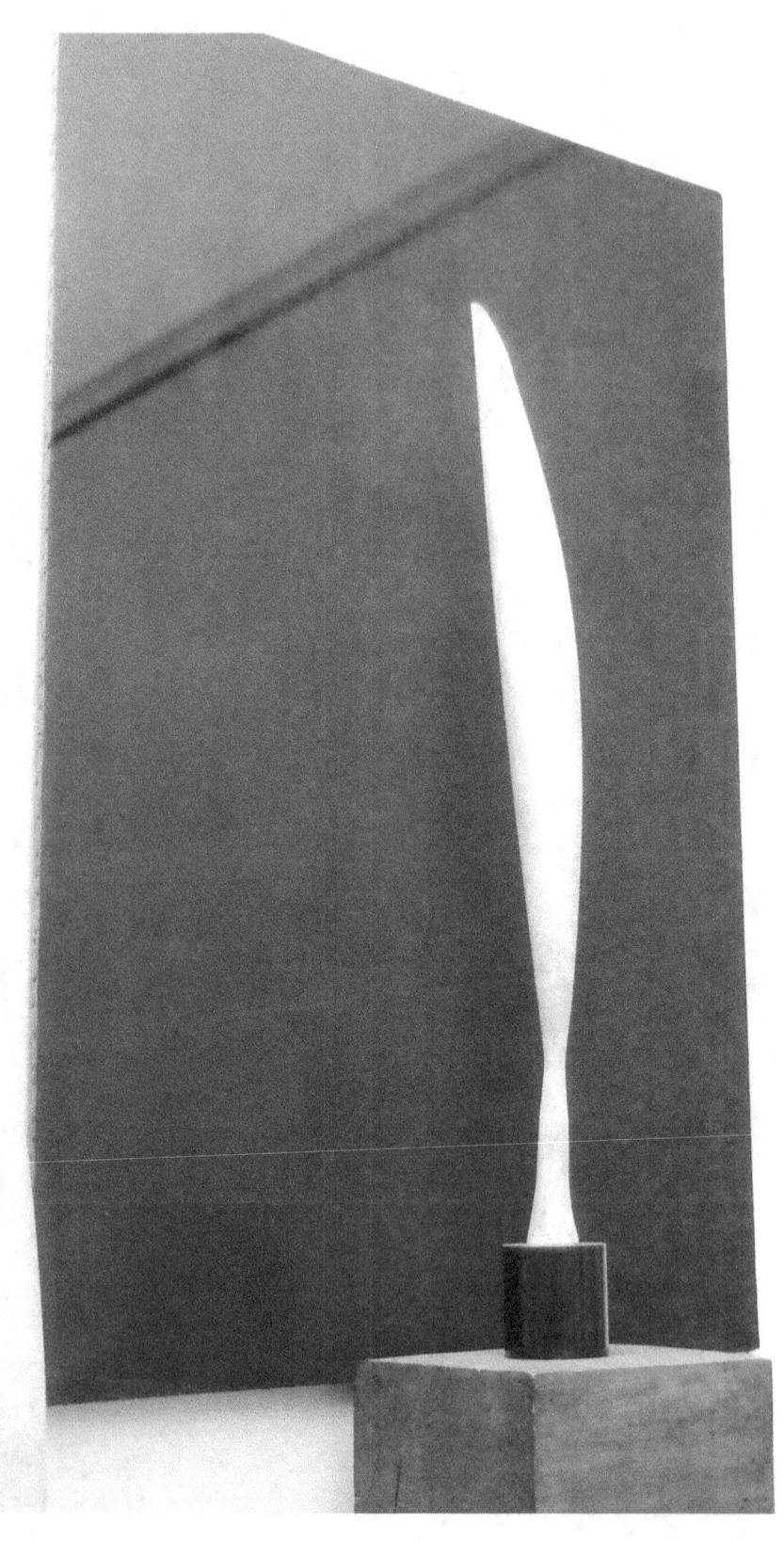

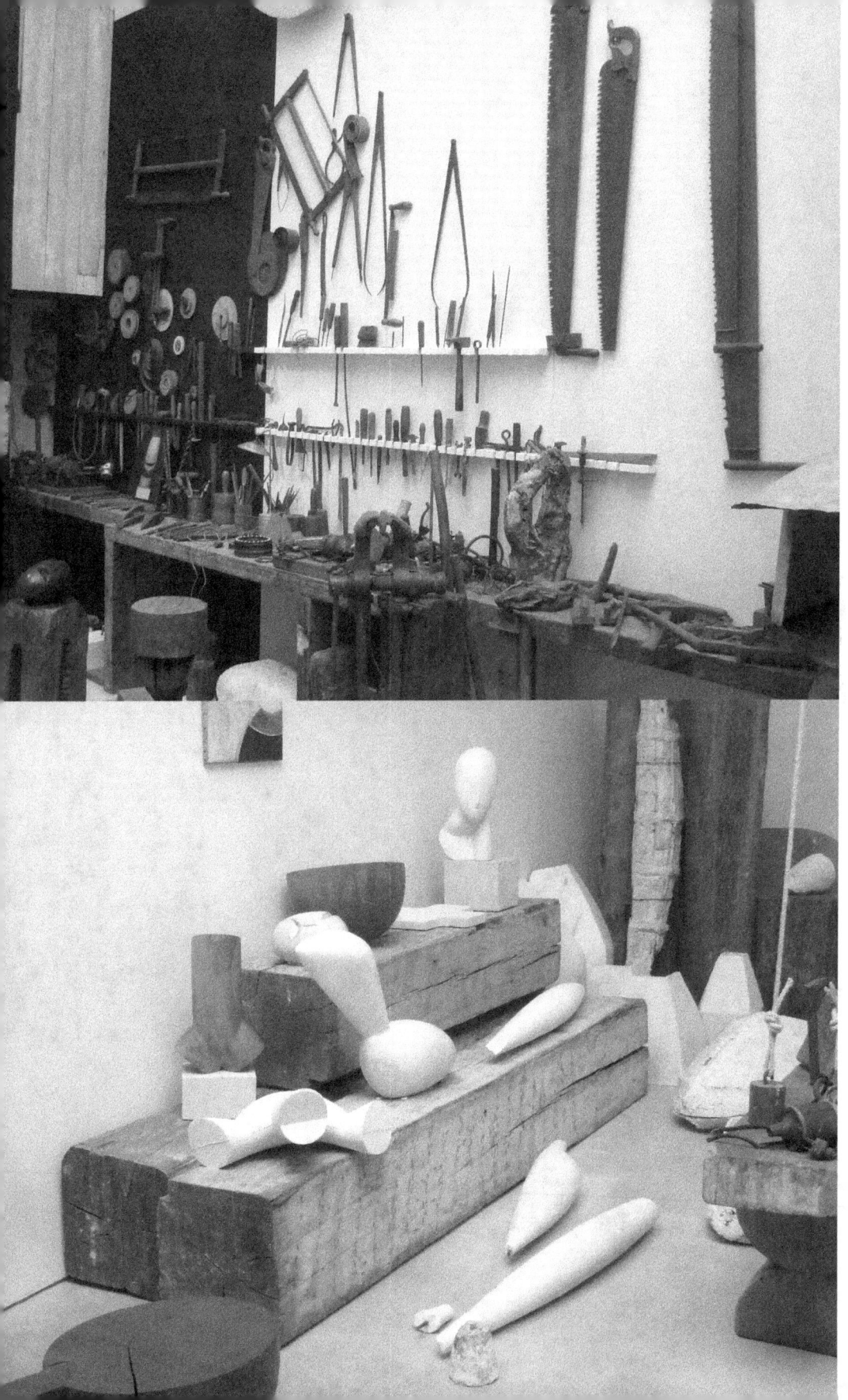

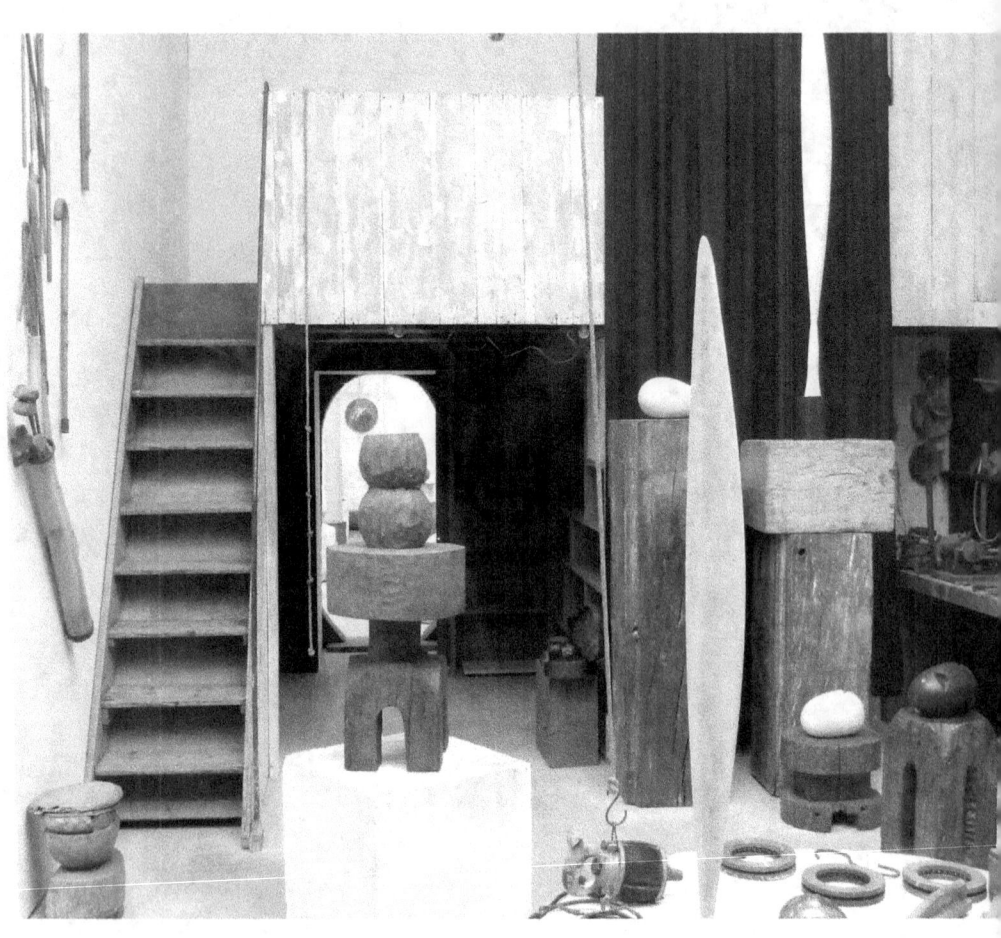

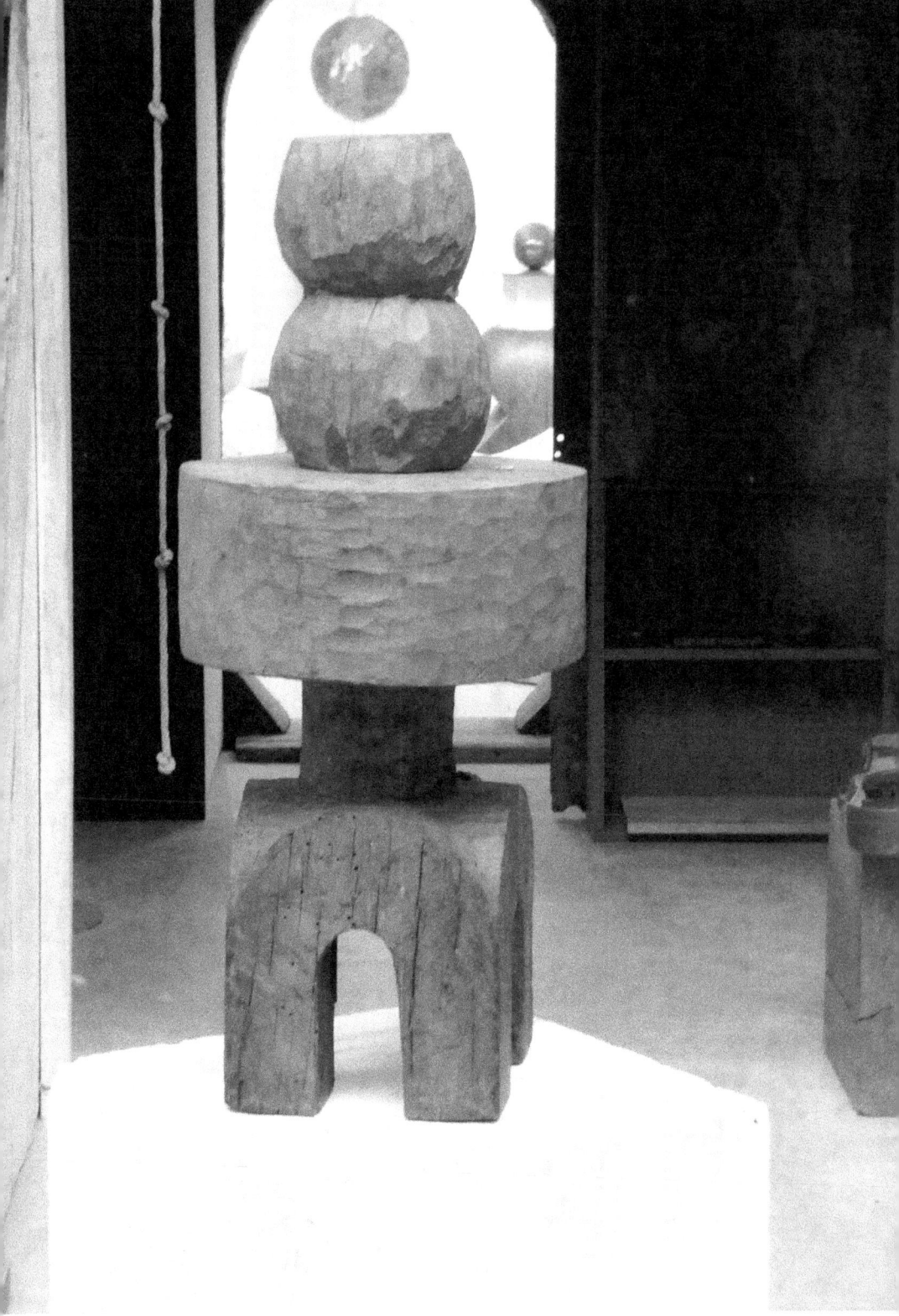

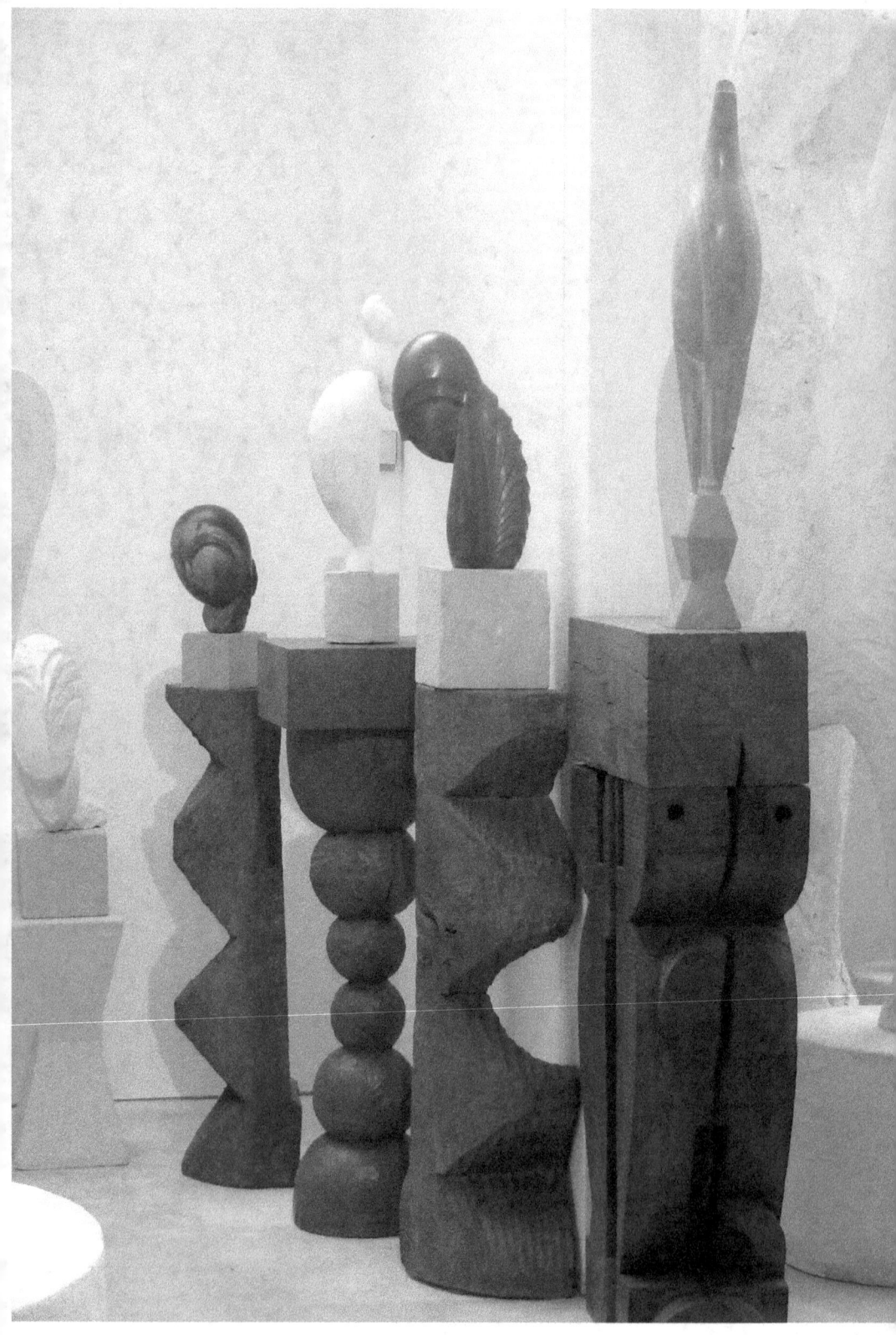

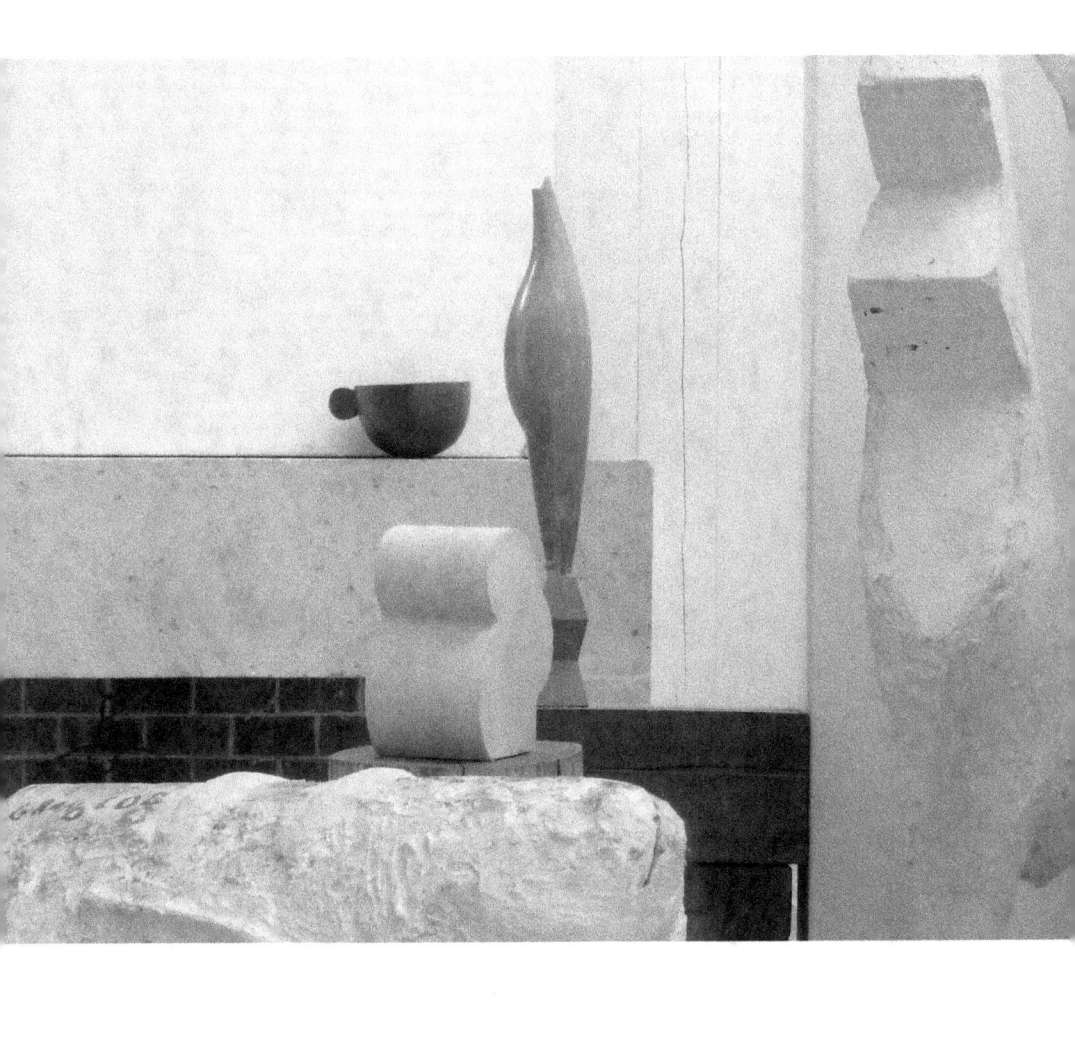

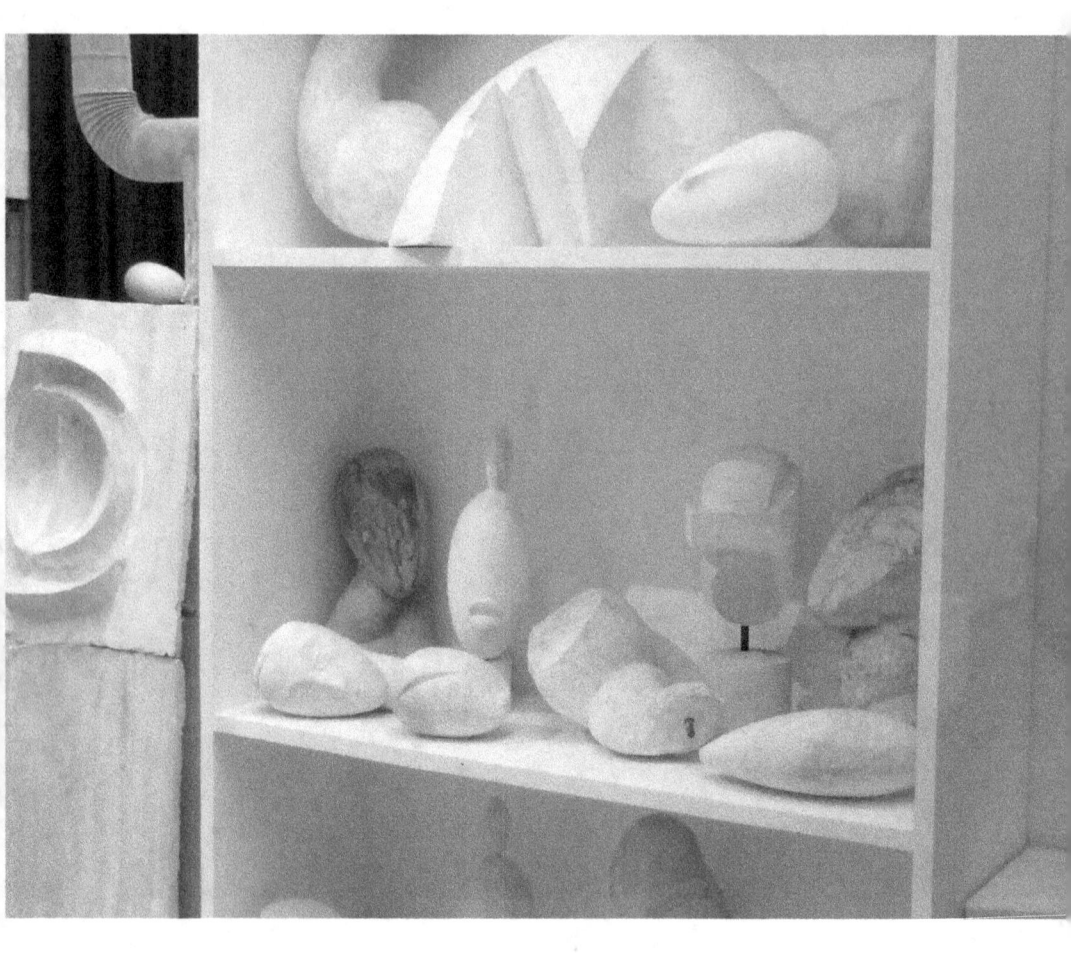

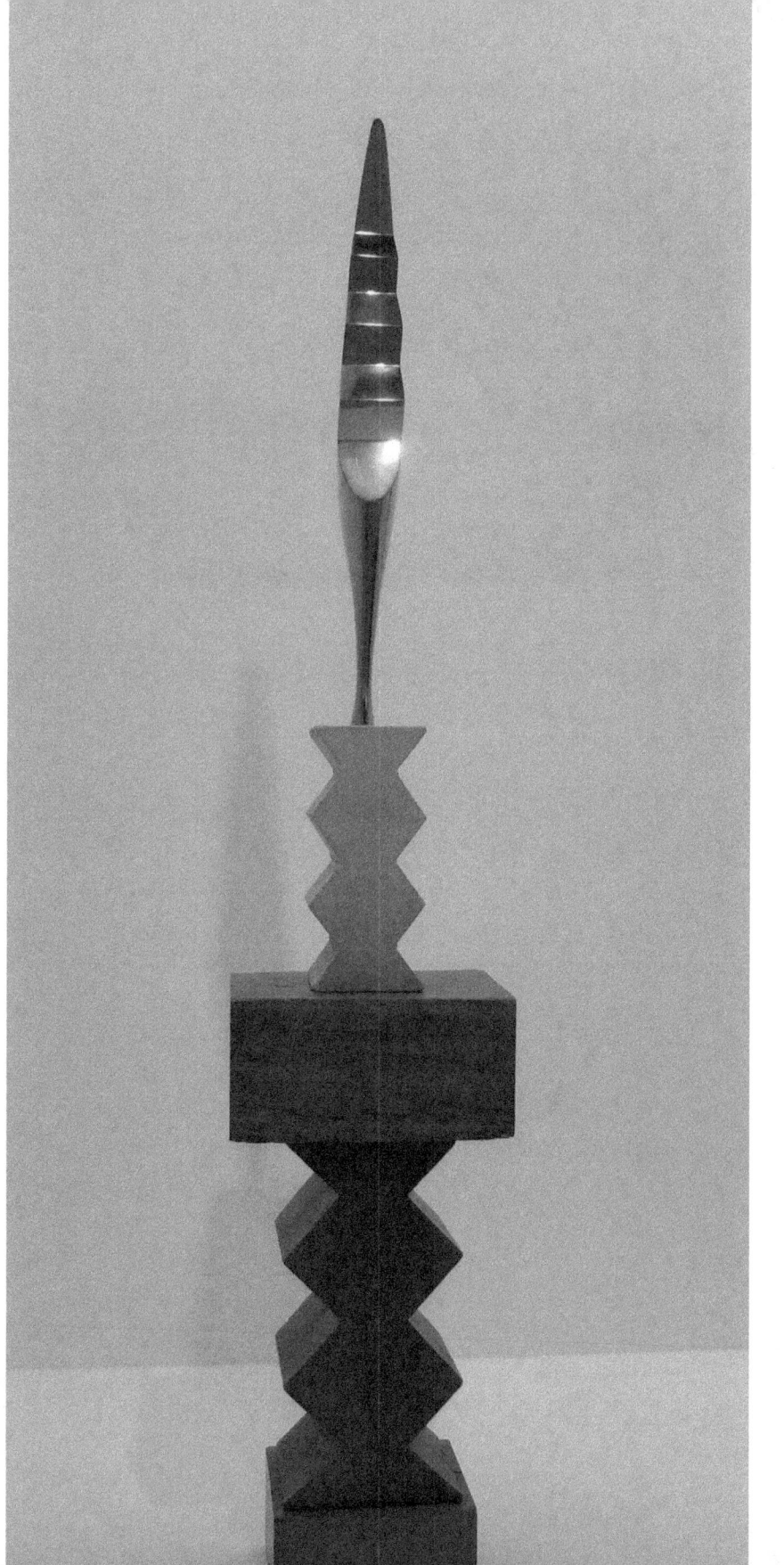

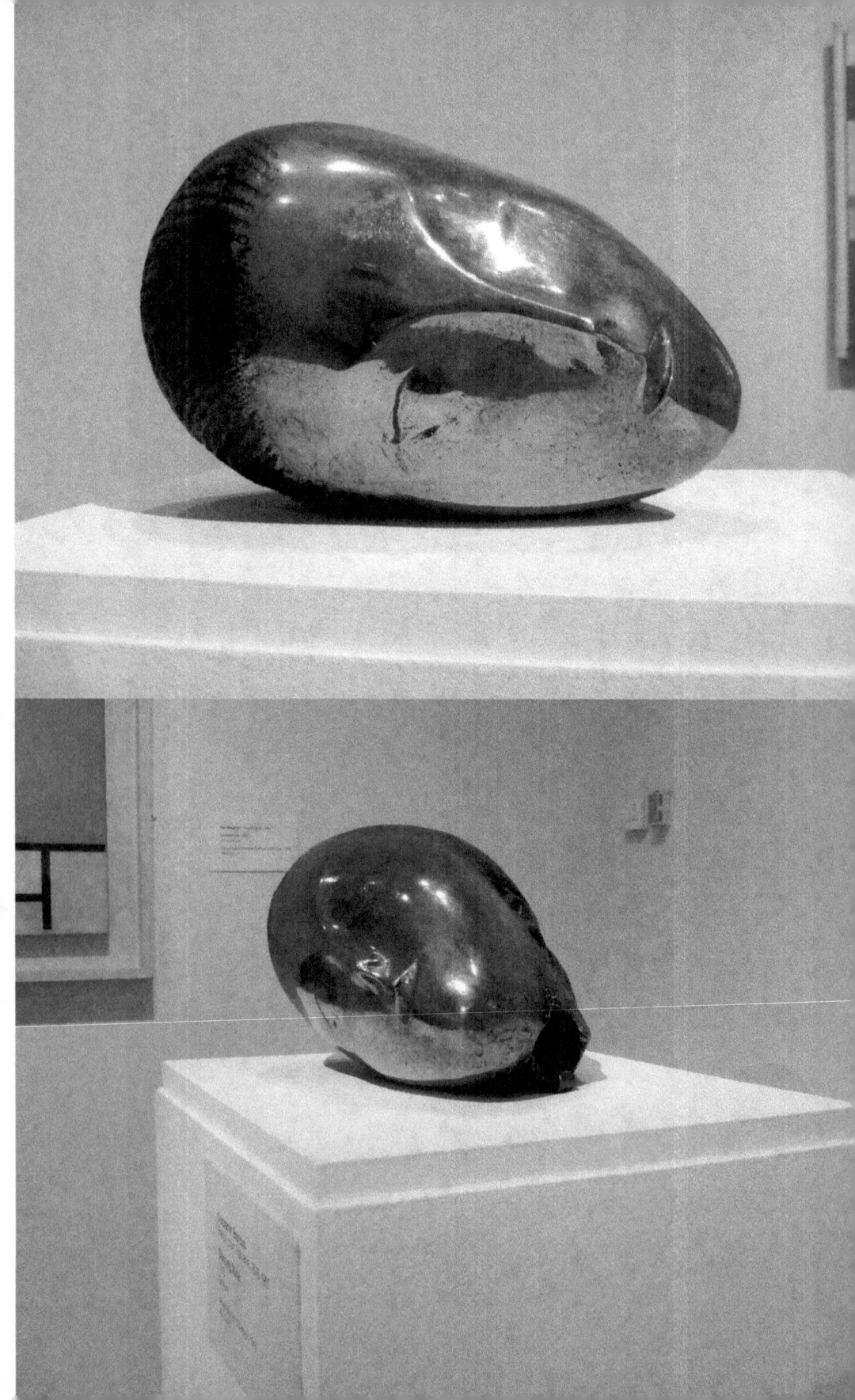

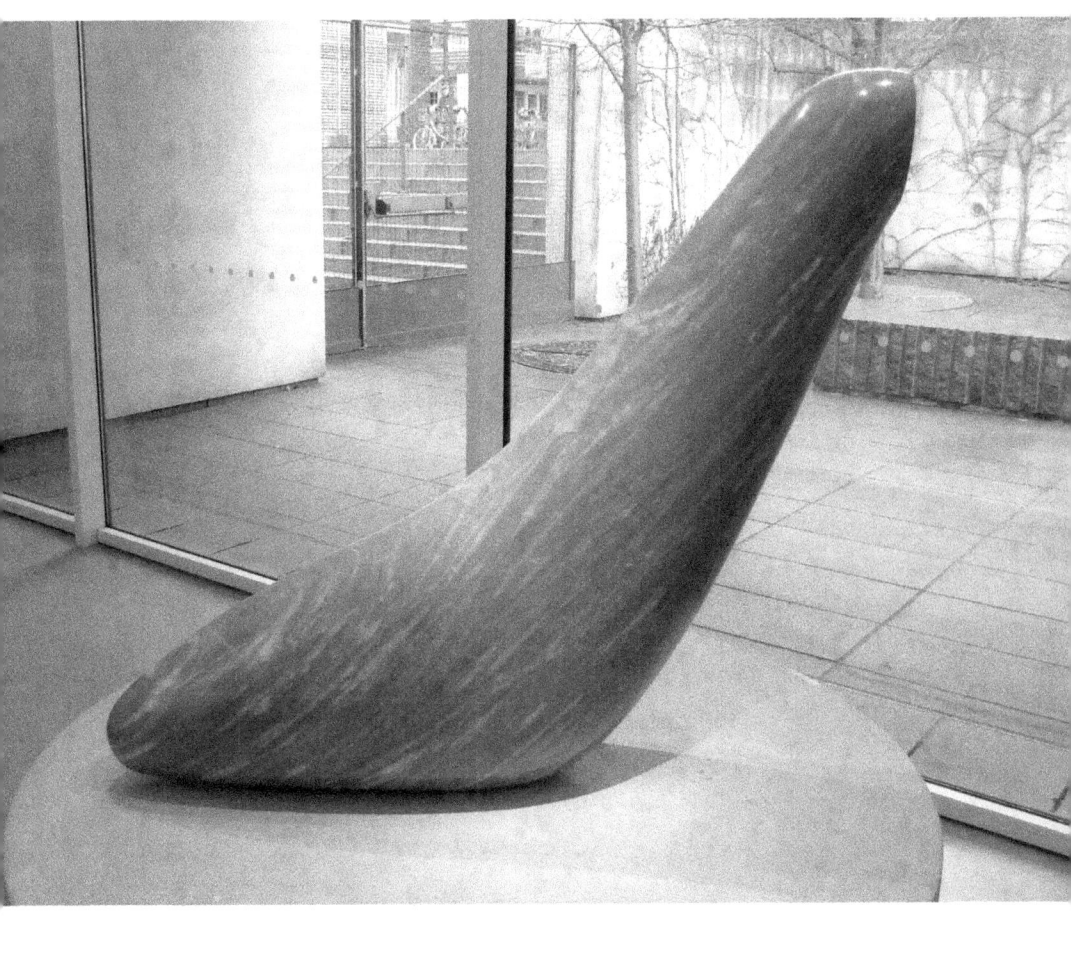

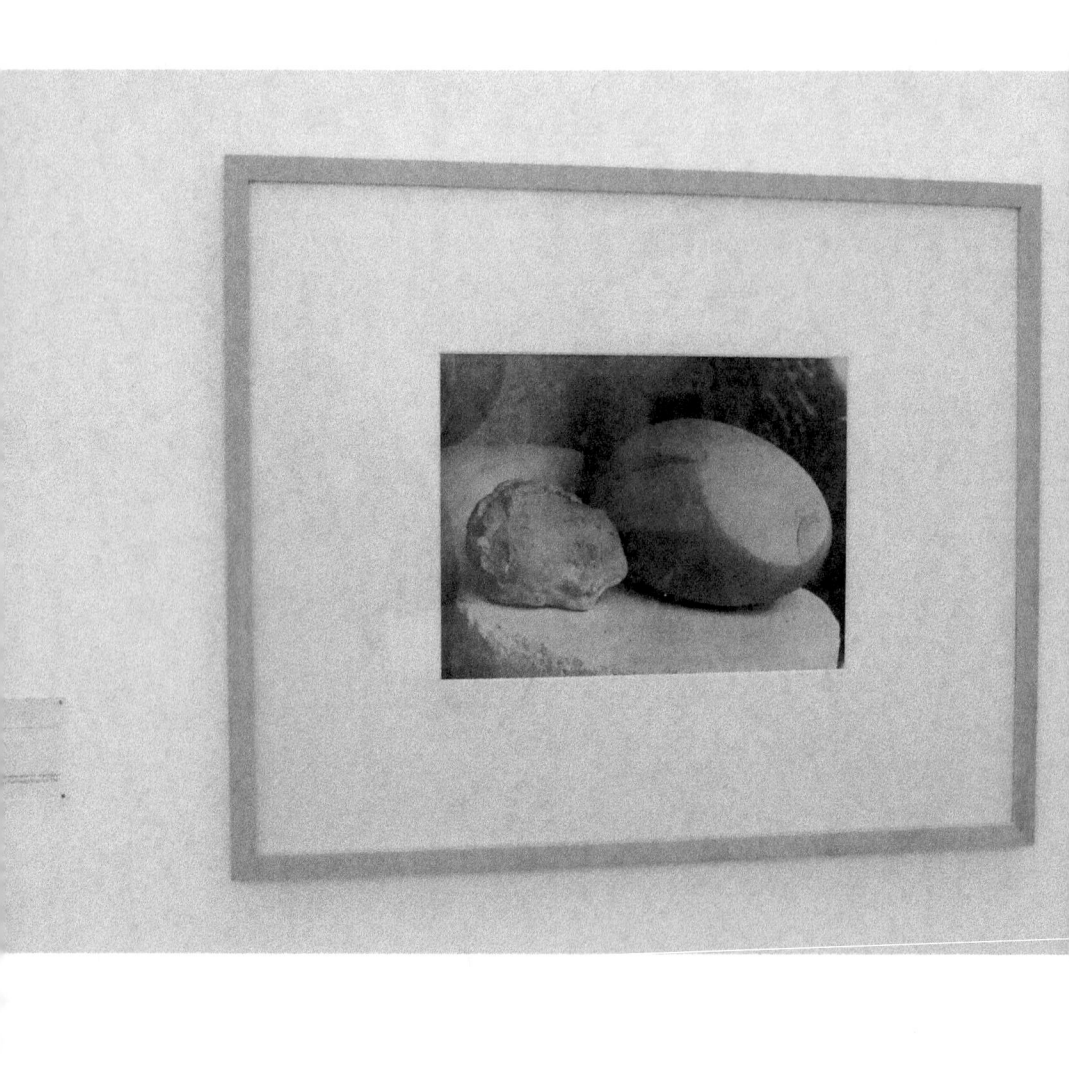

On the following pages, some of the contemporaries of
Constantin Brancusi, and some correspondences with
Brancusi's art in Eastern art.

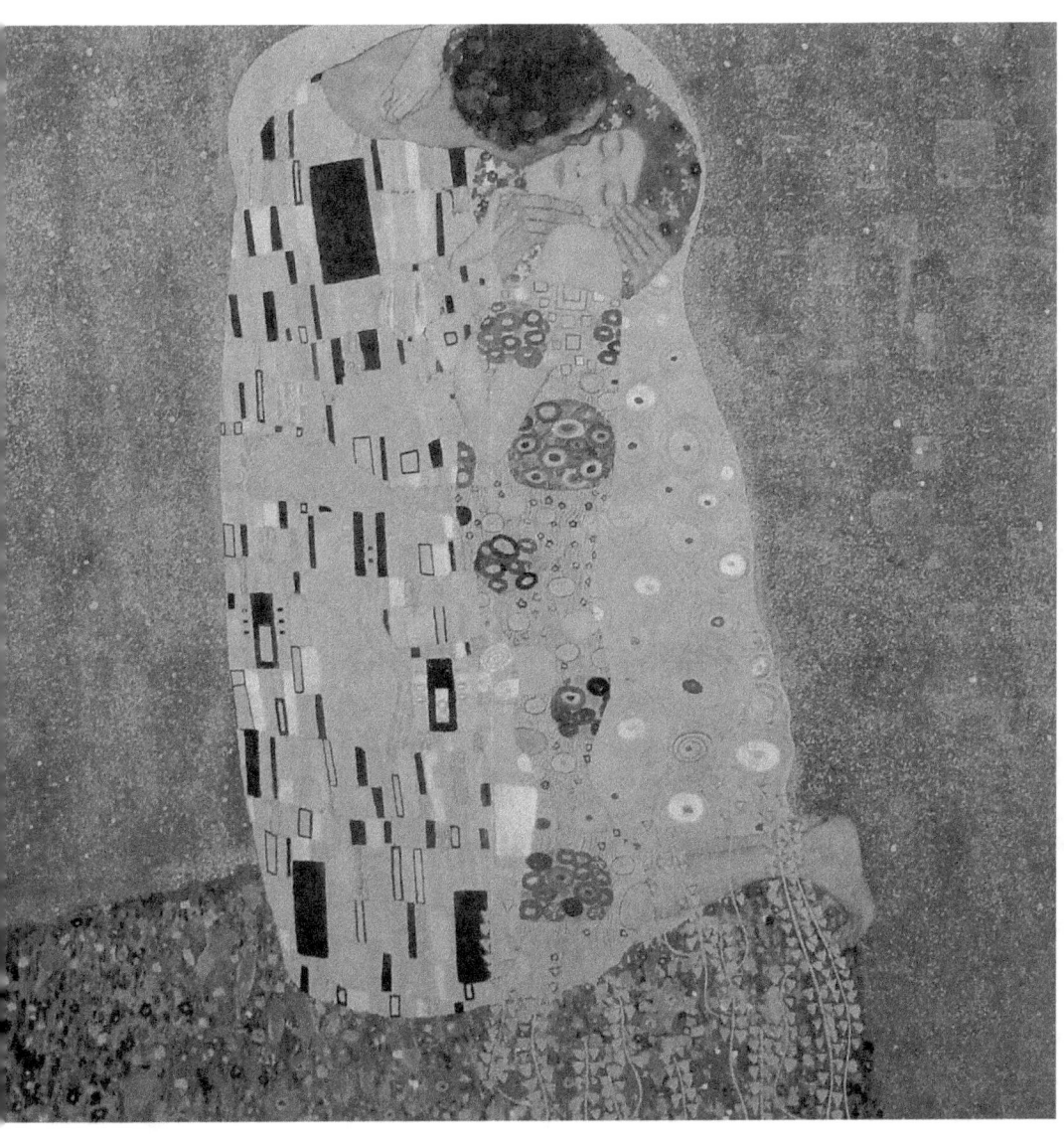

Gustav Klimt, The Kiss

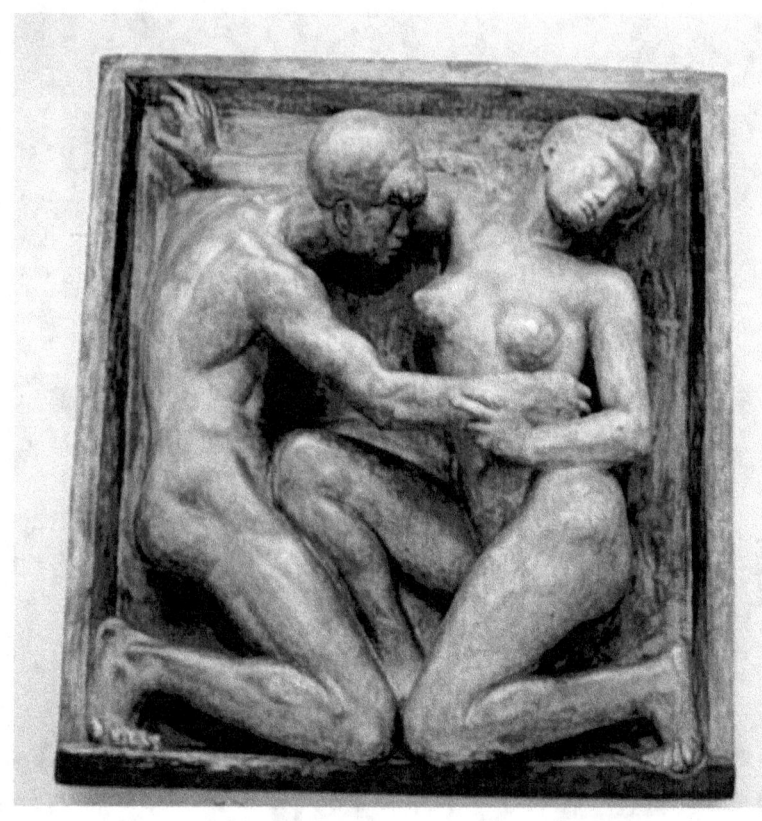

Aristide Maillol, Desire, 1908

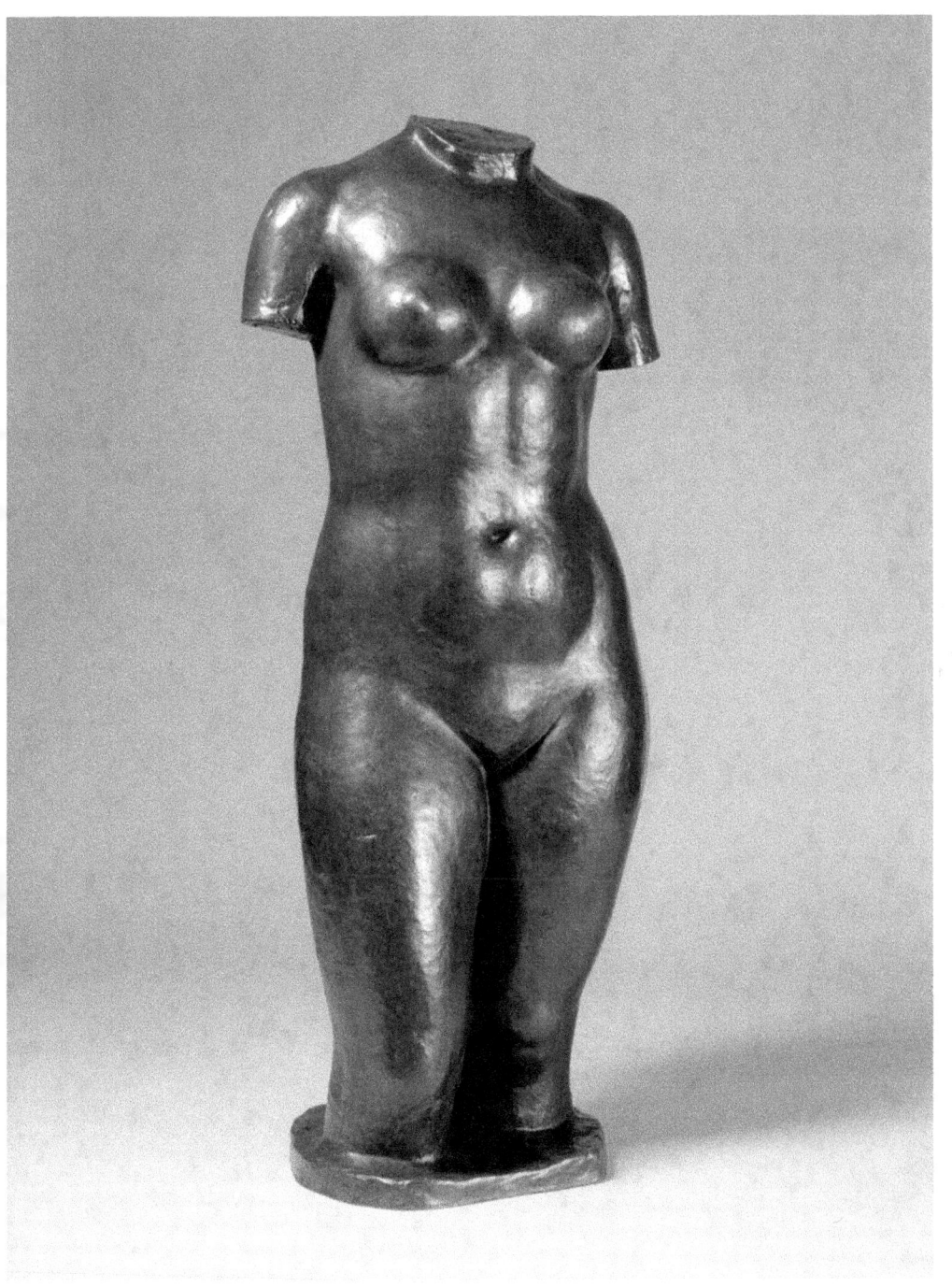

Aristide Maillol, Torso of a Young Woman, 1935,
Montreal Museum of Fine Arts

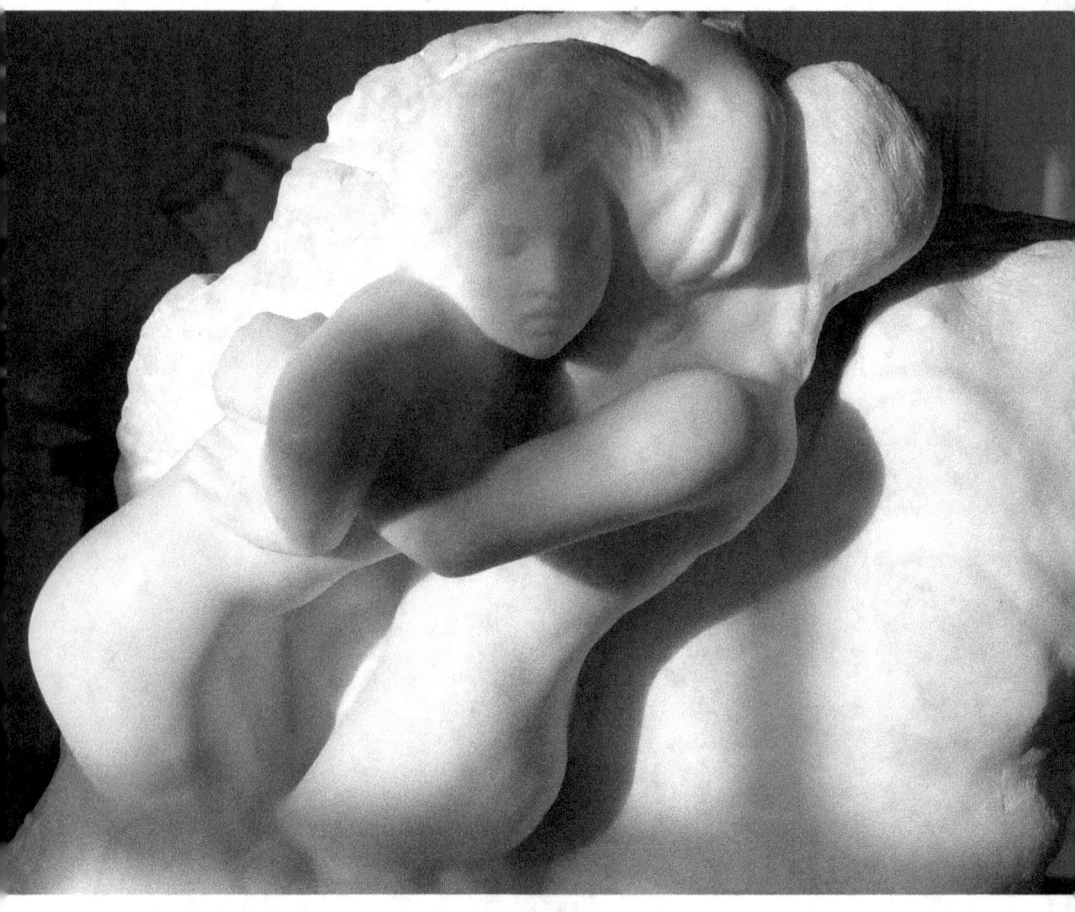

Auguste Rodin

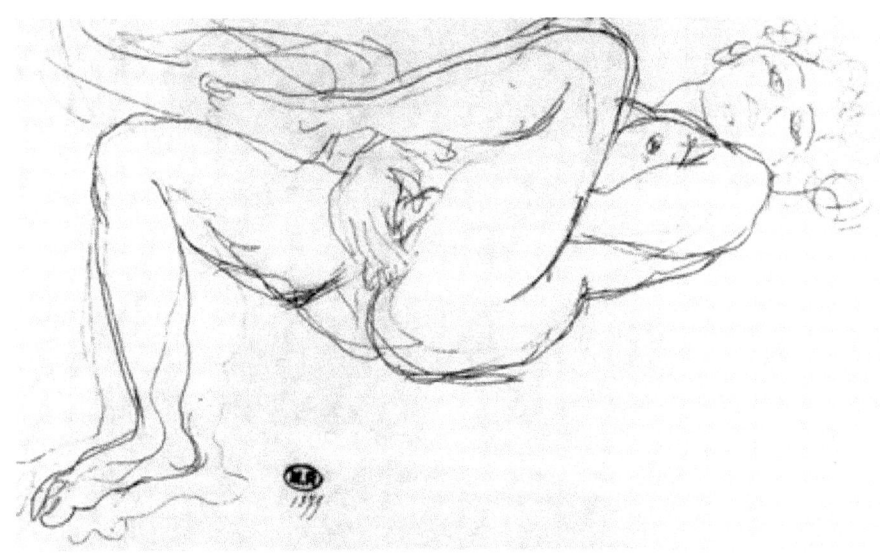

Auguste Rodin, drawings

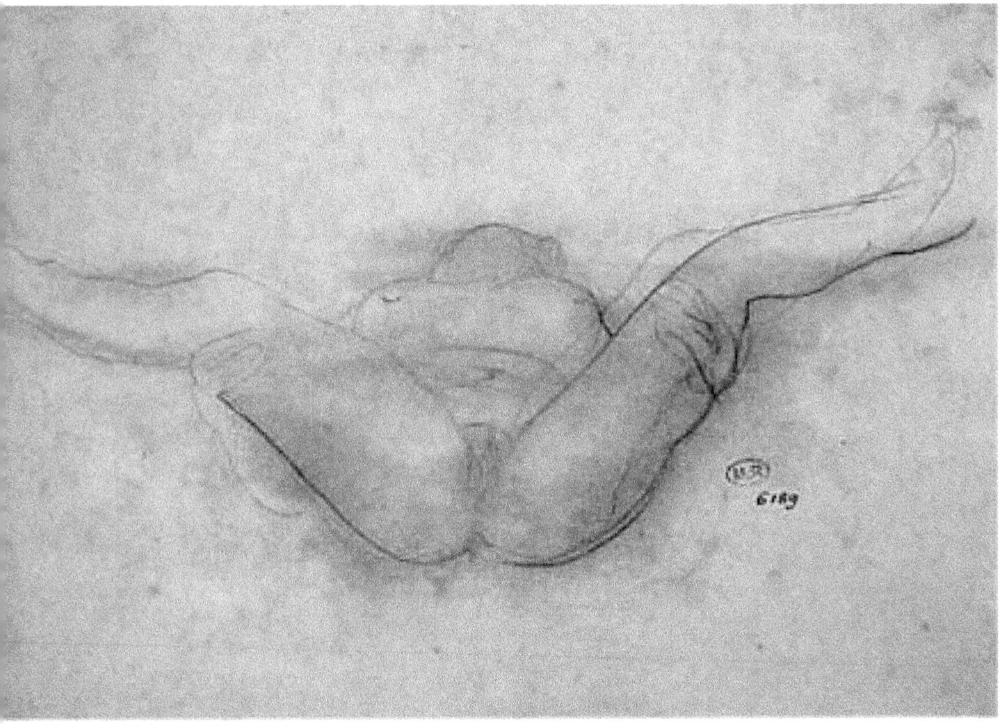

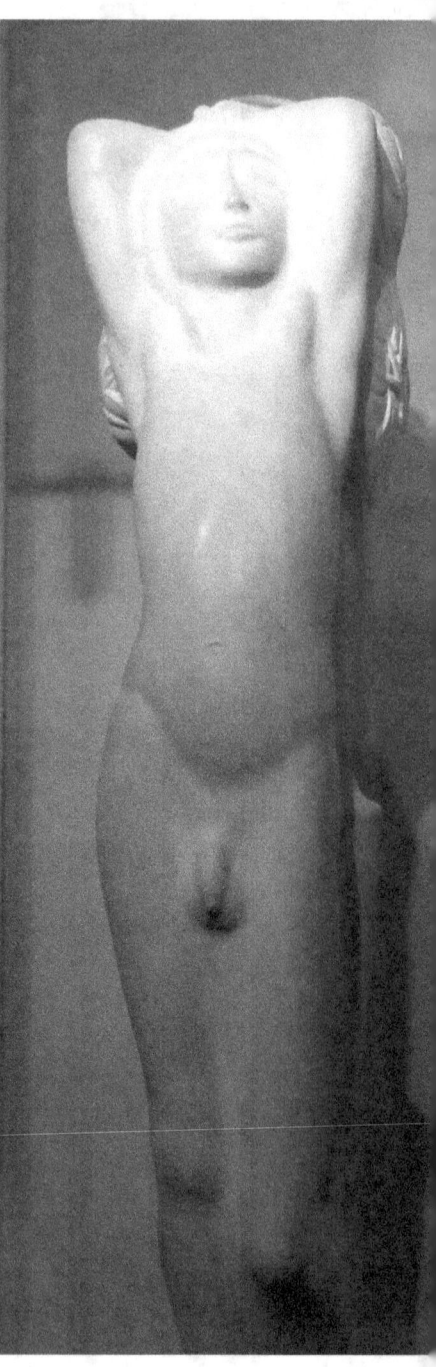

Eric Gill, St Sebastian,
1920, Victoria & Albert Museum,
London

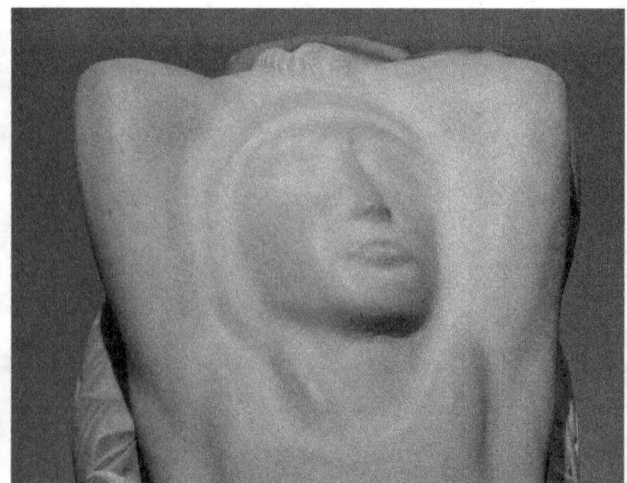

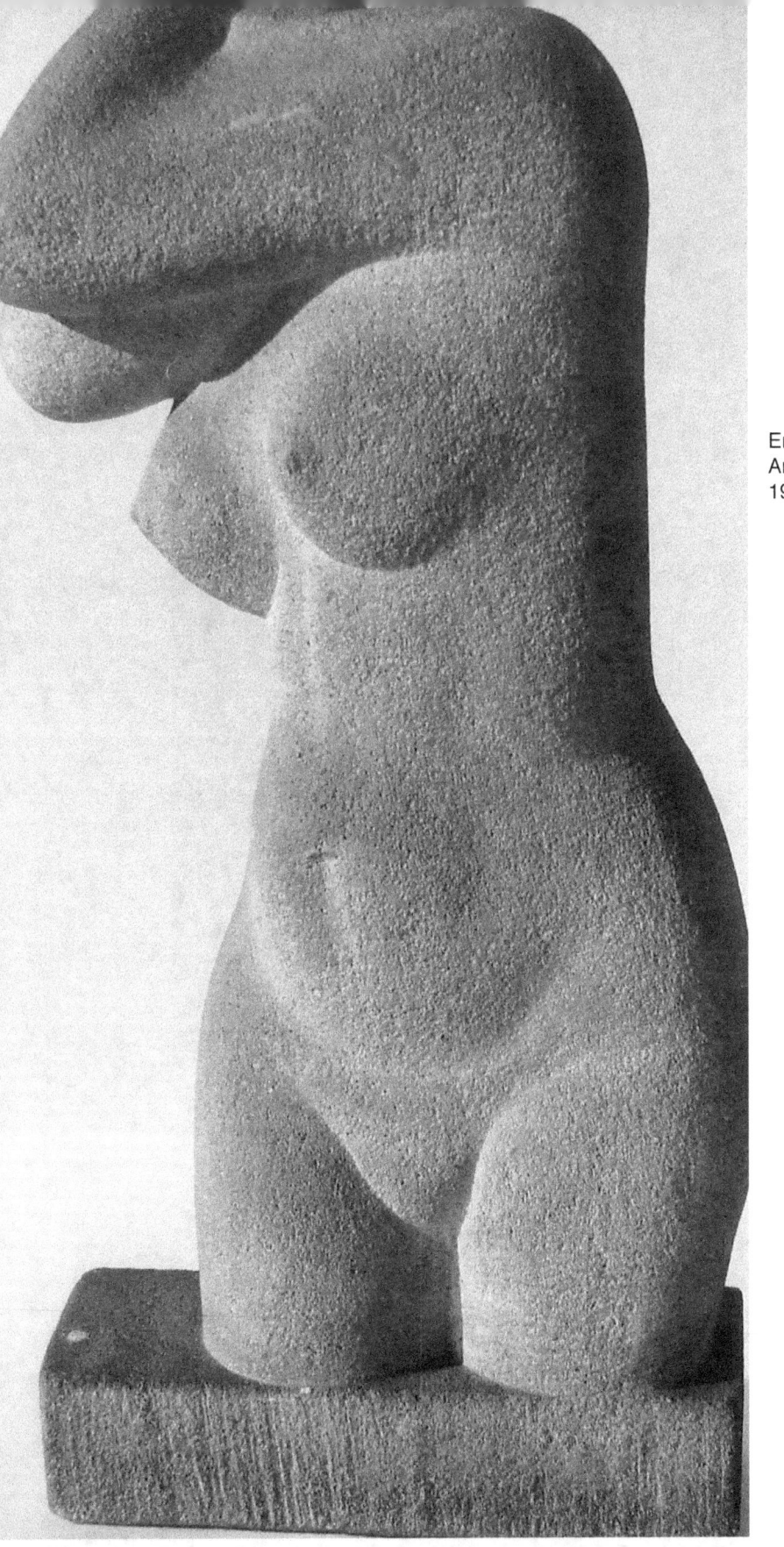

Eric Gill,
Anadyomene,
1920

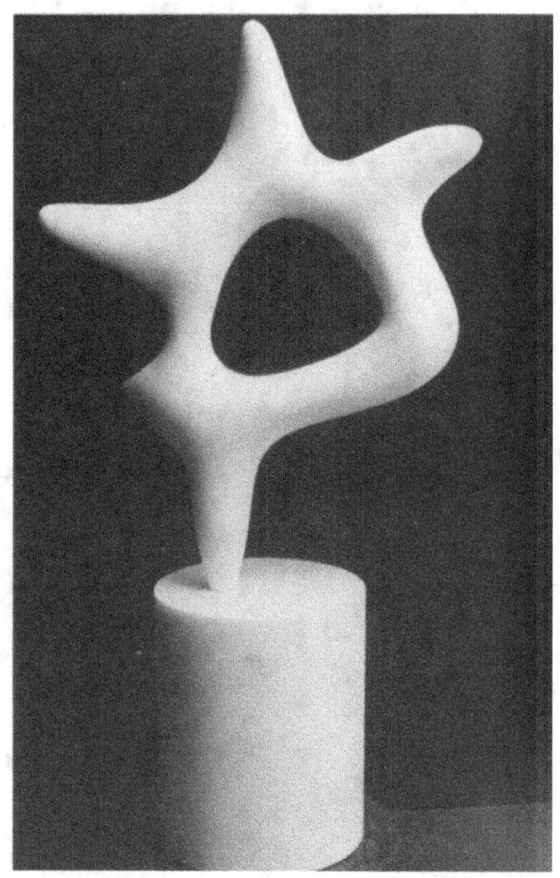

Jean Arp, Star

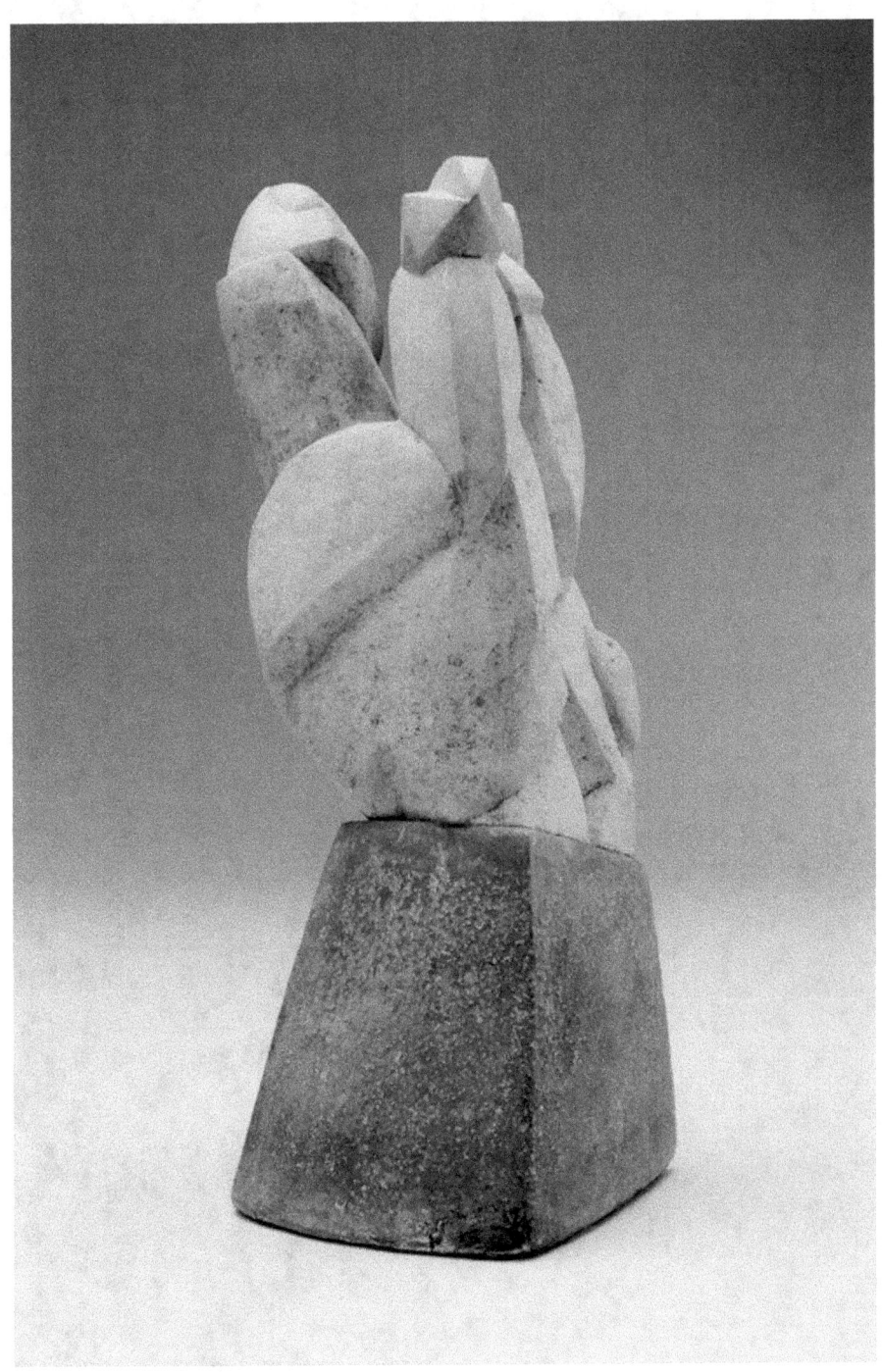

Henri Gaider-Brzeska

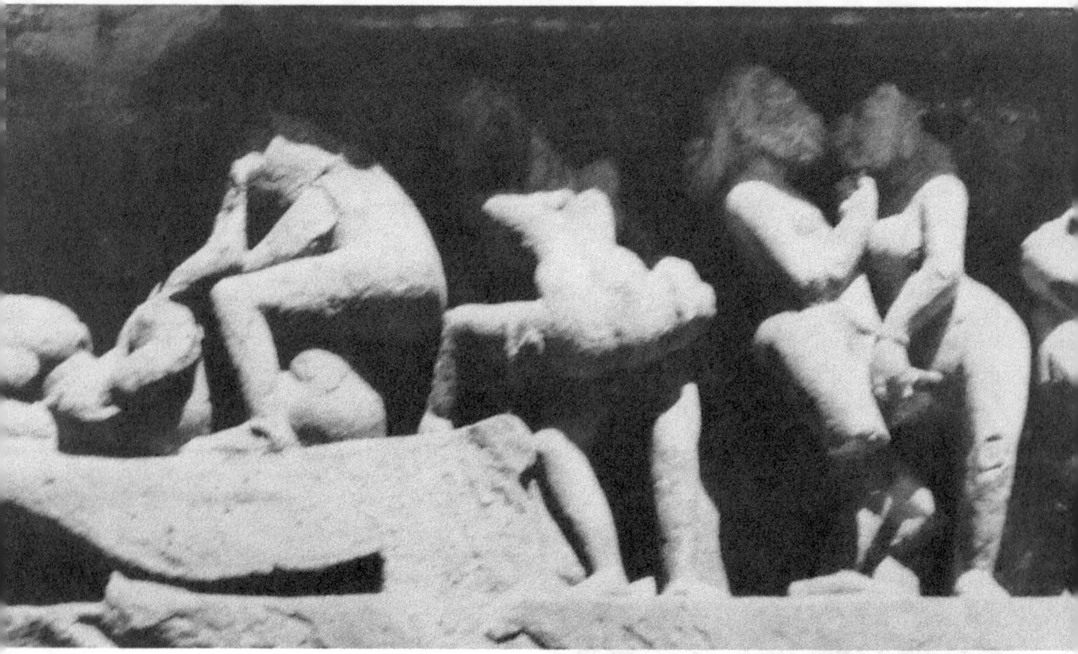

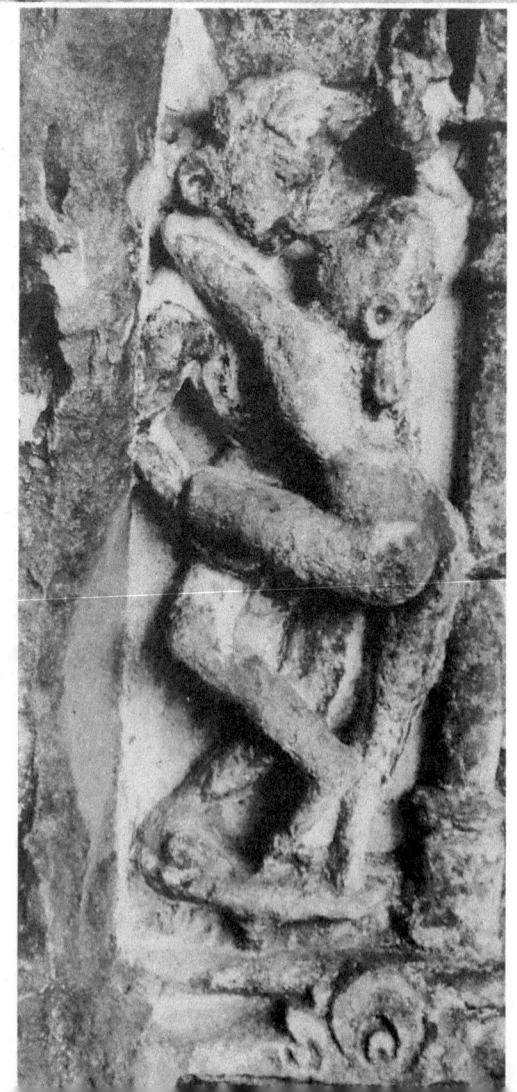

Khajuraho temple, 9-11 century, Northern India, right.

Temple, 11th century, Mount Abu area, Northern India

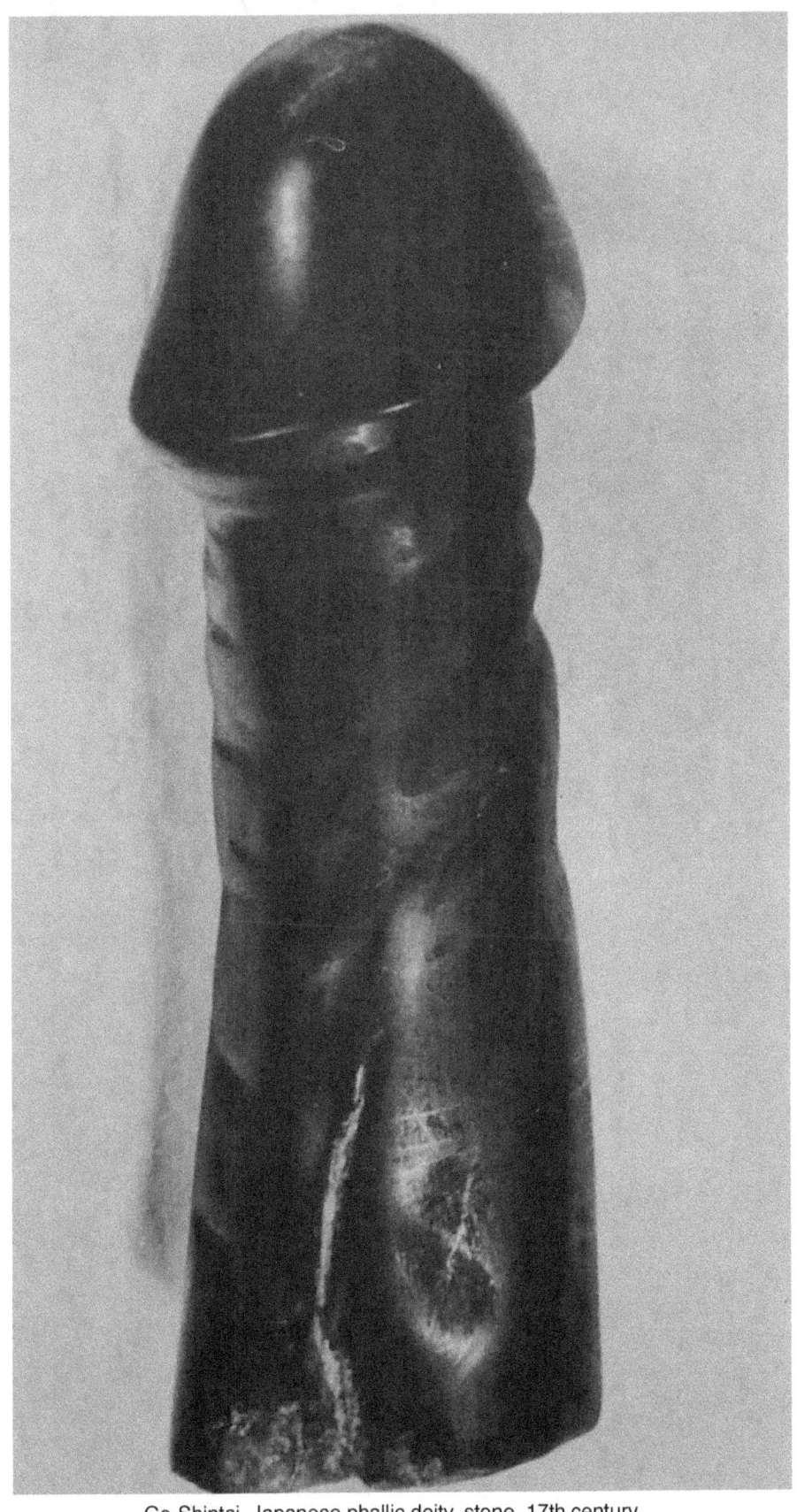

Go-Shintai, Japanese phallic deity, stone, 17th century

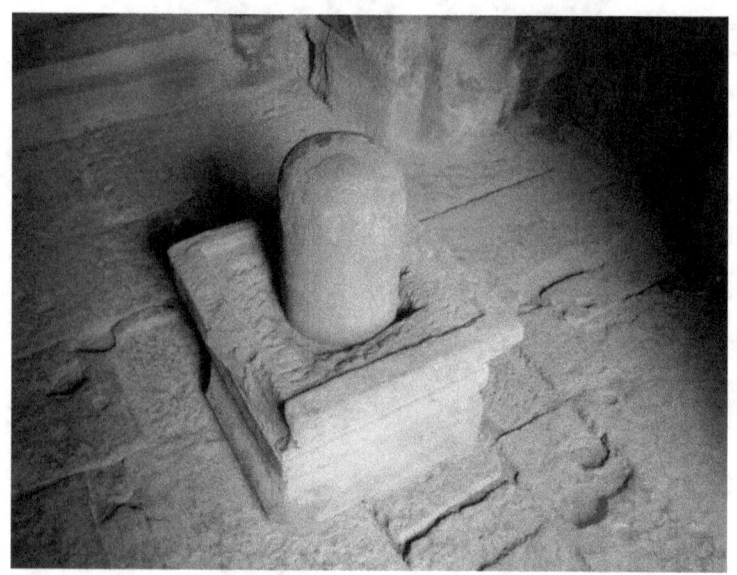

Lingam stone, Angkor, India

On the following pages, some artists who have been influenced
by Constantin Brancusi's art

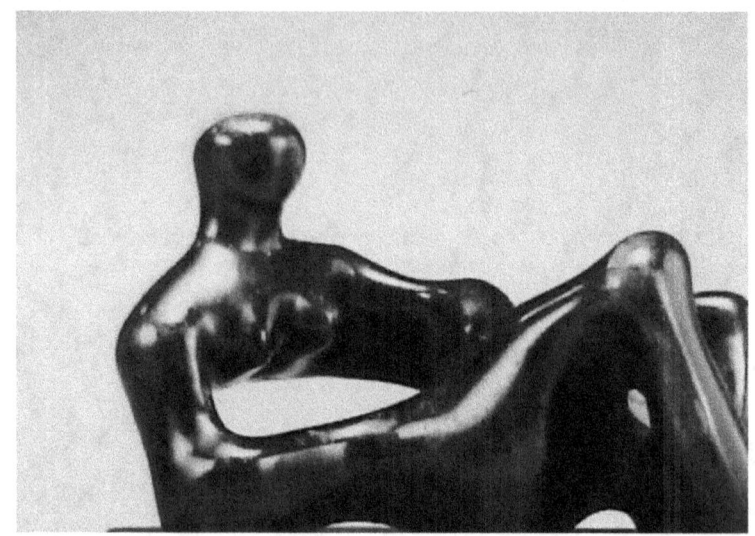

Henry Moore, Maquette For Recumbent Figure, 1938

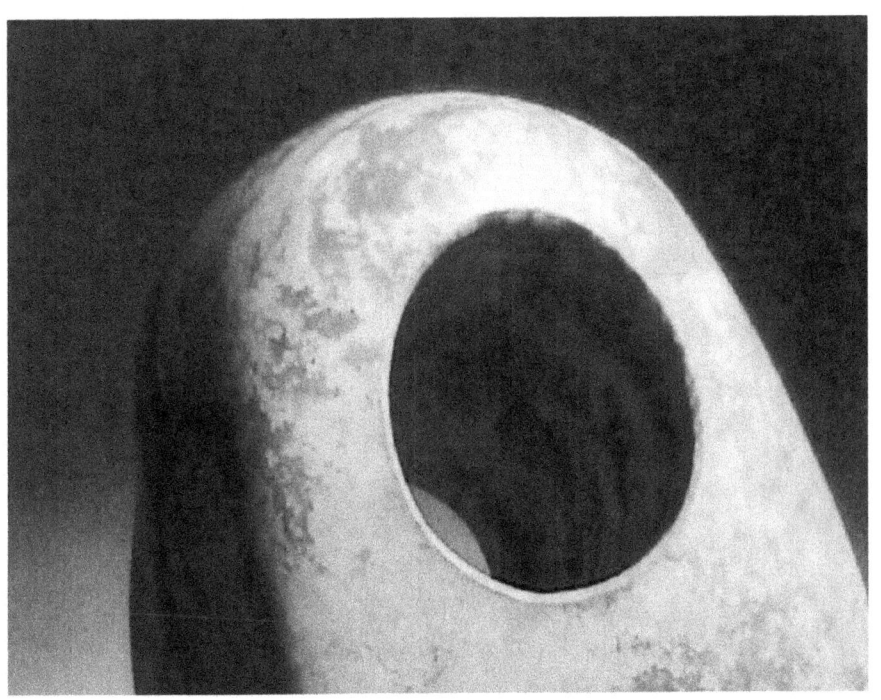

Barbara Hepworth, Pierced Form (April), 1968

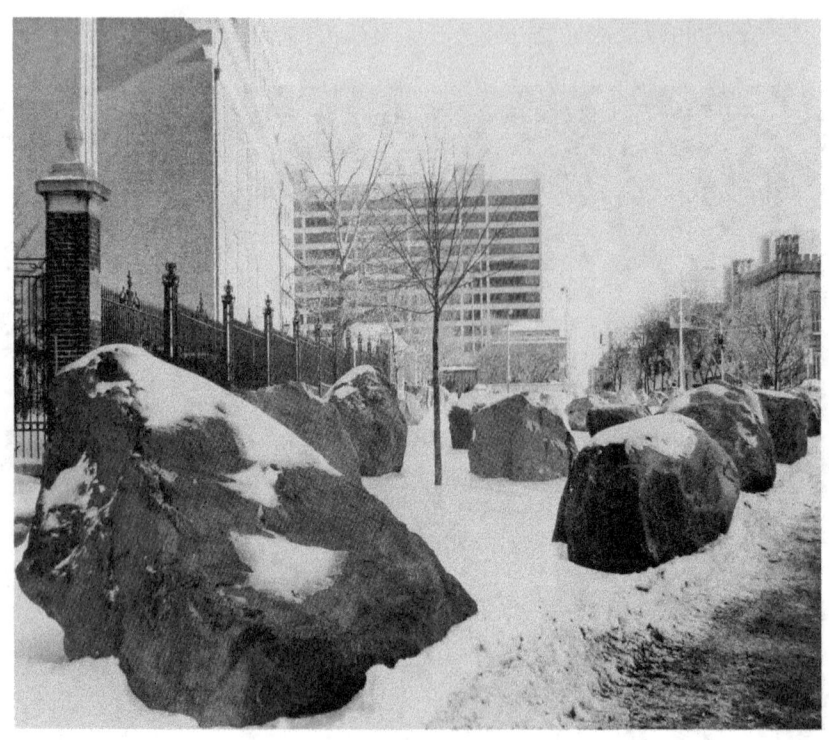

Carl Andre, Stone Field, 1977

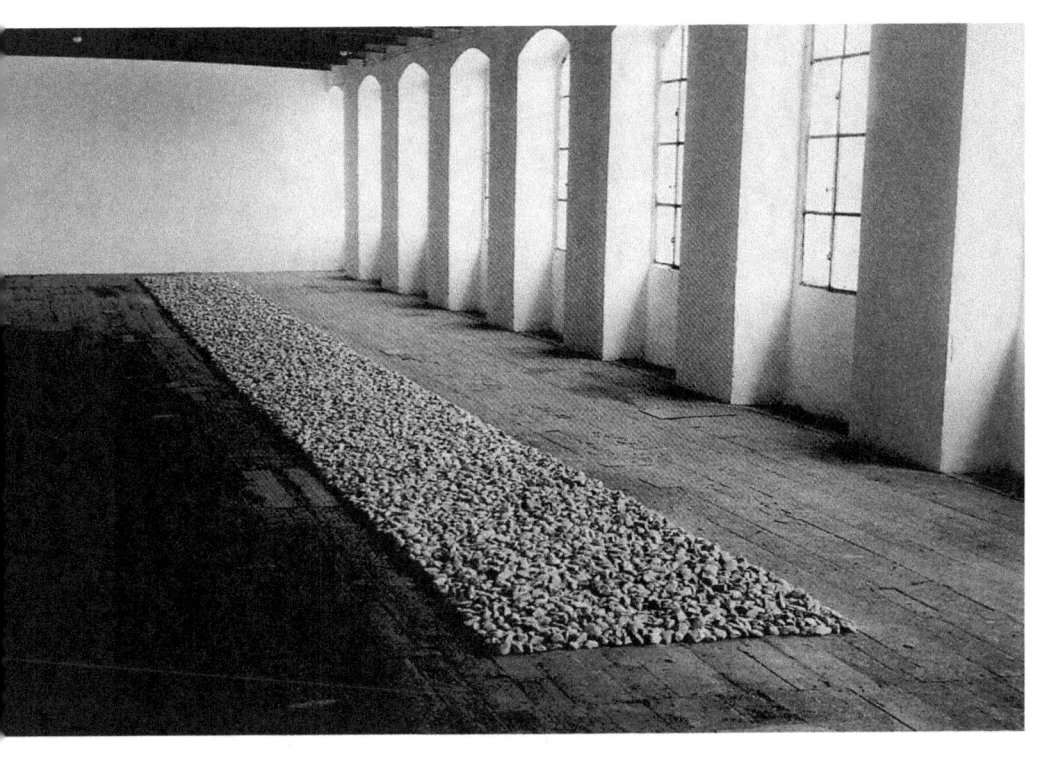

Richard Long, Stone Row

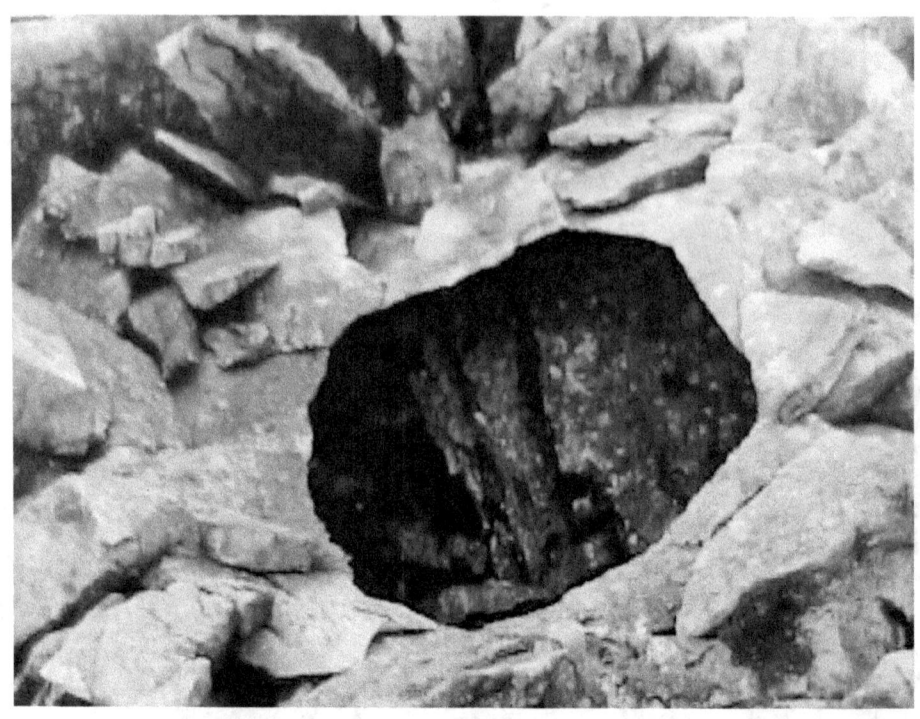

Andy Goldsworthy, Thin-edged Stones, 1980

7 / Column

The endpoint of Constantin Brancusi's creative search was his *Endless Column* (1937-38, cast iron, 96.2 ft x 35.4 x 35.4 in), a monumental structure at Tîrgu-Jiu in Romania.[1] Brancusi called it 'a stairway to heaven'.[2] The column – variously entitled *Column of Endless Remembrance*, *Infinite Column*, *The Column of Endless Memory* and *The Column of Endless Gratitude* – soars into space, literally and metaphorically, mythically and spiritually. Sidney Geist wrote:

> Marvellous is the fact that the elements of the *Column* do not diminish in size as they mount. The persistence of size and of shape, the constancy of the repetition, causes the *Column* to remain near to the mind as it moves off from the eye. We have here a poetry of the actual, without illusion or compensation, without tapering or entasis. (1968, 124-5)

Endless Column is, like the *Birds in Space*, a monument of magical, shamanic flight, a sculpture of pure ascension, which is pure desire. You don't need to have any time for the psychoanalysis of Sigmund Freud to see the phallic aspects of such towers, totem poles, minarets and columns. Brancusi's *Endless Column* and *Birds in Space* sculptures can be seen in Freudian, genital terms as phallic erections.

The shaman's dance, trance and magical journey, seen anthropologically, have erotic, phallic components. The shaman climbs up the World

Tree, itself another phallic symbol, a manifestation of phallic power. Further, dreaming (which is the key state of shamanism, for the shaman is the one who can dream magically), is associated with phallic energy, as Freud noted: during REM sleep erections occur (what some men refer to as their 'morning glory', a penis rising like the sun rising; dreaming has an erotic component for women, too, of course).

All these elements are caught up in Constantin Brancusi's sculptures of flight: shamanism, Cosmic Trees, phallic columns, erections, patriarchal power, and religious, mythic rebirth. Other forms of ithyphallic ascensions might include the Apollo moonshots, phallic rockets, flights in superhero movies, or even, at the heart of Western religion, Christ's Resurrection. This was a *bodily* resurrection from the tomb, as theologians have always stressed (like the immortality of ancient Egyptian religion – an eternity of the *body*, not only the *soul*). And all of the body means including the penis, as D.H. Lawrence noted: for Lawrence, Christ rose in the flesh, meaning complete with phallus, ready for a sexual life with a woman (as depicted in Lawrence's *The Escaped Cock*). The moment of resurrection-erection in *The Escaped Cock* is described thus:

> Himself bending over powerful and new like dawn.
> He crouched to her, and he felt the blaze of his manhood, his power rise up in his loins, magnificent.
> 'I am risen!'
> Magnificent, blazing indomitable in the depths of his loins, his own sun dawned and sent its fire running along his limbs, so that his face shone unconsciously. (1987, 596)

8 / Head

In sculptures such as *Sleep*, which is a softly rounded 'head' in sumptuous white marble, or the equally mysterious and ovoid *Sleeping Muse* (1909-10, Paris), and also his *Sleep* (1908, Romania Museum of Art, Bucharest), Constantin Brancusi came close to achieving that 'essence of things' which goes beyond form and content. 'This shape relates to growth and gestation,' wrote Peter Selz, 'and it is also a form of harmony and tranquillity' (85). For Brancusi, art should give an aesthetic shock that makes one realize one is alive, or as he put it: '[a]rt must give suddenly, all at once, the shock of life, the sensation of breathing'.[1]

Not a few sculptors since Constantin Brancusi's egg-shaped 'heads' and *Beginning of the World* have created rounded, 'abstract' forms, including Barbara Hepworth, Henry Moore, Louise Bourgeois, Tony Cragg, Martin Puryear, and Henri Matisse with his bulbous sculpture *Le Tiaré* (1930, Ahrenberg Collection, Sweden); Jean Lipchitz's *Song of Songs* (1945-48, private collection); and Jean Arp, who produced a number of forms based on smooth, rounded, organic forms, including yet another one of those headless, armless female torsos found in so much of patriarchal art (*Torse de Femme*, 1953, Wallraf Richartz Museum, Cologne, and *Human Concretion*, 1934, Paris).

The upward-thrusting, semi-organic shape of Constantin Brancusi's

Princess X occurs in the follower of Anthony Caro, William Tucker's work. Tucker's hand-modelled volumes (for example, *Gymnast III*, 1984-5 and *Okeanos*, 1987-88, both David McKee Gallery, New York) curve up into space, sculptural equivalents of Samuel Beckett's 'little body upright'. Tucker moved from tight, quasi-Minimal works in the 1960s to the looser, organic forms of the 1980s.[2]

9 / Kiss

Constantin Brancusi's most obviously erotic sculpture was one of his early pieces, which turned up in various forms: *The Kiss* (for example, 1907-08, stone, Museum of Art, Craiova, Romania and *The Kiss II*, c. 1908, private collection). Unlike Auguste Rodin's *tour-de-force* depiction of erotic passion, *The Kiss* (1886, Musée Rodin, Paris), Brancusi's *The Kiss* is a 'primitive', non-naturalistic square block of stone, very far indeed from the sculpture of Michelangelo Buonarroti, Gianlorenzo Bernini or Monsieur Rodin. For Brancusi *The Kiss* was his 'road to Damascus', a key work.[1]

Much of Auguste Rodin's art pivots around eroticism. Rodin produced drawings of women masturbating (for example, *Reclining Female Nude*, c. 1900, Musée Rodin, France), which influenced Gustav Klimt's images of auto-erotic women. Rodin's *Oceanides* (1905, Musée Rodin, Paris), like his *Gates of Hell*, depicts lovers entwining in a series of fluid lines and sensuous forms. Rodin's depictions of *The Kiss* centre around the voluptuousness of eroticism, on the beauty of bodies clasped together in complex poses. Rodin's *The Kiss* is the height of modern figurative sculpture, Michelangelo's art made modernist and more explicitly erotic.

Other sculptors produced similarly sensuous, entwined *Kisses*, with the man always on top, always bearing down onto the woman, always enveloping, always controlling the kiss (in M.L. Bégine's *The Embrace*

(1906), Jules Dalou's *The Kiss*, Edvard Munch's *The Kiss* (1895, private collection), Gustav Klimt's *The Kiss*, F. Voulot's *The Kiss* (1905), Pablo Picasso's *The Embrace* (1900), William Zorach's *The Embrace* (1933) and E. Derré's *La Grotte d'Amour* (1905)).

In Constantin Brancusi's art, the various versions of *The Kiss* aim to depict an intimate erotic experience of lovemaking, symbolized by a kiss. The two people – male and female, of course – are shown kissing face-on, their bodies fused together. It is a modern version of spiritual union, the dream of Plato, the love which is 'two-in-one', and celebrated through post-Classical Western history. The Platonic *syzygy* or 'two yolks (or souls) in one egg (life)' aspect is underlined by the fact that these *two* lovers are made out of *one* block of stone.

Constantin Brancusi's *The Kiss* is distinctly gendered, with many details that describe the man and the woman not apparent from just a brief glance. The hair, for instance, is parted on the woman but pulled back on the man; the man's hands are on her shoulders, while hers are pressed against the back of his head; the woman is clearly sexualized by her breasts, as ever in masculine art; the eyes and lips (there are no ears) seem to be the same, though the man is shorter than the woman. In subtle ways, Brancusi delineated the psychology of his male and female figures. They are at once flawed individuals and generalized (idealized) forms.

The variations on *The Kiss* (Constantin Brancusi regarded them all as one work) reveal interesting departures from that first, Craiova *The Kiss*. The 1908 Diamond *The Kiss* is much rougher, in its grey limestone, with the strokes of the chisel still visible, but the eyes bulge, with heavily-lined eyelids. These eyes became so enlarged in the later works they filled up the face until, in the late columns, all you can see is the great orbs of the eyes, fused together, in *The Gate of the Kiss* and *Column of the Kiss*[2]

These late *Kisses*, the column and the gate, are monumental versions of the Platonic *syzygy*, the Platonic soul union, but erotic and cosmological versions. The 'eyes' are biological 'cells', as Brancusi explained. They are the basic form of life, the organic cell, from which all life grows. These 'eyes' are also circles, and in *The Column of the Kiss* (c. 1933, plaster, 18 in high, Paris) and *The Gate of the Kiss* (1937-38, banpotoc travertine, 17 ft 3.5 in x 21 ft 7.2 in x 6 ft 6 in, Tirgu Jiu, Romania), Brancusi uses the circle as the prime symbol of life. He cuts it in two, and so those two semi-circles become the perfect symbol of the Platonic souls finding their 'other half'.

Circles split in two also have sexual associations, hinting at the genitals of men and women. The bisected circle can be, if you like, labia, or testes, or glans, etc. Constantin Brancusi explained the meaning of the 'eyes':

> What is left behind when you are no more? It is the memory of the eyes, of your looks that imparted love for man and people. These figures are a representation of the amalgamation of man and woman through love.[3]

It is worth noting, too, that above the pillars of *The Gate of the Kiss* are forty couples inscribed on the surface of the massive lintel. These couples are copulating, they are drawn like the full length bodies on the Montparnasse *The Kiss,* where legs and arms entwine in Tantric lovemaking. Brancusi's *The Gate of the Kiss* is thus an epic, monumental poem to erotic, human love, love made cosmic and mythic. The tenderness that writers such as D.H. Lawrence, William Shakespeare, Sappho, and André Gide thought of as essential in love is there in Brancusi's *Kissing Gate,* but made vast and monolithic.

The 1912/16 *The Kiss*, in limestone, is a further 'rationalization', as critics say, of the first *The Kiss*. There is a clear line marking the narrow space between the figures, who are shown down to the waist. The 1923-25 limestone *The Kiss* returns to the shortened version of 1908. It is rounded, making the two figures into an oval shape. In Constantin Brancusi's vision of the supreme erotic moment, the *unio mystica* or spiritual marriage as Catholic mystics and theologians call it, the two figures are clasped together so tightly nothing gets between them. It is a pure fusion of body and soul: their eyes touch, their faces touch, their mouths touch, and their bodies touch.

In later versions of *The Kiss*, such as the one in Montparnasse Cemetery (1909, stone, 35.2 in high, Paris), Constantin Brancusi showed the whole body of the two eternal, archetypal lovers. Sidney Geist wrote of the Montparnasse *The Kiss*:

> The initial innocence of *The Kiss* has given way to the image of pagan frankness. In the total embrace of the Montparnasse *Kiss* we witness a scene so sweet and stately that it is often not recognized for what it is. In all except primitive art, there is probably no representation of the sexual act that is at once so undisguised and so discreet. Although the lovers in this *Kiss* are revealed in a passional act, its intensity is mitigated by a new rigour of design and execution. The broad facade are, for all purposes, identical. (1978)

Constantin Brancusi's *The Kiss* motif has been influential, though not, perhaps, as influential as the *Birds in Space*, the eggs and heads, or the *Endless Column*. British artist Barry Flanagan has produced a sculpture of erotic figures carved into a chunk of square stone (*Tantric Figures*, 1973, collection: E.J. Power, London) that directly recalls Brancusi's *The Kiss*.

Constantin Brancusi's lovers recall the figures in Tantric art, where couples are shown erotically entwined with each other. In Oriental sex yoga and erotic literature, couples are depicted in a series of poses, which demonstrate how the cosmic energies, *yin* and *yang* or *Shiva* and *Shakti*, fuse together in an erotic-religious embrace. Brancusi's *The Kiss* makes the ephemeral nature of eroticism permanent: it is carved not in marble or bronze, but in stone, which gives the work a heavy, earthy, durable feel.

The Kiss is a sculpture that is meant to represent by its solid mass a timeless erotic union. *The Kiss* is nothing less than a representation of a central experience of society and culture – making love. It is a cosmic vision of togetherness, a vision that goes down to the fundamental, organic levels of life. Constantin Brancusi used the image of two halves melding into one in his monuments at Tirgu Jiu. Asking the American sculptor Malvina Hoffman what she thought of the columns, she replied: 'I see the forms of two cells that meet and create life. The beginning of life... through love. Am I right?' Brancusi replied:

> Yes, you are... and these columns are the result of years of searching. First came this group of two interlaced, seated figures in stone... then the symbol of the egg, then the thought grew into this gateway to a beyond. (1939, 53)

10 / Influence

Constantin Brancusi's influence on modern art has been enormous. Contemporary sculptors have often looked to the two great modern sculptors, Auguste Rodin and Constantin Brancusi, for inspiration. In the realm of abstract or non-figurative sculpture, Brancusi has remained influential (although of course he disliked the term 'abstract', claiming all his sculpture was 'realist', and his forms can be seen as figurative).

Sculptors who cite Brancusi as an influence include the British sculptors Henry Moore, Barry Flanagan, William Tucker, Andy Goldsworthy and Barbara Hepworth, and the American Minimal artists Donald Judd, Dan Flavin and Carl Andre.

In Barbara Hepworth's art, organic forms are not sexualized, as they are in so many other (male) sculptors. As with Brancusi's sculpture, Hepworth's art hovers between subjectivity and objectivity, between natural form and aesthetic abstraction (as in her *Two Forms* [1937, private collection], for example). Like Brancusi, Hepworth maintained that she always returned to nature, and took her inspiration from the natural world. For her, nature meant the Cornish landscape, and the human body. 'We return always to the human form – the human form in landscape', she remarked (1970, 50-53). Her sculpture stems from emotion and expression, from feeling: 'I rarely draw what I see – I draw what I feel in my body', she asserted.[1]

Barbara Hepworth's distinctive forms, with their smooth curves and holes, are clearly sensual objects.[2] Hepworth acknowledged the sensuality of sculptural forms (see the quote, above). In 1969 Elizabeth Catlett took the holed form of Hepworth and suppressed the erotic dimension to produce a political work that celebrated 'the struggle for liberation by black women in this country and everywhere'.[3]

The influence of Constantin Brancusi is apparent in Minimal, Arte Povera and Postminimal sculpture. Robert Morris, Donald Judd, Carl Andre and Dan Flavin (among others) acknowledged Brancusi's art, in particular his *Endless Column* (1918, 80 x 9.8 x 9.8 in, New York). Andre's early work *Last Ladder* (1959, Tate Gallery, London) is particularly like Brancusi's *Endless Column*. Andre described himself as 'a wood-carving disciple of Brancusi' in his early work. Andre explained his floor-standing sculptures, such as *Lever*, as 'putting Brancusi's *Endless Column* on the ground instead of in the sky'.[4]

The Brancusi ethics, of simplicity, purity, smoothness, interiority and organic form are found in the Minimal sculptors, as well as the Constructivist notion of working with materials in a 'natural' way, so that the material dictates the form you create with it. Barry Flanagan has commented that sculpture works directly with materials:

> The convention of painting has always bothered me. There always seemed to be a *way* of painting. With sculpture, you seemed to be working directly, with materials and with the physical world inventing your own organisations'.[5]

Minimal sculpture is certainly austere – 'cool', as some people call it. It is very ascetic, restrained, flat, exact, with its smooth surfaces and precise square edges and angles (detractors dubbed it blank, repetitive, soulless, and boring). The body seems to have been erased from cool Minimal art. There is no space for the body, and the spectator is also 'erased', in some way. The asceticism of Minimal art appears to deny the body (like early Christianity). Rosalind Krauss wrote:

> The art of [Rodin and Brancusi] represented a relocation of the point of origin of the body's meaning – from its inner core to its surface – a radical act of decentring that would include the space to which the body appeared and the time of its appearing. What I have been arguing is that the sculpture of our time continues this project of decentring through a vocabulary of form that is radically abstract. The abstractness of Minimalism makes it less easy to recognize the human body in those works and therefore less easy to project ourselves into the space of that sculpture with all of our settled prejudices left intact. Yet our bodies and our experience of our bodies continue to be the subject of this sculpture – even when a work is made of several hundred tons of earth. (279)

One can see the body written into, say, Barbara Hepworth's holed forms, or Constantin Brancusi's extraordinary egg shapes, but not, perhaps, in the giganticism of Michael Heizer's *Double Negative*, a huge cut in the Nevada desert. Yet, even here, the human body is present – if only by the way it is violently dwarfed by the scale of Heizer's earthwork (the body is also necessary to explore the artwork on foot).

The overpowering enormity of the American land artists is not something of which Constantin Brancusi would approve, one imagines. The enormous cuts into the earth's surface by Michael Heizer, or the long fences of Christo that run over many miles, seem at odds with Brancusi's philosophy. (Having said that, Brancusi did make a large piece of sculpture that can be seen as land art, the *Endless Column*).

When it suited him, Constantin Brancusi liked to make a powerful impact in a space. The site in Romania can be seen as an early work of land art, very much in the subjective, visionary vein of Sixties land art. Perhaps the land art of David Nash, Richard Long, Chris Drury and Andy Goldsworthy (among British artists) is more in tune with Brancusi's poetics, being much smaller in scale (though those British artists have also made very large works from time to time). (Incidentally, Christo is among the most famous of contemporary Eastern European artists, hailing from

Bulgaria).

Andy Goldsworthy, a contemporary British sculptor, has a sensitivity for natural or organic forms that is Brancusian, and he uses natural or 'found' materials, such as wood, stone, water and snow, of which Brancusi would approve. Goldsworthy's sculptures are marked by a number of elements familiar in land art: transience, domination, penetration, circular forms (globes, circles, spirals, snakes, cones) and nature mysticism. The ephemerality of the pieces, for instance, is a key component. Snow and ice will melt away, leaves will disintegrate, stones will be blown over. One of his best pieces, the delicious poppy covered boulder, has the title: *Poppy petals wrapped around a boulder held with water* (Sibobre, France, June 6, 1989). The petal-covered rock, with its brilliant red colour, nestles in some mossy boulders, looking very much like one of Brancusi's 'cosmic eggs'.

For Goldsworthy, the Romanian sculptor 'remains close both in his sculpture, his photography and the relationship between the two'. 'His work explains much about the way I feel for sculpture, time, atmosphere and light', Goldsworthy remarked.[6] Goldsworthy admired in particular the way that Brancusi photographed his sculptures in his Paris studio. Goldsworthy said that Brancusi would wait for exactly the right combination of light and shadow, so that his work 'comes alive at a particular time of day as the light momentarily touches it'.[7] For Goldsworthy, Brancusi's sculptures were at their best when they were photographed by the artist himself, rather than in the displays arranged by museums such as the Pompidou Centre in Paris or MOMA in Gotham.

Like Constantin Brancusi, Richard Long spoke in poetic, religious terms of his art – 'art should be a religious experience'.[8] Although Long's sculptures alter the world – no *physical object* can avoid altering the world – Long maintains that he takes his cue from the landscape, as Brancusi did, instead of imposing on it 'from outside', as it were: 'I use the world as I find it'.[9]

Like Constantin Brancusi's ideas on art, Richard Long's views have something in common with Zen Buddhism, Taoism, shamanism and Western magic.[10] The sculpture and the place are one, in a mystical relationship, as Long points out in his writings:

> The material and the idea are of the place; sculpture and place are one, the same. The place is as far as the eye can see from the sculpture. The place for a sculpture is found by walking. Some works are a succession of particular places along a walk, e.g. *Milestones*. In this work, the walking, the places and the stones all have equal importance.[11]

Constantin Brancusi walked from Munich to Paris in his youth (he'd run out of money), and later described the walking trip as ecstatic:

> I rambled through forests singing my joy and happiness... People don't realize how good it is to be alive; they don't know how to look at the wonders of nature.[12]

Richard Long has the *participation mystique* with the Earth, with places and atmospheres and organic materials, that the archaic peoples of the world had (and have). Constantin Brancusi too spoke of this primal, 'primitive' relationship with the world, which renders his sculpture 'archaic', for some people (although the term 'archaic' is used sometimes in the anthropological sense, but more often in the pseudo-psychological sense beloved of art critics). It is a pre-institutionalized, pre-pagan and pantheistic rapport with the world, deliberately eschewing dogma, doctrine and manifestos. For Richard Long is also part, as many commentators have noted, of a British Romantic tradition, that feeling for nature found in the art of William Blake, J.M.W. Turner, Percy Bysshe Shelley, John Constable, and others.[13]

For Constantin Brancusi, the connection is shaped only partly by the Parisian or modernist *avant garde*. In Brancusi's art, there is always a striving for some realm greater than his immediate *milieu* of the first half of the 20th century. The sculptural space for Brancusi is not that of the art of Michelangelo, Donatello, Bernini, Canova or Rodin, it is both fashionably 'primitive' in the *avant garde* Parisian sense, as found in the paintings of Pablo Picasso or Georges Braque, and also archaic, shamanic, magical, Platonic, mystical; a space where there is only *essence*, the 'essence of things'.

This is, finally, Constantin Brancusi's desired world, a paradise of 'essences'. An otherness that is utterly *real*, an abstraction that is pure reality. Nature not artifice, reality not fantasy, touch and objecthood, not ethereality and insubstantiality. In the sculpture of Brancusi, the emphasis is on the poetics of nature, not the nature of poetics, the mysticism of actualities, not the actualities of mysticism.

A paradox, in the end, for the more he stresses 'essence' and Platonic philosophy, the further Brancusi moves away from nature and reality. It is a paradox he celebrates, criticizes, reviews, has doubts about and continued to explore throughout his career. It is the paradox of all sculpture (and all art): the paradox between something being there (the art object) and something not being there, which is represented (the 'content', 'theme' or 'subject'). The paradox is a dichotomy never resolved into a (Platonic) unity. Yet Constantin Brancusi seems to have got closer than most to some kind of resolution, although he maintained, rightly, that no work of art is ever 'finished'.

Notes

1 / ESSENCE

1. Quoted in C. Giedion-Welcker, 1.
2. W. Kandinsky: "On the Problem of Form", *Der Blaue Reiter*, R. Piper, Munich, 1912, and in H. Chipp, 162.
3. C. Brancusi, in "Propos de Brancusi", 1957, 6.
4. In F. Merrill, 1926, 4E.
5. In P. James & H. Moore: *Henry Moore on Sculpture*, Viking Press, New York, NY, 1971, 60.
6. M. Eliade, in 1967, and 1984, 195-6.
7. C. Brancusi, 1957, 6.
8. R.M. Rilke, letter to 'une amie', Feb 3, 1923, quoted in *The Selected Poems of Rainer Maria Rilke*, tr. Stephan Mitchell, Picador, London, 1987, 299.
9. In ib., 215.
10. R.M. Rilke: *The Rodin-Book*, tr. G. Houston, Quartet, London, 1986, 46.
11. Quoted in A. Liberman, 48.
12. R.M. Rilke: *New Poems*, tr. J.B. Leishman, Hogarth Press, London, 1963, 57.
13. D.T. Suzuki: *The Basics of Buddhist Philosophy*, Allen & Unwin, London, 1957, quoted in R. Woods, ed. *Understanding Mysticism*, Athlone Press, London, 1980, 126.
14. Quoted in *Brancusi*, catalogue, Brummer Gallery, New York, NY, 1926.
15. C. Brancusi, in P. Pandrea, 120.
16. C. Brancusi, quoted in R. Howe, 124.
17. C. Brancusi, in M. Hoffman, 53.

2 / FISH

1. C. Brancusi, in M. Hoffman, 1939, 52.

3 / GENDER

1. Quoted in *This Quarter*, op.cit.
2. In D. Lewis, 1957, 28.

4 / PHALLUS

1. See P. Webb.
2. C. Brancusi, in R. Devigne, *L'Ere Nouvelle*, Jan 28, 1920.
3. J. Kristeva, *Revolution in Poetic Language*, 1986, 115.

5 / EGG

1. See Philip Rawsom, 1973, 193-7.
2. In ib., 194; *Egg of Brahman*, Benares, age unknown, stone, 7 in high; *Egg of Brahman*, Benares, age unknown, stone, 7 in high.
3. In D. Dudley, 127.

6 / BIRDS

1. In C. Giedin-Welcker, 1959, 220.
2. M. Eliade, 1972, 143; 1975, 100f.
3. In A. Atwater, 12.

7 / COLUMN

1. See S. Georgescu-Gorjan, 1964, 279-93; A. Parigoris, 1984, 76-84; S. Miller, 1980, 470-4; E. Balas, 1975-6, 94-104.
2. Quoted in B. Brezianu, 1976, 134.

8 / HEAD

1. Quoted in D. Dudley, 130.
2. See M. Kunz et al: *Starlit Waters: British Sculpture: An International Art, 1968-1988,* Tate Gallery, Liverpool 1988; M. Newman: "New Sculpture in Britain", *Art in America*, 70, 8, Sept, 1982.

9 / KISS

1. Quoted in H.P. Roche, 1957, 26f.
2. See S. Geist, 1973, 70-78.
3. C. Brancusi, in B. Brezianu, 1976, 143.

10 / INFLUENCE

1. Quoted in A.M. Hammacher, 98.
2. Barbara Hepworth: *Porthmeor: Sea Form*, 1958, bronze, Hirshhorn Museum and Sculpture Garden, Washington DC; *Pendour*, 1947, painted wood, Hirshhorn

Museum and Sculpture Garden, Washington DC, *Forms in Movement*, 1956, Barbara Hepworth Museum and Sculpture Garden, St Ives, Cornwall.

3. K. Petersen & J.J. Wilson, 142.

4. Carl Andre, quoted in Bourdon: "The Razed Sites of Carl Andre", in G. Battock, 103.

5. B. Flanagan, quoted in catalogue of *Entre el Objeto y la Imagen: Escultura británica contemporánea*, Palacio de Velasquez, Madrid, 1986, 233.

6. *Sheepfolds*, Michael Hue-Williams Gallery, London, 1996, 22.

7. *Réfuges d'Art*, Editions Artha, 2002, 85.

8. Quoted in D. Wheeler, 264.

9. R. Long: *Five, six, pick up sticks/ Seven, eight, lay them straight*, 1980, Anthony d'Offay Gallery, September 1980.

10. See A. Seymour: "El Estanque de Basho – una nueva perspectiva", in *Piedras Richard Long*, Ministerio de Cultura, Dirección general de Bellas Artes y Archivos and the British Council, 1986.

11. R. Long, quoted in E. Lucie-Smith, 1987, 121.

12. In I. Jianou, 30.

13. See A. Seymour, op.cit., S. Gablik, op.cit.

Bibliography

D. Adlow: "Brancusi", *Drawing and Design*, Feb 2, 1927

—. "Brancusi and Modern Sculpture", *Christian Science Monitor*, 26 Oct, 1955

A.L. Atwater: "A Recluse of Modern Art", *New York Herald Tribune Magazine*, 12 Jan, 1930

F.T. Bach: *Brancusi*, Du Mont, Cologne, 1987

—. *et al*: *Constantin Brancusi 1876-1957*, Philadelphia Museum of Art, 1995

—. *Constantin Brancusi*, 2000

E. Balas: "The Sculpture of Brancusi in the Light of His Rumanian Heritage", *Art Journal*, 35, no.2, Winter, 1975-6

—. "Object-Sculpture, Base and Assemblage in the Art of Constantin Brancusi", *Art Journal*, 18, Autumn, 1978

—. "Brancusi, Duchamp and Dada", *Gazette des Beaux-Arts*, 95, Apl, 1980

—. *Brancusi and His World*, 2008

G. Battock. "The Moral Integrity of Smudges", *New York Times*, Jan 25, 1968

—. *Idea Art*, Dutton, New York, NY, 1973

—. ed. *Minimal Art: A Critical Anthology*, University of California Press, Berkeley, CA, 1995

Ernest Beck. *Brancusi's Endless Column: Targu-Jiu, Romania (World Monuments Fund)*, 2007

C. Bell: "The Art of Brancusi", *Vogue*, 67, 1 June, 1926

M. Berger: *Labyrinths: Robert Morris, Minimalism and the 1960s*, Harper & Row, New York, NY, 1989

S. Boettger. *Earthworks*, University of California Press, Berkeley, 2002

A. Boime: "Brancusi in New York: Ab ovo ad infinitum", *Burlington Magazine*, 112, May, 1970

C. Brancusi: "Résponses de Brancusi; Aphorismes; Histoire de Brigands", *This Quarter*, 1, no.1, Paris, 1925

—. "Propos de Brancusi", *Prisme des Arts*, Paris, no. 12, May, 1957

—. "Aphorisms", *Rumanian Review*, 19, 1, 1965

B. Brezianu: "The Beginnings of Brancusi", *Art Journal*, 25, 1, Fall, 1965

—. *Brancusi: A Retrospective Exhibition*, Muzeul de Arta R.S.R, Bucharest, 1970

—. *Brancusi in Romania*, Editura Academiei R.S.R., Bucharest, Romantia, 1976

Elizabeth A. Brown. *Brancusi: Photographs*, 2003

J. Burnham: "Sculpture's Vanishing Base", *Artforum*, 6, Nov, 1967

—. *Beyond Modern Sculpture*, George Braziller, New York, NY, 1968

Pierre Cabanne. *Brancusi*, 2006

O. Chelimsky: "Memoir of Brancusi", *Arts Magazine*, 32, June, 1958

H.B. Chipp, ed. *Theories of Modern Art*, University Press of California, Los Angeles, 1968

F. Colpitt: *Minimal Art: The Critical Perspective*, University of Washington Press, Seattle, 1990

P. Comarnesco, M. Eliade and I. Jianou:*Témoignages sur Brancusi*, Arted, Paris, 1967

—. *Brancusi, Introduction, Témoignages*, Arted, Paris, 1982

D. Dudley: "Brancusi", *Dial*, 82, Feb, 1927

M. Eliade: *Myths. Dreams and Mysteries*, tr. P. Mairet, Harper & Row, New York, NY, 1975

—. "Brancusi and Mythology", in P.Comarnesco, 1967

—. *Shamanism: Archaic Techniques of Ecstasy*, Princeton University Press, 1972

—. *Ordeal by Labyrinth*, University of Chicago Press, Chicago, IL, 1984

—. *Symbolism, the Sacred and the Arts*, Crossroad, New York, NY, 1985

Jose Maria Faerna. *Brancusi*, 1997

S. Geist: *Brancusi: A Study of the Sculpture*, New York, 1968

—. *Constantin Brancusi, 1876-1957*, Guggenheim, New York, NY, 1969

—. "The Birds", *Artforum*, 9, Nov, 1970

—. "The Centrality of the Gate", *Artforum*, 12, Oct, 1973

—. *Brancusi: The Sculpture and Drawings*, Harry N. Abrams, New York, NY, 1975

—. *Brancusi: The Kiss*, Harper & Row, New York, NY, 1978

—. *Brancusi: A Study of the Sculpture*, Hacker, New York, NY, 1983

S. Georgescu-Gorjan: "The Genesis of the 'Column Without End', *Revue roumaine d'histoire de l'art*, Bucharest, no. 2, 1964

C. Giedion-Welcker: "Constantin Brancusi", *Horizon*, 19, Mch, 1949

—. *Constantin Brancusi*, George Braziller, New York, NY, 1959

—. *Contemporary Sculpture: An Evolution in Volume and Space*, Wittenborn, New York, NY, 1964

C. Gimenez & Matthew Gale. *Constantin Brancusi: The Essence of Things*, 2004

T. Godfrey. *Conceptual Art*, Phaidon, London, 1998

R. Goldwater & Marco Treves, eds. *Artists on Art*, John Murray, 1975

—. *What is Modern Sculpture?*, Museum of Modern Art, New York, NY, 1969

M. Gooding & W. Furlong. *Song of the Earth*, Thames and Hudson, 2002

D. Grigorescu: *Brancusi and the Romanian Roots of His Art*, tr. M. Chitoran, Meridiane, Bucharest, 1984

A.M. Hammacher: *The Evolution of Modern Sculpture*, Abrams, New York, NY, 1969

B. Hepworth: *Barbara Hepworth, Carvings and Drawings*, Lund Humphries, London, 1952

—. *Pictorial Autobiography*, Praeger, New York, NY, 1970

M. Hoffman: *Sculpture Inside and Out*, Norton, New York, NY, 1939

R.W. Howe: "The Man Who Doesn't Like Michelangelo", *Apollo*, 49, May, 1949

R. Hughes. *Nothing If Not Critical: Selected Essays on Art and Artists*, Collins Harvill, London, 1990

—. *The Shock of the New*, Thames & Hudson, London, 1991

P. Hulten *et al*: *Brancusi*, Harry N. Abrams, New York, NY, 1987

I. Jianou: *Brancusi*, Tudor Publishing, New York, NY, 1963

D. Judd: *Complete Writings 1975-1986*, Van Abbemuseum, Eindhoven, Netherlands, 1987

N. Konstam: *Sculpture: The Art and the Practice*, Collins, London, 1984

R.E. Krauss: *Passages in Modern Sculpture*, Thames & Hudson, London, 1977

—. "Sculpture in the Expanded Field", *October*, 8, Spring 1979, 31-44

—. "Sense and Sensibility: Reflection on Post '60s Sculpture", *Artforum*, 12, Nov, 1973, 43-53

J. Kristeva: *The Kristeva Reader*, ed. T. Moi, Blackwell, 1986

—. *Desire in Language: A Semiotic Approach to Literature and Art*, ed. Leon Roudiez, tr. T. Gora *et al*, Blackwell, 1982

—. *Revolution in Poetic Language*, tr. M. Walker, Columbia University Press, New York, NY, 1984

D.H. Lawrence: *A Selection from Phoenix*, ed. A.A.H. Inglis, Penguin, London, 1971

—. *Selected Essays*, Penguin, London, 1950

—. *The Complete Short Novels*, ed. Keith Sagar & Melissa Partridge, Penguin 1982/87

D. Lewis: *Constantin Brancusi*, Wittenborn, New York, NY, 1937

—. *Constantin Brancusi*, St Martin's Press, New York, NY, 1974

A. Liberman. *The Artist In His Studio*, Viking, New York, NY, 1960

E. Lucie-Smith: *Sculpture Since 1945*, Phaidon, 1987

—. *Sexuality in Western Art*, Thames & Hudson, London, 1991

F. Merrill. "Brancusi, the Sculptor of the Spirit", *New York World*, Oct 3, 1926

H.C. Merillat: *Modern Sculpture: The New Old Masters*, Dod, Mead & Co, New York, NY, 1974

S. Miller: "Brancusi's 'Column of the Infinite'", *Burlington Magazine*, 122, July, 1980

K. Millett: *Sexual Politics*, Doubleday, New York, NY, 1970

H. Moore: "The Sculptor Speaks", *The Listener*, XVIII, 18 Aug, 1937

H. Morphy & M. Boles, eds. *Art from the Land*, University of Washington Press, 2000

L. Nead: *Female Nude: Art, Obscenity and Sexuality*, Routledge, London, 1992

I. Noguchi. *A Sculptor's World*, Harper & Row, NY, 1968

P. Pandrea: "The Laws of Craiova", *Portraits and Controversies*, Bucharest, Romania 194 vol. 1

A. Parigoris: "Brancusi at Tirgu-Jiu: The Return of the 'Prodigal Son'", *Burlington Magazine*, 126, Feb, 1984

K. Petersen & J.J. Wilson: *Women Artists: Recognition and Reappraisal from the Early Middle Ages to the Twentieth Century* Women's Press, London, 1978

R. Pollack: "Brancusi's Sculpture vs. His Homemade Legend", *Artnews*, 48, Feb, 1960

P. Rawson: *The Art of Tantra*, Thames & Hudson, London, 1973

A.C. Ritchie: *Sculpture in the Twentieth Century*, Museum of Modern Art, New York, NY, 1952

C. Robins, ed: *The Pluralist Era: American Art 1968-1981*, Harper & Row, New York, NY, 1984

H.P. Roche: "L'Enterrement de Brancusi", *Homage de la Sculpture à Brancusi*, Paris, 1957

Margit Rowell. *Brancusi vs. United States: The Historic Trial, 1928*, 2001

A. Saarinen: "The Strange Story of Brancusi", *New York Times Magazine*, 23 Oct, 1955

I. Sandler. "The New Cool-Art", *Art in America*, 53, 1, Feb, 1967

—. *The Triumph of American Painting*, Harper & Row, New York, NY, 1970

—. *American Art of the 1960s*, Harper & Row, New York, NY, 1988

—. *Art of the Postmodern Era: From the 1960s to the Early 1990s*, HarperCollins, London, 1997

P. Selz: *Art in Our Times: A Pictorial History 1890-1980*, Thames & Hudson, London, 1982

E. Shanes: *Constantin Brancusi*, Abbeville, New York, NY, 1989

G. Shapiro. *Earthworks: Robert Smithson and After After Babel*, University of California Press, Berkeley, CA, 1995

A.T. Spear: "A Contribution to Brancusi Chronology", *Arts Bulletin*, 48, Mch, 1966

—. *Brancusi's Birds*, New York University Press, New York, NY, 1969

F. Stella: *Working Space*, Harvard University Press, Cambridge, MA, 1986

K. Stiles & P. Selz, eds. *Theories & Documents of Contemporary Art: A Sourcebook of Artists' Writings*, University of California Press, Berkeley, CA, 1996

J.J. Sweeney: "The Brancusi Touch", *Artnews*, 54, Nov, 1955

D. Sylvester: *About Modern Art*, Chatto & Windus, London, 1996

M. Tabart & I. Monod-Fontaine: *Brancusi, Photographer*, Agrinde, New York, NY, 1979

—. & Paola Mola. *Brancusi: The White Work*, 2005

W. Tucker: *The Language of Sculpture*, Thames & Hudson, London, 1974

—. *Early Modern Sculpture: Rodin, Degas, Matisse, Brancusi, Picasso, Gonzalez*, Oxford University Press, New York, NY, 1974

—. "The Road to Târgu-Jiu", *Art in America*, 64, Nov, 1976

R. Varia: "Constantin Brancusi: Sculptor Roman", *Contemporanul*, Bucharest, 4, Jan, 1925

—. *Brancusi*, Rizzoli, New York, NY, 1987

—. *Brancusi*, 2003

P. Webb: *The Erotic Arts*, Secker & Warburg, London, 1983

D. Wheeler: *Art Since Mid-Century: 1945 to the Present*, Thames & Hudson, London, 1991

Richard Williams. *After Modern Sculpture: Art in the United States and Europe 1965-70*, Manchester University Press, Manchester, 2000

W. Zorach: "The Sculpture of Constantin Brancusi", *Arts*, 9, Mch, 1926

WEBSITES

There are good websites for Constantin Brancusi material at the Philadelphia Museum of Art, the Museum of Modern Art in Gotham, and the Pompidou Centre in Paris.

THE ART OF
ANDY GOLDSWORTHY

COMPLETE WORKS: SPECIAL EDITION
(PAPERBACK and HARDBACK)

by William Malpas

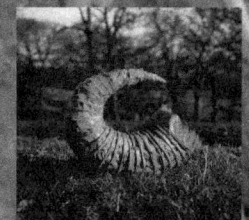

A new, special edition of the study of the contemporary British sculptor,
Andy Goldsworthy, including a new introduction, new bibliography and many
new illustrations.

This is the most comprehensive, up-to-date, well-researched and in-depth
account of Goldsworthy's art available anywhere.

Andy Goldsworthy makes land art. His sculpture is a sensitive, intuitive
response to nature, light, time, growth, the seasons and the earth. Goldsworthy's environmental art is becoming ever more popular: 1993's art book
Stone was a bestseller; the press raved about Goldsworthy taking over a
number of London West End art galleries in 1994; during 1995 Goldsworthy
designed a set of Royal Mail stamps and had a show at the British Museum.
Malpas surveys all of Goldsworthy's art, and analyzes his relation with other
land artists such as Robert Smithson, Walter de Maria, Richard Long and
David Nash, and his place in the contemporary British art scene.

The Art of Andy Goldsworthy discusses all of Goldsworthy's important and
recent exhibitions and books, including the *Sheepfolds* project; the TV docu-
mentaries; *Wood* (1996); the New York Holocaust memorial (2003); and
Goldsworthy's collaboration on a dance performance.

Illustrations: 70 b/w, 1 colour. 330 pages. New, special, 2nd edition.
Publisher: Crescent Moon Publishing. Distributor: Gardners Books.

ISBN 1-86171-059-3 (9781861710598) (Paperback) £25.00 / $44.00

ISBN 1-86171-080-1 (9781861710802) (Hardback) £60.00 / $105.00

ANDY GOLDSWORTHY
IN CLOSE-UP

SPECIAL EDITION (HARDBACK and PAPERBACK)

by William Malpas

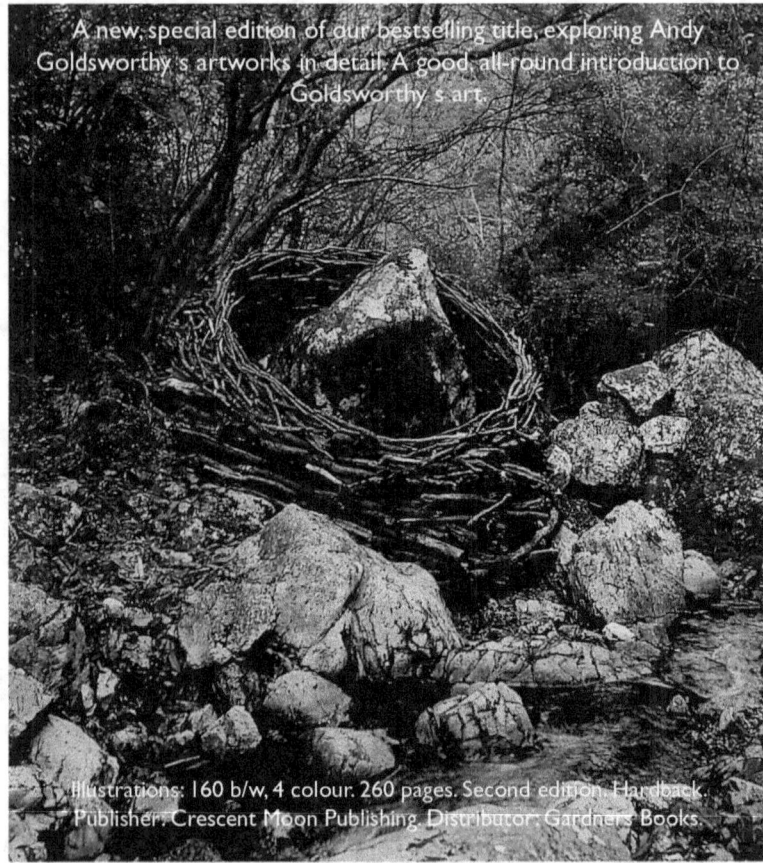

A new, special edition of our bestselling title, exploring Andy Goldsworthy's artworks in detail. A good, all-round introduction to Goldsworthy's art.

Illustrations: 160 b/w, 4 colour. 260 pages. Second edition. Hardback. Publisher: Crescent Moon Publishing. Distributor: Gardners Books.

ISBN 1-86171-094-1 (9781861710949) (Hbk) £60.00 / $105.00

ISBN 1-86171-091-7 (9781861710919) (Pbk) £25.00 / $44.00

Available from bookstores. amazon.com, play.com, tesco.com, and other web-sites.
In the United States from Baker & Taylor, (800) 7753760 or (800) 7751100 or (908) 5417062. electser@btol.com or btinfo@btol.com.

ANDY GOLDSWORTHY

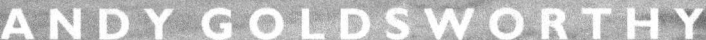

TOUCHING NATURE:
SPECIAL EDITION

(PAPERBACK and HARDBACK)

by William Malpas

A new, special and updated edition of our bestselling title, providing
an excellent general introduction to the art of Andy Goldsworthy.

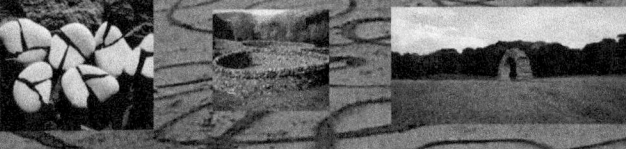

Illustrations: 75 b/w, 2 colour. 354 pages. Third edition. Paperback.

Publisher: Crescent Moon Publishing. Distributor: Gardners Books.

ISBN 1-86171-056-9 (9781861717) (Paperback) £25.00 / $44.00

ISBN 1-86171-087-9 (9781861710871) (Hardback) £60.00 / $105.00

THE ART OF
RICHARD LONG

COMPLETE WORKS : SPECIAL EDITION
(HARDBACK and PAPERBACK)

by William Malpas

A new study of the British artist Richard Long, an important contemporary international artist. The most detailed, in-depth exploration of Richard Long's art currently available.

Illustrations: 48 b/w, 2 colour. 439 pages.
First edition. Hardback and paperback editions.

Publisher: Crescent Moon Publishing. Distributor: Gardners Books.

ISBN 1-86171-079-8 (9781861710796) (Hardback) £60.00 / $105.00

ISBN 1-86171-081-X (9781861710819) (Paperback) £25.00 / $44.00

LAND ART

A COMPLETE GUIDE TO LANDSCAPE, ENVIRONMENTAL, EARTHWORKS, NATURE, SCULPTURE AND INSTALLATION ART

by William Malpas

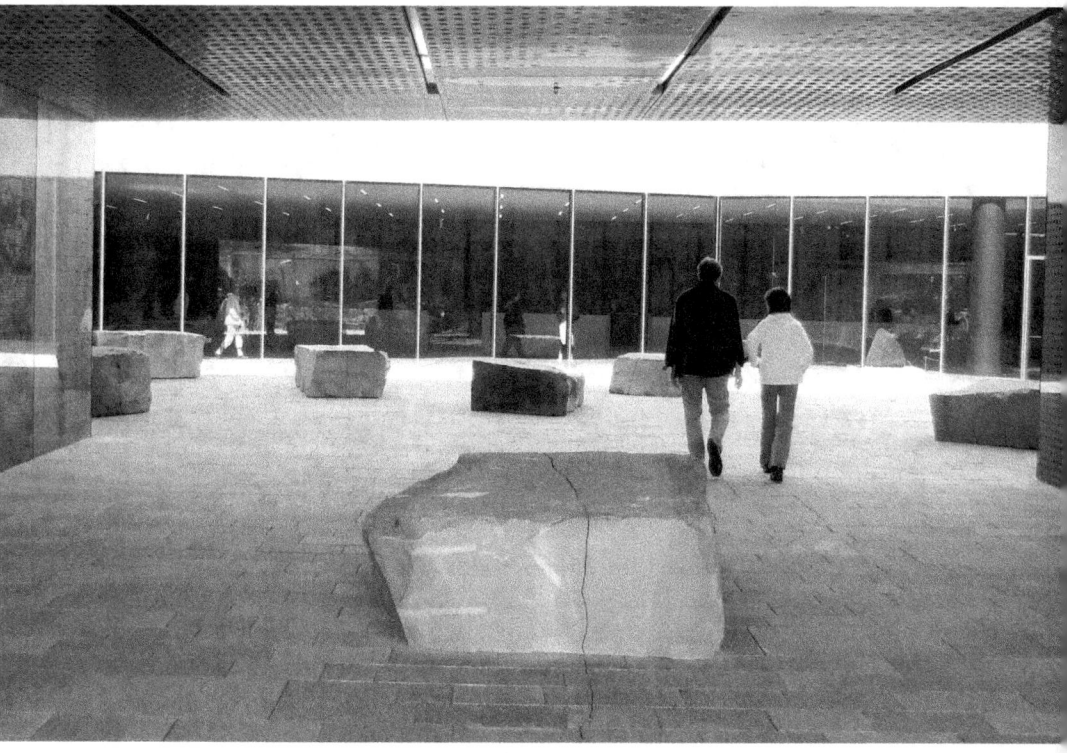

A new, special edition of our popular book on land art.
Chapters on land artists such as Robert Smithson, Walter de Maria, Christo,
Michael Heizer, Richard Long and Andy Goldsworthy.

Illustrations: 35 b/w, 2 colour. 314 pages. First edition. Paperback.

Publisher: Crescent Moon Publishing. Distributor: Gardners Books.

ISBN 1-86171-062-3 (9781861710628) £25.00 / $44.00

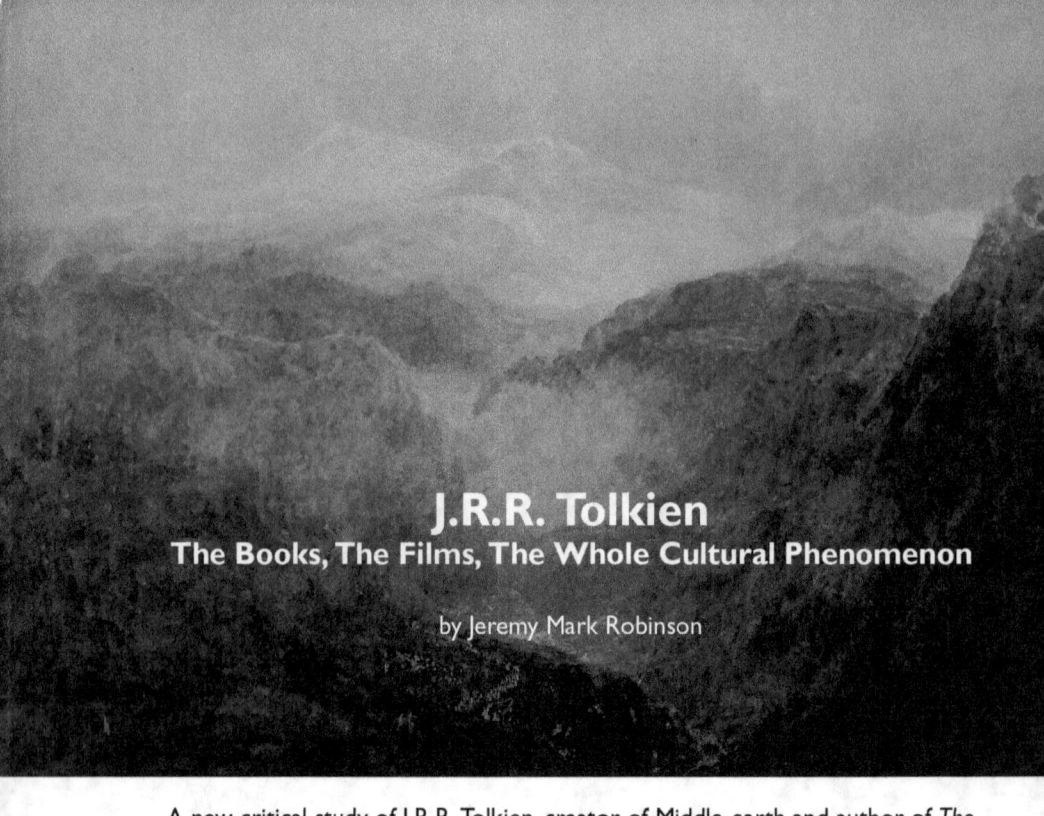

J.R.R. Tolkien
The Books, The Films, The Whole Cultural Phenomenon

by Jeremy Mark Robinson

A new critical study of J.R.R. Tolkien, creator of Middle-earth and author of *The Lord of the Rings, The Hobbit* and *The Silmarillion*, among other books.

This new critical study explores Tolkien's major writings (*The Lord of the Rings, The Hobbit, Beowulf: The Monster and the Critics, The Letters, The Silmarillion* and *The History of Middle-earth* volumes); Tolkien and fairy tales; the mythological, political and religious aspects of Tolkien's Middle-earth; the critics' response to Tolkien's fiction over the decades; the Tolkien industry (merchandizing, toys, role-playing games, posters, Tolkien societies, conferences and the like); Tolkien in visual and fantasy art; the cultural aspects of The Lord of the Rings (from the 1950s to the present); Tolkien's fiction's relationship with other fantasy fiction, such as C.S. Lewis and *Harry Potter*; and the TV, radio and film versions of Tolkien's books, including the 2001-03 Hollywood interpretations of *The Lord of the Rings*.

This new book draws on contemporary cultural theory and analysis and offers a sympathetic and illuminating (and sceptical) account of the Tolkien phenomenon. This book is designed to appeal to the general reader (and viewer) of Tolkien: it is written in a clear, jargon-free and easily-accessible style.

754pp ISBN 1-86171-057-7 £25.00 / $37.50

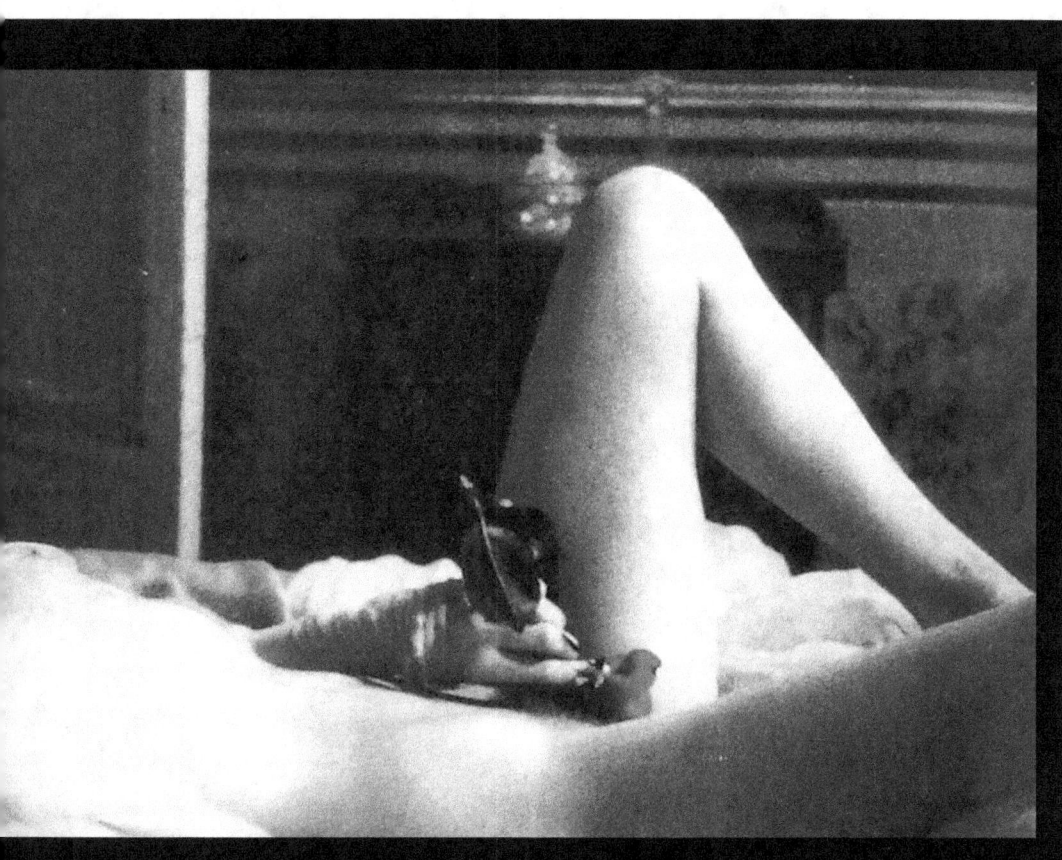

Walerian Borowczyk

Cinema of Erotic Dreams

by Jeremy Mark Robinson

Walerian Borowczyk (1923-2006) was a Polish artist, animator and filmmaker who lived in France for much of his life. He is the author of European art cinema masterpieces Goto: Island of Love, Blanche and Immoral Tales, some surreal animated shorts, and controversial films such as The Beast. This new book concentrates on Borowczyk's feature films, from Goto to Love Rites, which contain some of the most extraordinary images and scenes in recent cinema. Erotica for some, porn for others, Borowczyk's films are highly idiosyncratic and unforgettable.

Bibliography, notes, illustrations   240pp.
Paperback   ISBN 9781861712301   £15.00 / $30.00

Jean-Luc Godard

The Passion of Cinema /
Le Passion de Cinéma

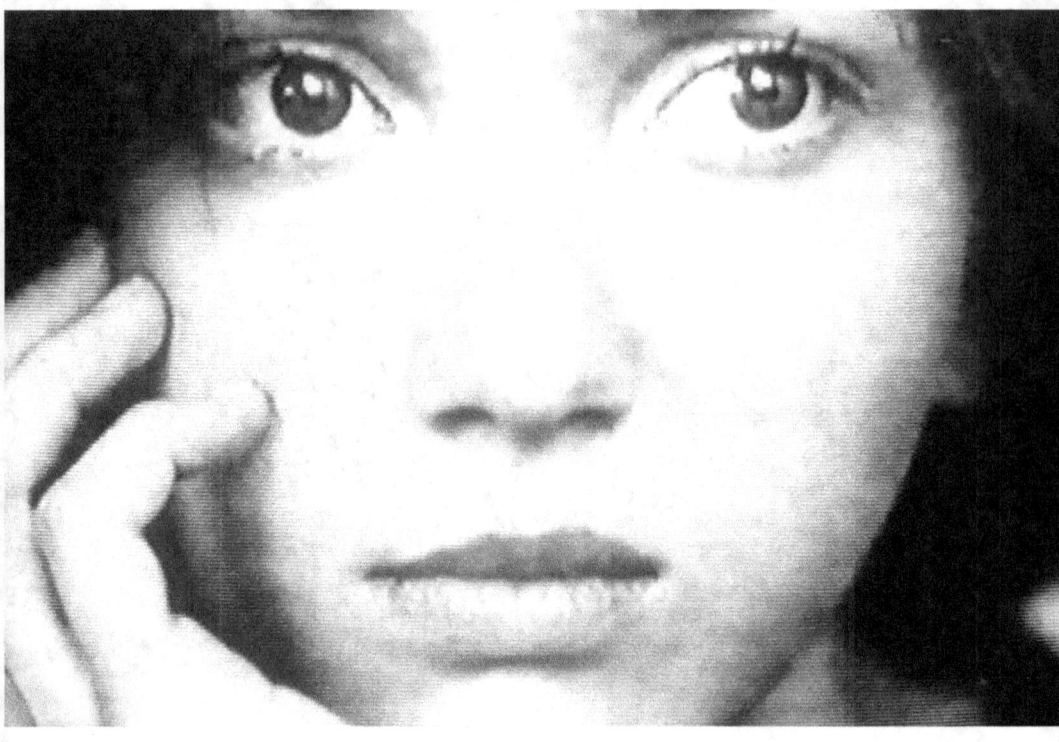

by Jeremy Mark Robinson

A new study of the French filmmaker Jean-Luc Godard (b. 1930),
director of iconic films such as *Breathless, Weekend, Pierrot le Fou,
Passion* and *Vivre Sa vie*. This book explores 27 of Godard's major films,
from *Breathless* to *Notre Musique*, and includes a scene by scene
analysis of Godard's controversial 1985 movie of the Virgin Mary,
Je Vous Salue, Marie.

Bibliography, notes, illustrations   420pp
Hardback   ISBN 9781761712271   £50.00 / $100.00

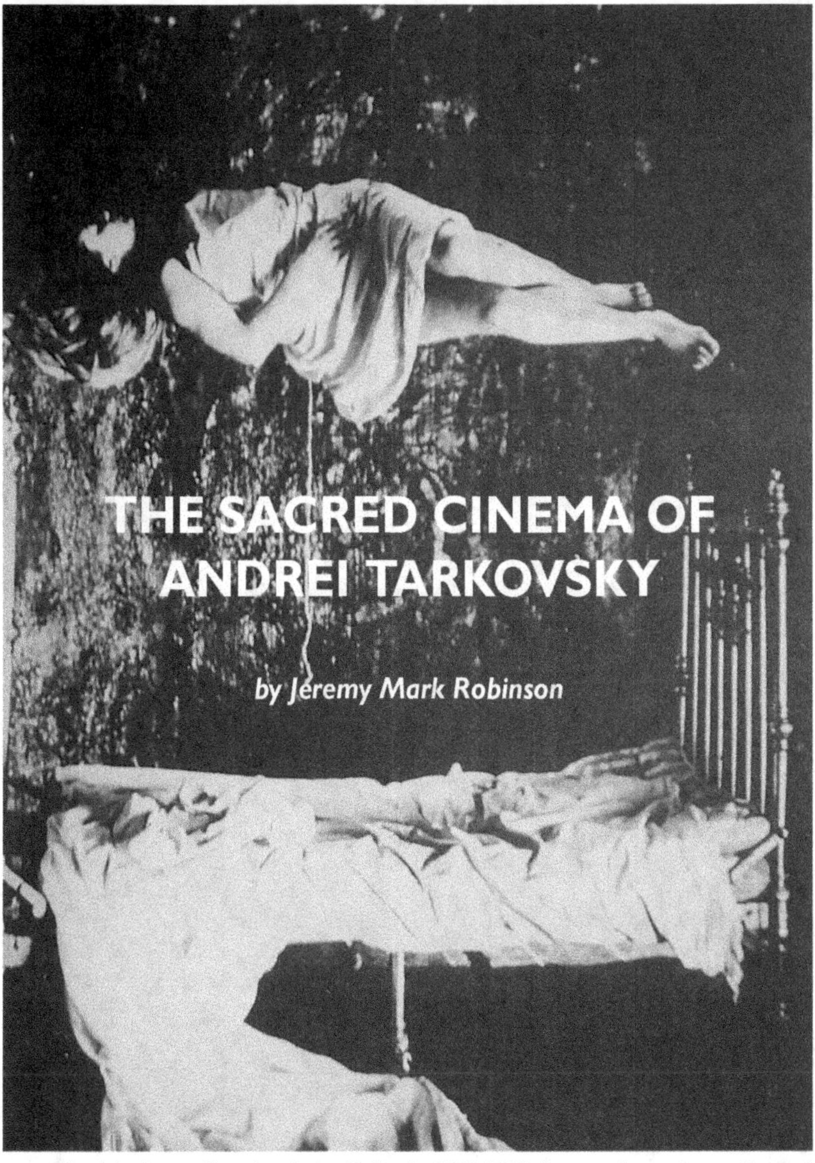

THE SACRED CINEMA OF
ANDREI TARKOVSKY

by Jeremy Mark Robinson

A new study of the Russian filmmaker Andrei Tarkovsky (1932-1986), director of seven feature films, including *Andrei Roublyov, Mirror, Solaris, Stalker* and *The Sacrifice*.

This is one of the most comprehensive and detailed studies of Tarkovsky's cinema available. Every film is explored in depth, with scene-by-scene analyses. All aspects of Tarkovsky's output are critiqued, including editing, camera, staging, script, budget, collaborations, production, sound, music, performance and spirituality. Tarkovsky is placed with a European New Wave tradition of filmmaking, alongside directors like Ingmar Bergman, Carl Theodor Dreyer, Pier Paolo Pasolini and Robert Bresson.

An essential addition to film studies.

Illustrations: 150 b/w, 4 colour. 682 pages. First edition. Hardback.

Publisher: Crescent Moon Publishing. Distributor: Gardners Books.

ISBN 1-86171-096-8 (9781861710963) £60.00 / $105.00

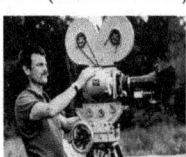

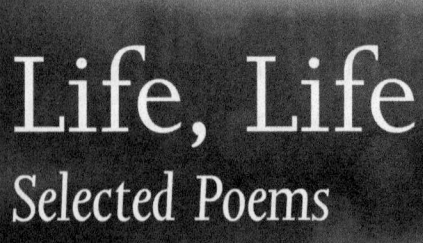

Life, Life
Selected Poems

Arseny Tarkovsky

translated and edited by Virginia Rounding

Arseny Tarkovsky is the neglected Russian poet, father of the acclaimed film director
Andrei Tarkovsky. This new book gathers together many of Tarkovsky's most lyrical
and heartfelt poems, in Rounding's clear, new translations. Many of Tarkovsky's poems
appeared in his son's films, such as *Mirror, Stalker, Nostalghia* and *The Sacrifice*.
There is an introduction by Rounding, and a bibliography of both Arseny and Andrei Tarkovsky.

Bibliography and notes   110pp   2nd ed   ISBN 1-86171-114-X   £10.00 / $20.00

In the Dim Void

Samuel Beckett's Late Trilogy:
Company, Ill Seen, Ill Said and *Worstward Ho*

by Gregory Johns

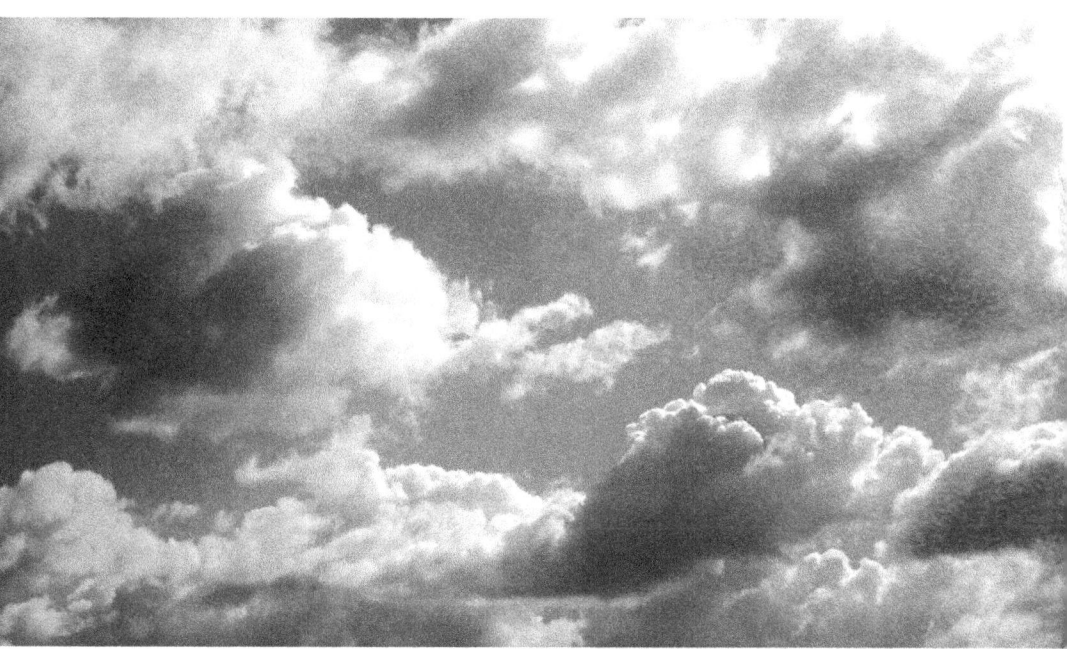

This book discusses the luminous beauty and dense, rigorous poetry of Beckett's late works, *Company, Ill Seen, Ill Said* and *Worstward Ho*. Johns looks back over Beckett's long writing career, charting the development from the *Molloy-Malone Dies-Unnamable* trilogy through the 'fizzles' of the 1960s to the elegiac lyricism of the *Company* series. Johns compares the trilogy with late plays such as *Ghosts, Footfalls* and *Rockaby*.

Bibliography, notes.   120pp
ISBN 1861710712 and ISBN 1861712356   £10.00 / $20.00

CRESCENT MOON PUBLISHING

ARTS, PAINTING, SCULPTURE

The Art of Andy Goldsworthy: Complete Works
Andy Goldsworthy: Touching Nature
Andy Goldsworthy in Close-Up
Andy Goldsworthy: Pocket Guide
Andy Goldsworthy In America
Land Art: A Complete Guide
Richard Long: The Art of Walking
The Art of Richard Long: Complete Works
Richard Long in Close-Up
Richard Long: Pocket Guide
Land Art In the UK
Land Art in Close-Up
Land Art In the U.S.A.
Land Art: Pocket Guide
Installation Art in Close-Up
Minimal Art and Artists In the 1960s and After
Colourfield Painting
Land Art DVD, TV documentary
Andy Goldsworthy DVD, TV documentary
The Erotic Object: Sexuality in Sculpture From Prehistory to the Present Day
Sex in Art: Pornography and Pleasure in Painting and Sculpture
Postwar Art
Sacred Gardens: The Garden in Myth, Religion and Art
Glorification: Religious Abstraction in Renaissance and 20th Century Art
Early Netherlandish Painting
Leonardo da Vinci
Piero della Francesca
Giovanni Bellini
Fra Angelico: Art and Religion in the Renaissance
Mark Rothko: The Art of Transcendence
Frank Stella: American Abstract Artist
Jasper Johns: Painting By Numbers
Brice Marden
Alison Wilding: The Embrace of Sculpture
Vincent van Gogh: Visionary Landscapes
Eric Gill: Nuptials of God
Constantin Brancusi: Sculpting the Essence of Things
Max Beckmann
Egon Schiele: Sex and Death In Purple Stockings
Delizioso Fotografico Fervore: Works In Process 1
Sacro Cuore: Works In Process 2
The Light Eternal: J.M.W. Turner
The Madonna Glorified: Karen Arthurs

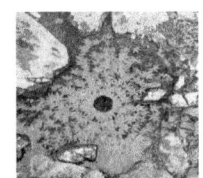
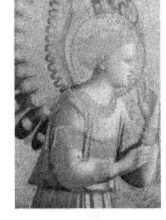

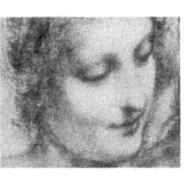
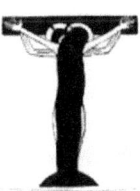
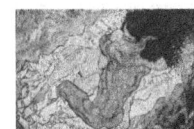

LITERATURE

J.R.R. Tolkien: The Books, The Films, The Whole Cultural Phenomenon
The *Earthsea* Books of Ursula Le Guin
Beauties, Beasts and Enchantment: Classic French Fairy Tales
Tolkien's Heroic Quest
Sexing Hardy: Thomas Hardy and Feminism
Thomas Hardy's *Tess of the d'Urbervilles*
Thomas Hardy's *Jude the Obscure*
Thomas Hardy: The Tragic Novels
Love and Tragedy: Thomas Hardy
The Poetry of Landscape in Hardy
Wessex Revisited: Thomas Hardy and John Cowper Powys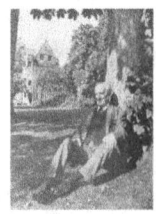
Wolfgang Iser: Essays
Petrarch, Dante and the Troubadours
Maurice Sendak and the Art of Children's Book Illustration
Andrea Dworkin
Cixous, Irigaray, Kristeva: The *Jouissance* of French Feminism
Julia Kristeva: Art, Love, Melancholy, Philosophy, Semiotics and Psychoanalysis
Hélene Cixous I Love You: The *Jouissance* of Writing
Luce Irigaray: Lips, Kissing, and the Politics of Sexual Difference
Peter Redgrove: Here Comes the Flood
Peter Redgrove: Sex-Magic-Poetry-Cornwall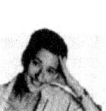
Lawrence Durrell: Between Love and Death, East and West
Love, Culture & Poetry: Lawrence Durrell
Cavafy: Anatomy of a Soul
German Romantic Poetry: Goethe, Novalis, Heine, Hölderlin
Feminism and Shakespeare
Shakespeare: Love, Poetry & Magic
The Passion of D.H. Lawrence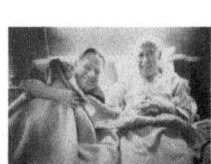
D.H. Lawrence: Symbolic Landscapes
D.H. Lawrence: Infinite Sensual Violence
Rimbaud: Arthur Rimbaud and the Magic of Poetry
The Ecstasies of John Cowper Powys
Sensualism and Mythology: The Wessex Novels of John Cowper Powys
Amorous Life: John Cowper Powys and the Manifestation of Affectivity (H.W. Fawkner)
Postmodern Powys: New Essays on John Cowper Powys (Joe Boulter)
Rethinking Powys: Critical Essays on John Cowper Powys
Paul Bowles & Bernardo Bertolucci
Rainer Maria Rilke
Joseph Conrad: *Heart of Darkness*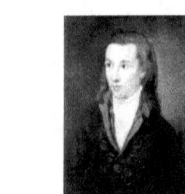
In the Dim Void: Samuel Beckett
Samuel Beckett Goes into the Silence
André Gide: Fiction and Fervour
Jackie Collins and the Blockbuster Novel
Blinded By Her Light: The Love-Poetry of Robert Graves
The Passion of Colours: Travels In Mediterranean Lands
Poetic Forms

POETRY

Ursula Le Guin: Walking In Cornwall
The Best of Peter Redgrove's Poetry
Peter Redgrove: Here Comes The Flood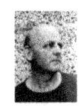
Peter Redgrove: Sex-Magic-Poetry-Cornwall
Dante: Selections From the Vita Nuova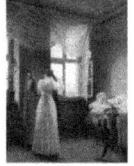
Petrarch, Dante and the Troubadours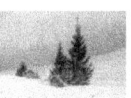
William Shakespeare: Sonnets
William Shakespeare: Complete Poems
Blinded By Her Light: The Love-Poetry of Robert Graves
Emily Dickinson: Selected Poems
Emily Brontë: Poems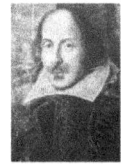
Thomas Hardy: Selected Poems
Percy Bysshe Shelley: Poems
John Keats: Selected Poems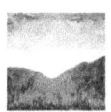
D.H. Lawrence: Selected Poems
Edmund Spenser: Poems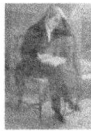
Edmund Spenser: Amoretti
John Donne: Poems
Henry Vaughan: Poems
Sir Thomas Wyatt: Poems
Robert Herrick: Selected Poems
Rilke: Space, Essence and Angels in the Poetry of Rainer Maria Rilke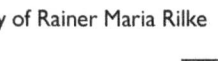
Rainer Maria Rilke: Selected Poems
Friedrich Hölderlin: Selected Poems
Arseny Tarkovsky: Selected Poems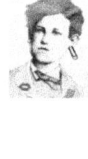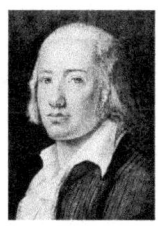
Arthur Rimbaud: Selected Poems
Arthur Rimbaud: A Season in Hell
Arthur Rimbaud and the Magic of Poetry
Novalis: Hymns To the Night
Paul Verlaine: Selected Poems
D.J. Enright: By-Blows
Jeremy Reed: Brigitte's Blue Heart
Jeremy Reed: Claudia Schiffer's Red Shoes
Gorgeous Little Orpheus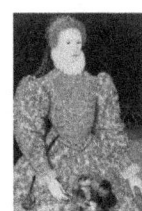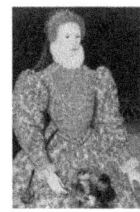
Radiance: New Poems
Crescent Moon Book of Nature Poetry
Crescent Moon Book of Love Poetry
Crescent Moon Book of Mystical Poetry
Crescent Moon Book of Elizabethan Love Poetry
Crescent Moon Book of Metaphysical Poetry
Crescent Moon Book of Romantic Poetry
Pagan America: New American Poetry

MEDIA, CINEMA, FEMINISM and CULTURAL STUDIES

J.R.R. Tolkien: The Books, The Films, The Whole Cultural Phenomenon
Cixous, Irigaray, Kristeva: The *Jouissance* of French Feminism
Julia Kristeva: Art, Love, Melancholy, Philosophy, Semiotics and Psychoanalysis
Luce Irigaray: Lips, Kissing, and the Politics of Sexual Difference
Hélene Cixous I Love You: The *Jouissance* of Writing
Andrea Dworkin
'Cosmo Woman': The World of Women's Magazines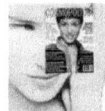
Women in Pop Music
Discovering the Goddess (Geoffrey Ashe)
The Poetry of Cinema
The Sacred Cinema of Andrei Tarkovsky
Walerian Borowczyk: Cinema of Erotic Dreams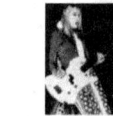
Jean-Luc Godard: The Passion of Cinema
John Hughes and Eighties Cinema
The Cinema of Richard Linklater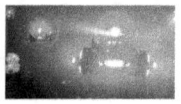
Liv Tyler: Star In Ascendance
The Cinema of Donald Cammell
The Cinema of Hayao Miyazaki
Blade Runner and the Films of Philip K. Dick
Paul Bowles and Bernardo Bertolucci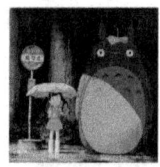
Media Hell: Radio, TV and the Press
An Open Letter to the BBC
Detonation Britain: Nuclear War in the UK
Feminism and Shakespeare
Wild Zones: Pornography, Art and Feminism
Sex in Art: Pornography and Pleasure in Painting and Sculpture
Sexing Hardy: Thomas Hardy and Feminism

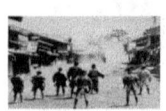 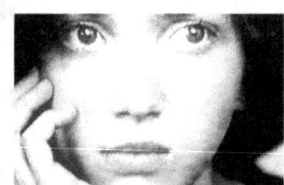 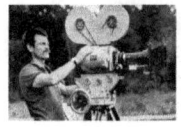

In my view *The Light Eternal* is among the very best of all the material I read on Turner. (Douglas Graham, director of the Turner Museum, Denver, Colorado)

The Light Eternal is a model monograph, an exemplary job. The subject matter of the book is beautifully organised and dead on beam. (Lawrence Durrell)

It is amazing for me to see my work treated with such passion and respect. (Andrea Dworkin)

Sex-Magic-Poetry-Cornwall is a very rich essay... It is like a brightly-lighted box. (Peter Redgrove)

CRESCENT MOON PUBLISHING
P.O. Box 393, Maidstone, Kent, ME14 5XU, United Kingdom.
01622-729593 (UK) 01144-1622-729593 (US) 0044-1622-729593 (other territories)
cresmopub@yahoo.co.uk   www.crescentmoon.org.uk

www.ingramcontent.com/pod-product-compliance
Lightning Source LLC
Chambersburg PA
CBHW071303220526
45468CB00001B/258